A HOP, A SKIP AND A JUMP

A HISTORY OF AUSTRALIAN CHILDHOOD AMUSEMENTS

WARREN FAHEY

BOODGIE BOOKS

Copyright © 2026 by Warren Fahey

All rights reserved.

No part of this book may be reproduced in any form or by any electronic or mechanical means, including information storage and retrieval systems, without written permission from the author, except for the use of brief quotations in a book review.

'A Hop, a Skip and a Jump' final edit by Denis Tracey.

Bodgie Books offers a catalogue of books and recordings exploring Australian folklore, curious history and music.

bodgieproductions@gmail.com

❀ Formatted with Vellum

CONTENTS

Australian Childhood   v

1. All At Sea   1
2. Indigenous Play   50
3. Playtime In The Bush and City   79
4. Singing The Baby To Sleep   120
5. Word Games   154
6. The Playground   190
7. Wonder And Excitement   240
8. Girls Will Be Girls   273
9. Secret Boy's Business   302
10. Dressing Up And Down   325
11. Getting Mobile   342
12. Bowerbirds   366
13. Merrily Around the Maypole   395
14. Very Australian Songs, War Cries & Stories   404
15. Play Songs, Taunts And Parodies   455

Index   477
Notes   481

AUSTRALIAN CHILDHOOD

This collection aims unashamedly to press nostalgia buttons for Australians born in the twentieth century. It will, I trust, also provoke curiosity in those born later. It is a miscellany of odds and ends, mostly reminders of earlier, simpler times when children mostly entertained themselves with word games, board games, homemade toys, dressing up, collecting everything from bugs to swap cards, playing energetic chasing games, and, generally, creating fun times out of very little.

This is not to say today's children are not creative - because they are. However, there is little doubt that, in many ways, we have become a nation of people who get entertained rather than entertain each other. We have become the product of a consumer society that dictates our behaviour from the cradle to the grave. In many ways, children have been robbed of their childhood. The desire to create has too often been replaced with the desire to want - even to the point where very young children demand mobile phones!

The collection has plundered personal memories in diaries, books, newspaper reports, and oral histories. It also tracks the changes in childhood amusements: pastimes that have disappeared, crazes and fashions. There are also examples that disappear and magically reappear fifty or so years later. If you discover a rhyme or game you remember, but it's different - good! - for this is the essence of the treasure chest which is folklore.

Above all, it celebrates Australian childhood and the constantly surprising creativity of children at play. Children find wonder and magic everywhere - because they look for it. They happily follow Alice down and down into Wonderland, fly up and up with Peter Pan, or skip merrily through their childhood—because they can.

This book is dedicated to the early collectors of Australian children's folklore - Dorothy Howard, Ian Turner, June Factor, Gwenda Davey, Judy McKinty and Wendy Lowenstein. It is also testament to the pioneering work of the Australian Children's Folklore Collection of Museums Victoria and its continuing interest in Australian childhood.

Warren Fahey

1
ALL AT SEA

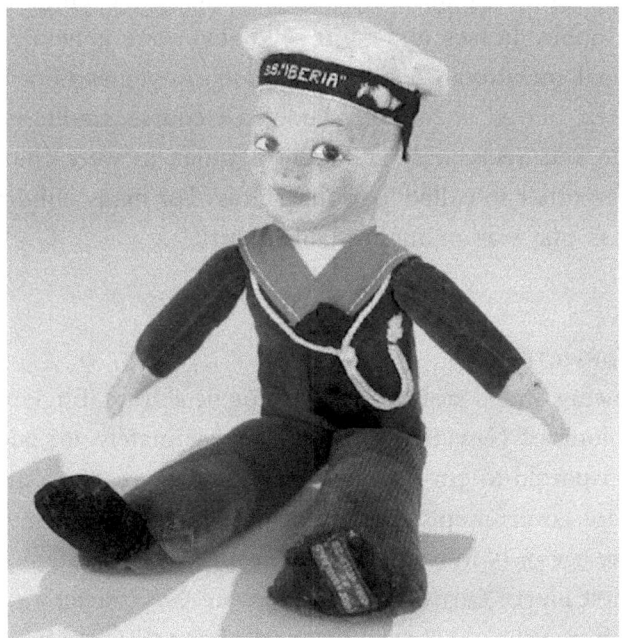

Souvenir doll from *S.S. Iberia*. Victorian Maritime Centre made by Norah Wellings. *Museums Victoria*

The sea has always been mysterious: a place of great battles, astonishing discovery and the fathomless realm of marine creatures great and small. A place of escapism and adventure, where imagination runs wild and free, especially in the minds of the young.

During the first one-hundred and fifty years of European settlement in Australia, from the convict era to the mid-twentieth century, mass migration programs saw hundreds of thousands of children arrive by ship. The voyage was long, sometimes dangerous, and generally dull. Children, however entertained, if at all, generally do not cope well with confinement.

Social order determined Victorian-era children's play. Poor children often made their own toys, such as rag balls, or, if they were lucky, bought cheap penny toys or roughly fashioned hoops. Wealthier children played with dolls with wax or china faces, toy soldiers, hobby horses and train sets. Toys were generally seen as educational, including wood blocks and jigsaw games associated with Noah's Ark, played at Sunday school. Of course, traditional games like 'Hide and Seek' and 'Tag' were popular, as were charade-type games and other so-called 'parlour games'. For many children of the lower class, play was an unaffordable luxury.

CHILD CONVICTS

Following the decision to send convicts from England to the penal colony of New South Wales, approximately 168,000 people were transported to our colonies over some 80 years. Court records and various government reports provide evidence that many children under the age of 15 were transported as part of the system. Included in the First Fleet's harrowing journey were two convict girls aged 13 and 14, a nine-year-old convict boy, and a baby who had been born in Lincoln Gaol.

It is difficult to imagine how desperate England's main cities, particularly London, Liverpool and Manchester, were at this time. Poverty and disease were widespread. Alcohol abuse often led to homelessness. Survival, for many, depended on stealth and bravado. Children of the time, often seen as a source of cheap labour and seemingly appearing innocent, were used as pickpockets and worse. The unlucky ones caught were considered no different from adult criminals.

George Cruikshank. 1848. First illustration in *The Drunkard's Children*. Folio. London.

Child criminals were mainly lower-class unfortunates convicted of petty crimes like 'opportunistic theft' and other minor crimes against personal property. Mary Haydock, 13, was pretty typical; sentenced to seven year's transportation for being 'found with a horse that was not her own. By today's standards the severity of punishment rarely matched the crime.

Thirteen-year-old Elizabeth Hayward was the youngest female convict on the First Fleet. In January 1787, she was sentenced to seven years' transportation at the Old Bailey for stealing clothes from her employer, a clog maker. Elizabeth was confined on board the *Lady Penrhyn* for about three and a half months *before* the ship sailed.

Anne Mather was another young offender, possibly no more than 14 years old at the time of her trial at the Old Bailey on 18 April 1787. She was charged with feloniously stealing 'one pair of velvet breeches value 4s, two cloth waist-coats value 1s, being the property of John Carter'.

At nine years old, John Hudson, a sometime chimney sweep and the youngest First Fleet convict at the time of sentencing, was tried at the Old Bailey London on 10 December 1783 and sentenced to seven years transportation for a felony, but, strangely, not for burglary. John's crime was breaking into the dwelling of William Holdsworth in East Smithfield and stealing 'one linen shirt, valued at 10 shillings, five silk stockings, valued at 5 shillings, one pistol, valued 5 shillings, and two aprons, valued at 2 shillings'.

Transportation peaked in the 1830s. But in 1837, thirteen children under ten were sentenced to transportation, the youngest being eight years old. Their crimes included stealing a loaf of bread, a handkerchief, butter, coal, a pair of shoes, and spoons. Fifteen per cent of all transported convicts were under the age of eighteen.

Convicted children were treated much the same as the most hardened, older prisoners, which, by all accounts, was often inhumane. They travelled below deck chained to each other 24/7 and rarely, if ever, saw sunlight or exercised or inhaled fresh air. One shudders at how the young boys and girls would have been treated and abused on such voyages. And bear in mind that the first transport ships took an extremely long time to make the voyage. The First Fleet took over three months.

Conditions onboard the convict ships

Convicts, including child convicts, were taken onboard in chains and shackles. Once aboard, these were unlocked. A hatch was opened, the convicts went below to the prison deck, and the hatch was locked. They were sometimes kept in chains, behind bars, and on deck. They were often chained in groups when the ship was at capacity. There was little ventilation, and the air was stale and filthy. Later journeys allowed for some limited time on deck where they could get exercise and fresh air, still chained together.

Seasickness, stomach upsets, and measles were common. However, most ships, particularly later voyages, were kept reasonably clean under the supervision of the ship's surgeon.

A Hop, a Skip and a Jump

But in the early days particularly, discipline was brutal, with regular use of the lash. In later days, if the convicts misbehaved, they would be 'boxed'—put in a small confined space in the bow, in which a man could neither lie down nor stand. Discipline knew no favours, and children were treated as adults. One suspects that any attempt at play would not have been tolerated.

Worse still were the chilling accounts of the voyages' desperation, starvation and exhaustion. In 1801 a young man, Thomas Milburn, incarcerated on the *Neptune*, wrote, in 1801, to his parents of his horror at having remained chained to a dead man for over a week. He had kept quiet so as to recieve his rations until he could not bear the stench any longer. [1]

John Acton Wroth, transported in the 1840s, described the ship's quarters.[2]

> ...with bunks along either side of the deck, each separated from its neighbour by a ten-inch high board. Four berths of the lower and upper tiers formed a mess, constructed so four men could sit around a table. These men occupying midship slept in hammocks, slung up each night over the tables. Younger men and boys had these. Each bed had a mattress, pillow and two blankets. The hammock had two blankets.

Convicts, including several young boys, destined for transportation to Botany Bay.

Convict Gaol Nursery. Brixton Library Service.

Very young children also accompanied their convict mothers on female transport ships.[3] Some had been born in prison and, with no other means of support, had remained in the gaol or asylum for years, awaiting the mother's transportation. Female convict Rebecca Boulton conceived and bore her child while in Lincoln Goal. The gaoler in Spilsby, Lincolnshire, wrote to the authorities on 30 December 1786 seeking permission for Rebecca to take her baby onto the First Fleet. He wrote, 'She has a female child about eight months old, and I should be glad you'd inform me whether the child can go with the mother, she being desirous of taking it'. Permission was granted on 22 March 1787, just in time to keep them both together. Sadly, four months after arriving at Botany Bay, both mother and baby died in the same week.

Despite the efforts of ship's surgeons and more conscientious officers and crews, hygiene on convict ships was poor to hideous, and many fell to disease. Dreadful reports exist of ship crews taking advantage of the female convicts. There were also many shipwrecks, including two instances where entire female transport ships were lost. One female transport ship, cruising off Tasmania, took 54 children to their deaths.

. . .

THE VOYAGE WAS OFTEN a terrifying experience for the weak. One young lad came out on a ship where youth gangs ruled, and the younger children were referred to as 'pigs'. The gangs would take the food from the little boys, eat the best bits, and throw them back the offal, which they called 'feeding their pigs.'

The determination to survive would have been the main distraction for young children on convict ships. Although thoughts of play would seem to have been the furthest thing from their minds, young children have imaginations and can create play even under the worst stress. Hopefully, these children found some solace in whatever play they devised.

Life in the Colonies

On arrival, the female convicts and their children were usually assigned to settlers as servants or sent to the Female Factories at Parramatta or Hobart, where they were expected to work washing, mending and making clothes. Some girls were lucky and sent to families who often regarded the child convict as a member of their own family. Others were less fortunate and were sent to homes that saw them severely overworked. Exhaustion replaced playtime.

During the early 1830s, many male convict children were sent to Tasmania's Point Puer (Latin for 'boy'), which was situated near the well-known and notorious Port Arthur adult prison. These boys were usually aged 9 to 18 and were considered to be too weak to work for settlers, as many were suffering from malnutrition or a diagnosed illness.

Point Puer Peninsula and buildings can be seen in the background in this sketch by N Remand, 'Etablissement penitentiare de Port Arthur'

The establishment at Point Puer was built *by* young boys in 1834. It was the first British purpose-built reforming institution for criminal boys. This was to be achieved by separating them from adult convicts, with education, trade training and religious instruction being the vehicles to change immoral habits. The number of boys sent to Point Puer steadily increased, and a daily routine was established. At 5 am, they were to wake and stow their hammocks and bedding. Next, overseers supervised them while they washed outdoors in tanks of ice-cold water. The typical morning continued with prayers, breakfast and an assembly. They attended classes and workshops where they were taught a trade. They were given an hour's play at midday, followed by lunch. We have no full reports on what these boys played, but it would likely have been physical with improvised football, cricket, and games like leapfrog. Half the boys went to school while the other half worked on the prison farms from 2 pm until 5:30 pm. There was another hour's play until dinner at 6:30 pm. Inmates were expected to read before bed, as reading was seen as one of the paths to enlightenment. Lights went out at 9 pm. [4]

Boys who misbehaved were placed in morbid solitary confinement, chained or given thirty strokes of the lash. One of the most serious cases of child rebellion was of two 14-year-old boys who murdered their overseer by stoning him. Some boys attempted to escape Point Puer, although most were unsuccessful and several drowned.

Point Puer Convicts working. *AOT. Libraries Tasmania*

Child Convicts and Young 'Bolters'

Although young convicts were usually indentured to families where they were expected to work for the benefit of their protector, many were treated little better than slaves. Remember that this was the same era when young children, sometimes as young as six, worked in British mills and mines. Child labour was seen as a normal part of life. In England, if they refused to work, they were flogged and deprived of food. Treatment in the colonies was rarely as wicked, although often hard, seemingly endless and tiring. There was little time for play. Occasionally, escape to the bush was seen as a better option for survival.[5]

> *Two Dollars Reward!*
>
> FOR *the apprehension of a Vagrant Boy. A servant of mine, probably seduced from my service, having absconded: all persons harbouring or detaining him after this Notice, will be prosecuted according to law; he is bound for a term of years over to my service by his parents, who are servants of James Busby, Esq., in New Zealand.*
>
> *Description - Patrick Moore, born in Dublin, Catholic, 13 years of age, a well-looking, stout, intelligent, and rather talkative lad; brown hair, hazel eyes, and good teeth, ruddy complexion;—had on when he went away, a blue striped shirt, brown corduroy trowsers, dark striped waistcoat, a straw hat, and laced boots, rather big;—Any Person returning him to my house, Castlereagh-street, opposite Captain Lamb, will receive a Reward of TWO DOLLARS*

> ABSCONDED from his Home, without any just cause or provocation, JOHN CONDER, a Boy, between the ages of 9 and 10, of a fair complexion, with flaxen hair. Whoever is found harbouring him, will be dealt with according to the utmost Rigour of the Law.
> ESTHER CONDER, Pitt-street.

Many of the convicts sent to New South Wales in the early years were already diseased, and many died from typhoid and cholera on the ships. Because of the number of epidemics that swept the colony and the general abuse of alcohol, a lot of children became orphans. The young colony was often a miserable place, and it was not unusual to see abandoned and orphaned children living on the streets. By 1801, there were 2000 children in the colony. A school was decided to be built to 'improve children's chances in life'.

One of the earliest schools established in New South Wales was the Female Orphan Institution, founded by Governor King and his wife in 1800 and opened a year later with 31 girls aged between 7 and 14 years of age. By 1829, the residents of the institution numbered 152, including some abandoned Aboriginal children. The girls were taught sewing and spinning and attended classes in reading and writing. Much of the work was in training the girls to be useful as farm and house help. Some critics of the school claimed it was nothing more than a training ground for domestic slavery. A Boy's Orphan School was opened in 1819. Numerous benevolent societies followed, many with strange names like the Ragged Children's Society and the Society for the Relief of Destitute Children. Playtime at these establishments was regimented and supervised.

FEMALE ORPHAN INSTITUTION: Sydney, 7th November, 1818.[6]

> *WANTED, a respectable and well-qualified Man and Woman, for the Situations of Master and Matron of the Female Orphan Institution, which will become Vacant on the first of January next, by the Resignations of Mr. and Mrs. Hosking.—None but a married Couple need apply; and they will be required to give perfect Satisfaction as to their Qualifications, as prescribed by the lately published Rules and Regulations of the Instruction; and the most ample Testimonials of good Character and Conduct.*

By the 1830s, England removed children from working in mines and other dangerous environments. There were positive moves to send young children to the colonies for a better life.

SAVING **young souls through apprenticeship.**[7]

Sydney Gazette. The scheme consists in the importation of children, from nine or ten to twelve or fourteen years of age, from the poorhouses, asylums for orphans, &c., which abound in England, and to apprentice them to the farmers and others for a reasonable period. It is presumed that, in the several manufacturing towns in Great Britain, there are hundreds of families reduced to such distress that it is not improbable many of them would consent to part with their starving offspring if proper security could be given for their safety and protection; and being received into a household at so tender an age, they would, it is supposed, in a few years, differ in nothing from the children of the soil. They would thus serve an apprenticeship to the climate, the seasons, and all the peculiarities of colonial life.

It is surprising to read advertisements offering work to children as young as ten.

ALL WORK **and No Play** [8]

WANTED, several Apprentices, whose treatment will be liberal. Boys from 10 to 14 years will be accepted. Apply to Mr. GLAYLAND, Parramatta.

A Genteel and very useful little Girl, about 12 years of age, lately from England, wants a Situation in a respectable family, where her mother may rely upon her being treated well.—Apply at the Gazette Office.

WANTED, in a respectable Family in Town, a Girl, about 10 or 12 years old, to nurse an Infant.—Apply at the Gazette Office.

> WANTED, a COLONIAL GIRL, from 12 to 14 years of age, from industrious Parents; one from the Country, or Parramatta, will be preferred. Liberal wages will be given; her principal employment will be in the house, and with children---Apply to Mrs. WILLSHIRE, Brickfield Hill, Sydney.

> WANTED, a BOY to wait in a respectable Public-house and Shop.—A Youth having had some little education, and destitute of friends, would be preferred.—Also, an aged WOMAN, as Servant of All-work.—Apply to Mr. WM. KEMPTON, Sign of the King George, Clarence-street, Sydney.

But despite these improvements, people generally believed that poor children should work. Girls' most common employment was as domestic servants from the age of ten to twelve. They began their day's work early, before the household had awoken, and continued working until night. Other girls took up apprenticeships in the textile industry or worked in shops and laundries. At ten, boys could become apprentices in a wide selection of trades. In most cases, they lived in the home of the craftsperson to whom they were apprenticed. A craftsperson held the authority to administer and punish an apprentice for clumsiness, laziness, or anything else they thought suitable. Abuse was common.

Children too young to serve apprenticeships or work as servants helped look after horses, ran errands and opened carriage doors with the expectation of receiving a tip. Some children as young as six were employed to undertake minor tasks on farms. However, wealthy children were not expected to work - instead, they received an education.

Children also accompanied government officials who were sent to administer the colonies. There were also free settler families. Many of these families, typical of the era, had five or six children, sometimes more. The first free settlers came in 1793 on HMS *The Bellona*, which also transported convicts.

The early colonial days of Australia must have been rough for children - though no doubt preferable in many ways to life in English urban slums. By the late 1830s, the population of NSW had reached about 50,000. The convict population was about half that figure; of the free men, about 17,000 had once been convicts. Both the convict and free societies brought children into this strange world.

As the colony grew, the government realised it needed to encourage free settlers, especially single women. The Emigration Committee, searching for women to emigrate to Australia, offered a bounty on the sea passage.[9] Families were also encouraged. Bricklayer William Bloomfield, married to Frances Jane Meares, had eleven children, including six girls, and an assisted passage to a new life must have been quite an attraction. In 1833 the Bloomfield family sailed to Australia, the children scattered throughout the ship. As steerage passengers, they would have had to take their own provisions to cover the long voyage.

On board 1875. *State Library Victoria*

Golden Children

The discovery of gold in 1851 led to more than a million people travelling to Australia in the short space of twenty years. Ships typically had three classes: first, second and steerage. Children were not particularly catered for and were encouraged to remain with the family unit for much of the voyage. Disease and disaster were still commonplace, and it was not unusual for an entire family to die, often of measles, typhoid, diarrhoea or scarlet fever. In 1852, at the beginning of the Victorian gold rush, Edward Grimes, the immigration officer at Melbourne, recorded that 15,477 people had passed through the port, and that 849 deaths had occurred during the voyage. Hundreds more died after the ships docked. Overall, one out of every five children died on the outward voyage.[10]

Skinner Prout's 'On board an Australian Emigrant Ship. *The Illustrated London News 1849*

In 1852, approximately twelve thousand children lived in the Victorian goldfields. It would have been a strange life. Schooling was virtually non-existent, and a child's day was mostly occupied with chores like fetching clean water, washing, gathering firewood, looking after livestock and younger children, cooking, and helping in the search for gold. Children would be expected to wash mud to find a small nugget, rock the miner's cradle (another form of sluicing for gold specks) and generally be helpful. Mining families moved from goldfield to goldfield, responding to rumours of better golden opportunities.

As the goldfield towns grew, so did the population's appetite for entertainment. Larger towns typically had a venue for concerts and theatrical performances, and these venues also arranged special shows for children. At home, when not working, children played with improvised and purchased toys or played musical instruments. Board games were popular, and one such game was based on the search for gold. Children chased hoops down dusty lanes, played hopscotch, skipped, flew kites and played ball games.

~

Sumner Family outside their Teetotal Shop, Ballarat. *Museums Victoria*

THE EMIGRANTS

By the time of the second wave of the gold rush, around 1860, the Britain to Australia voyage had been reduced to 80 - 90 days, but it was still a long time for a child to be restricted to a ship.

It is not difficult to imagine scenes of children running around the deck, dodging working sailors, ropes, barrels, and other equipment, or exploring below deck, running along corridors, around public spaces, and even down to the livestock pens. Undoubtedly, many hours were spent creating games like 'hide and seek' and 'catch-me-if-you-can'.

Playtime opportunities on board ships depended very much on your class of passage. Well-off children had a safer environment, sometimes a nanny, and dedicated school and play schedules. Lower classes lived in cramped conditions, and children had work obligations, so play was usually unscheduled. One imagines these children had more opportunities to 'explore' and have fun. It would have been a combination of absolute boredom and occasional hectic fun.

Ocean travel in the twenty-first century has become luxurious. Commercial and naval sailors receive quality accommodation with all the trappings of modern life, including good food, wine and the

Internet. Not so the travellers of the eighteenth and nineteenth centuries when millions crisscrossed the seas, including those making the voyage to and from Australia, in conditions far from acceptable.

Preparing for the voyage.
Illustrated Sydney News
1885

Following emigration opportunities, particularly in the 1870s and 80s, many British and Irish families set out for a new life in the colonies. The voyage to Australia was generally uncomfortable with shared accommodation. By 1870, the faster ships were making the crossing in around eight weeks. Most ships completed the journey without any stops. Diaries indicate the voyages proved arduous for emigrants and especially dangerous for young children. Many ships operated by opportunistic companies were severely overcrowded and barely seaworthy.

Drawings from the time show passengers herded into shared accommodation, often an entire family of five restricted to one open bunk, double-decker dormitory style. Cabin passengers, typically one in ten, had exclusive use of the poop deck. Steerage passengers were usually confined to the lower deck areas. Steerage was further separated by class, gender and marital status. Single men were separated from married couples and children. Passengers often referred to themselves and other steerage passengers as 'prisoners'.

Emigrants plot their progress on board a ship bound for Australia. *Hulton Archive. Museums Victoria*

On a typical journey, emigrants had to be out of bed by 7 am, with all the children washed and dressed before breakfast at 8 am, then, afterwards, they were sent off to school. At 9 am, the decks were cleaned, and groups were assigned to clean areas of the ship that didn't belong to a particular mess. Dinner was at 1 pm, tea at 6 pm and lights out at 8 pm. Government regulations determined the daily routine on British emigrant ships and many private ships leaving English ports. Steerage passengers were required to clean their berths (as were some second and third-class passengers), which was how most emigrants started their day. Regulations also dictated the timing of religious services and weekly musters for inspections by the Surgeon Superintendent, wash days and daily cleaning of the 'coppers'. It would have been a very long day for most children.

Women and children waiting waiting waiting

Afternoons were usually free for emigrants to do as they liked. Depending on the weather, leisure time was spent sewing, reading or writing letters and diaries. Passengers fell into a routine of eating, drinking, and sleeping with occasional organised or impromptu amusements. Children were typically left to their own devices; however, many families tended to be protective, lest the children got into trouble. Adult and young passengers had to make their own entertainment. The main activities included reading, writing, talking, riddling, joking, singing and playing music.

TRIP DIARIES, like today's blogs, covered everyday life at sea. Seasickness, whether their own or their fellow passengers, was a reoccurring subject. As the voyage progressed, passengers recorded sighting islands, phosphorus water, the heat, crossing the equator, being stuck in the doldrums and, as they headed south, freezing weather and icebergs, sharks, flying fish and birds. Many ships printed a weekly newspaper containing poems, stories, passenger details, riddles, announcements and songs.

RELIGIOUS SERVICES WERE CONDUCTED on all ships, and the sounds of hymns reminded emigrants of home and safety. Attendance was also seen as an important part of a child's education. Sunday school for children, depending on their religion, often included games, songs, and magic lantern shows based on Bible stories.

A family on the crossing. *Sydney Illustrated News* 1875

The deck offered fresh air and a chance to move. *Museums Victoria*

Singing was an accepted part of early Victorian-era life and an important part of ship life, being part of the sailor's everyday work. Children must have been captivated by the shouts of the shantyman and the call-and-response shanties that steered the great ships, turned the capstan wheel and sent the sails ripping through the wind. Shanties like 'Haul on the Bowline', 'We're All Bound Away', 'Whiskey Johnny' and 'Rio Grande' are typical. One wonders if the salty sailors, known for their love of bawdry, censored their shanties in the presence of children.

Sailors singing below deck. ANMM

Racquet games like badminton were a popular pastime.
Illustrated News

THE SHIP'S drawing-room piano was usually well-prized, and regular singing sessions of parlour songs, music hall, and light opera were programmed. Amateur theatrical shows, including plays written and featuring the passengers, were also enjoyed. From the 1850s onwards, amateur blackface minstrel shows included the latest songs, dance tunes, and monologues.

Postcard featuring a game of deck cricket on a P&O ship, 1915.
A.F.U.

Deck games included cricket, quoits, badminton and tug-of-war contests. Singalongs and dancing were popular.

Tug-a-war Cunard *Franconia*. A.F.U.

Boys playing greasy pole, *T. S. S. Beltana, 1925*. Museums Victoria

As shipping developed, conditions changed, and impressive clippers such as the *Marco Polo* brought a certain luxury to sea travel. Once again, they reduced the travel time, improved conditions, and saw some interest in entertaining children. Later, ocean liners also revolutionised sea travel, including employing an officer or matron to look after the 'children's program'.

Some ships were better than others, as this passenger on the *Royal Mail Alameda* reported in 1897:[11]

> The entire trip was a pleasant one, and the numerous passengers thoroughly enjoyed themselves with the usual ship's sports and other amusements. A novel amusement for the children was given by a troupe of performing ponies. They walked up on the deck of the mailboat and gave the little ones a

daily ride. These ponies, much to the regret of all, landed at Honolulu.

Games like jigsaws, Ludo and deck quoits helped pass the long days. Many lines produced their own sets. *A.F.U.*

In a newspaper article in 1928[12], the French steamer *Isle de France* was described as a 'Wonder upon Wonder' with a merry-go-round and a Punch and Judy theatre. It is interesting to speculate whether one of the ship's crew assumed the role of 'manning' the Punch and Judy puppet show or whether they had a general entertainer assigned for such a role.

British porcelain Punch, Judy and Toby figurenes.

Isle de France in full steam. Ship's Archive.

Steamers also provided more space for recreation by adding the promenade and boat decks above the main deck. Most people took advantage of warmer weather by lazing around in deck chairs. When the weather was mild, passengers spent most of their time walking the deck and playing deck games. Quoits, indoor cricket, shuttlecock, badminton, table tennis or ping-pong, and shuffleboard were all played to pass the time, amuse the children and keep the passengers fit.

The games of Chuck Penny and Cavendish are mentioned as being played on emigrant ships and also in the early colonies. Any form of gambling, including games, were viewed as suspicious.

F. FOWLER, in his 1859 book *Southern Lights and Shadows*, noted:[13]

> The Australian boy is a slim, dark-eyed, olive-complexioned young rascal, fond of cavendish, cricket and chuck penny, and systematically insolent to all servant girls, policemen, and new chums. He baptises female emigrants after the names of the ships in which they arrived, such as Susan Red Rover and Matilda Agamemnon. He is Christian, in turn, a gum sucker and a cornstalk.

A game of deck quoits. *Sydney Illustrated News*

Empress of Ireland with children onboard. *Canadian Pacific Steamships Archive*

In 1906, a newspaper reported on children's entertainment on the *Empress of Ireland*, a Canadian Pacific Steamship Company luxury vessel on the Australian run. One feature of the deck included a large, fenced sandbox for children. The mighty ship, sometimes called Canada's Titanic', sank after a collision in 1914. One hundred and thirty-three children died in the shipwreck.

> Trees and Castles on an Ocean Liner. [14] A playground for children is a feature of the magnificent steamer *Empress of Ireland*. The playground is for the children's amusement in the third class only. A vast space on the deck is set apart entirely for the youngsters. Trees are planted in pots, and there are heaps of sand, spades and buckets so that the youngsters can pretend they are all seaside and living at sea.

A Hop, a Skip and a Jump

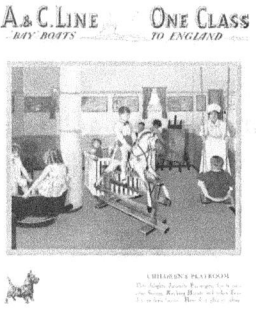

Advertisement showing nursery room

Crowded deck 1911. *State Library Victoria*

Chuck Farthing. Some ships discouraged gambling, but it remained popular with young boys, especially chuck-farthing, a game that originated in the United Kingdom. The rules of the game were described in the nineteenth century as follows: '

Each competitor starts with the same number of coins. They pitch their coins one at a time from a mark at a given distance towards a hole in the ground. The competitors are ranked based on how close they come to the hole. The competitor closest to the hole receives all of the coins and proceeds to a second mark nearer to the hole, from which he throws all of the coins at once towards the hole. All of the coins that remain in the hole are his to keep. The remainder of the coins are given to the next closest competitor, and the process is repeated until no coins remain.

Many deck games, including gambling games, were straight from the streets of English cities and considered the property of the lower class. Of course, this didn't stop children from playing them.

A VARIATION of the game called chuck-hole or chuck-penny was played similarly, except that if the coins rolled outside a ring drawn around the hole, it was declared a "dead heat," and each competitor reclaimed his coin. The coins were usually small denominations, farthings, halfpence, or pennies. Sometimes, rough-cast leaden markers called dumps were used. Game wowsers frowned on such frivolous pursuits.[15]

> If parents wish to see their children prosper, let them admonish them against the innocent amusement of chuck farthing—because, chuck farthing resembles gaming, and gaming is not included in the Kit of Virtues; but on the contrary supports a very fair pretension to rank highly in the catalogue of Vices which disgrace mankind.

Deck quoits and similar games must have been a challenge in rough seas. *Maritime Museum Tasmania*

Passengers were intrigued by the crew and workings of the great ships, and many sea diaries detail daily life and the jobs of various crew members. Many passengers, including children, sketched the sailors and officers. Some ships arranged drawing classes for children.

Word games were extremely popular on sea voyages. They didn't require anything other than keen players.

A typical Victorian-era word game was called 'The Ship's Alphabet'. It is easy to see how such a game helped children learn their alphabet. One player is elected 'Captain', and he or she asks each player a question - based on the alphabet commencing with A.

'Daddy at the wheel' - a passenger sketch *S S Sobroan*. *National Library of Australia*

> *Captain: The name of the letter?*
> *Player 1: A*
> *Captain: The name if the ship?*
> *Player 2: Atheneum*
> *Captain: The name of the captain?*
> *Player 3: Albert*
> *Captain: The name of the port she hails from?*
> *Player 4: America*
> *Captain: The place she is bound for?*
> *Player 5: Australia*
> *Captain: The name of the letter?*
> *Player 1: B, etc.....through the entire alphabet*

Reading

Young readers treasured books on long sea voyages. Favourites for boys included *Moby Dick* (or *The Whale*) by Herman Melville, *Captains Courageous* by Rudyard Kipling, *Robinson Crusoe* by Daniel

Defoe, and *Treasure Island* by Robert Louis Stephenson. Girls favoured the escapism and romance of works by the Bronte sisters: *Wuthering Heights, Jane Eyre, Agnes Grey* and *The Tenant of Wildfell Hall.*

The daring Grace Darling to the rescue. *Grace Darling Museum.*

IT WAS common for later ships to maintain a lending library.

Readings from Samuel Taylor Coleridge's *The Rime of the Ancient Mariner*, Homer's Iliad, Swineburne and Wordsworth's poems of *Grace Darling*, and Felicia Dorothea Hemans' *The Boy Stood on the Burning Deck* (aka *Casabianca*) sparked travellers' literary appetites.

CHALK WAS indispensable for nineteenth-century children. They used it at school and in play. When chalk was not available, charcoal came in handy for drawing and in games like hopscotch, where the general rule is to toss a small object into chalk-numbered triangles of a pattern of rectangles outlined on the ground and then hop or jump through the spaces to retrieve the object. Chalk was also used to draw game boards on the decks of ships.

The game of 'Scotch-Hoppers'. *Juvenile Games for the Four Seasons.*

Hop-Scotch. Is an old game, definitely seventeenth century, possibly earlier. The original game was called 'Scotch Hoppers' and was played by both girls and boys. The drawn board has various designs. The game was referenced in sea diaries as being played on board during calm weather. One could imagine it being quite a feat if played during rough seas. A manuscript[16] compiled between 1635 and 1672 refers to 'Scotch Hoppers'

> 'They play with a piece of tile or a little flat piece of lead, upon a boarded floor, or any area divided into oblong figures like boards'.

'Cup and Ball' was another popular Victorian-era game that went to sea. It could be played solo or in groups. Essentially, it was a game of skill and, as they say, 'good for hours of fun.'[17]

The game of 'Cup and Ball'. *Juvenile Games for the Four Seasons*

Settlement and young colonials

Once across the treacherous seas to a new life in Australia, families settled down and got on with the business of settlement. Pioneering in either the rough townships or rugged bush was a trial. The birth of 'young colonials' was met with joy and satisfaction. There was always a lot of work to be done: animals to tend, soil to be prepared for planting, needlework, cooking and cleaning. Children were expected to do their fair share, including the older children looking after the younger ones.

Advertisements in the early colonial newspapers announced the arrival of toys, especially around the Christmas period. The main imports were dolls, skipping ropes, tin drums, hoops, music boxes, board games, bats and balls, and musical instruments. Toys with moveable parts, especially dolls, tin soldiers, and animals, were particularly favoured, as per this 1804 advertisement.[18]

'A large and very handsome Assortment of Toys, comprising every Article for the amusement of Children, viz. Dolls drest and undrest, among which are a few beautiful imitations of nature, in wax; Fiddles Tamborines, and music boxes, set irregular airs, Battledores and shuttlecocks.'

With God's Will. Religious beliefs in the second half of the nineteenth century limited playtime. In stricter families, toys were put away on Saturday evening in preparation for the Sabbath, when no playing or toys were allowed. Sunday school, for some liberal religions, was seen as a healthy opportunity and as entertainment. Preachers used games, charades, magic lanterns, and playtime. Many of the lantern shows were based on biblical storytelling and nursery rhymes.

Lost Children

For over a century, religious and charitable bodies organised child emigration, especially to Canada and Australia. The Children's Friend Society, established in 1830, sent its first party of child migrants to Australia in 1832. In 1844, the Ragged School Movement began, and 150 children were sent to New South Wales in 1849. In

1850, Parliament legalised Poor Law Guardians to fund the emigration of children to the colonies.

Nowadays it is accepted that all children deserve a happy upbringing with a balanced education, including playtime, but this was not always so. From the very earliest of times, the colonial government became concerned with the number of children living on the streets. Mortality was high in both children and adults and during the rum-soaked days of the convict system, orphaned or abandoned children were common. Many adults and children died from diseases on the voyage to Australia, and sometimes, children arrived at the docks parentless. There was also concern for the children of convicts. If Britain had a problem with its bulging gaols, it also had a problem with vagrant children and children rescued from workhouses in all its main cities. Concerned citizens recommended these children would be better off in the colonies, and from an early date, young children were shipped out to Australia. An Orphan School was established near Prospect, close to Parramatta. Over the years, other organisations assumed responsibility for the protection of children. Despite these good motives, many young children between the ages of 9 and 13 arrived here or were collected here and put to work as farm hands, family help and other work.

Sunday school. *London Illustrated News* 1872

There was little consideration for play.

As society developed, so did its social conscience. The second half of the nineteenth century saw the establishment of numerous organisations to protect children. The Female Orphan Institute, The Orphan Home For Girls, The Blind, Deaf and Dumb Institute, The Crippled Children Society, The Preventorium Institution for Ailing Children and the Model Boys' Home. There were many Industrial Schools for both boys and girls, mostly for juvenile troublemakers who had been to court and sentenced to an institution.

The first part of the twentieth century saw a continuing need for these institutions, especially after WWI and even as late as the 1930s when capital cities had child vagrants abandoned because of the Depression.

The Empire Society, established in 1922, fostered over 200,000 British people to Australia, including young children, and the Big Brother Movement, founded in 1925, sent 12,264 boys and young men in the course of a decade.

LITTLE SAILOR BOYS. *The Vernon* Training Ship for Boys was one of the most famous and successful institutions. It was established in 1867 using a decommissioned sailing ship, *The Vernon*, anchored at Sydney's Cockatoo Island. Naval life was seen as disciplined, and the concept of 'young sailor boys' fitted Victorian and Edwardian ideals.

The *Vernon* was replaced by the *Sobraon* in 1892. It was three times bigger than the *Vernon,* and approximately 4000 boys passed under its sails until decommissioned in 1927. Boys were raised as 'little sailors' living and learning on the ship.

Little sailor boys on the training ship *Vernon*. *State Archives NSW*

A Hop, a Skip and a Jump

Little sailors boys on *The Sobroan*. State Archives NSW

Cockatoo Island also had an institution for wayward girls when the Biloela Industrial School for Girls was established in the 1870s. Both institutions were operated by the government as reform schools.

Lifeboat drill. Children with life vests. 1918. SLV

Post Federation migration

After Federation in 1901, Australia increased its immigration programs and again, post WWI, the country stepped up to take thousands of young children, including orphans. The White Australia Policy was enforced.

Children posing with lifeboat on *Oriana*. Museums Victoria

It must have been quite a challenge to muster and control hundreds of confused and excited children on long voyages like this one from 1950.[19]

New Australia's nurse keeps 400 children amused.

Children's nurse on *New Australia*, Mrs. H. Jones, had a big job ahead when the ship sailed from Southampton with over 400 children aboard. But Mrs Jones, who has been nursing children for 15 years, coped admirably. With only a playroom roughly twice the size of a normal bedroom, one toy boat, one slide, one see-saw, one miniature navigating bridge, and about 6 chairs at her disposal, she managed to keep all the young migrants amused most of the time, and most of them amused all the time. With the help of one stewardess she organised a tea party, fancy dress ball, hung rope swings from beams, held singing classes and provided white chalk for hopscotch and prizes for competitions and guessing games. She also set up a stage in the lounge and the children entertained the adults with a well-rehearsed concert. A passenger conducted school for the elder children in the mornings, and at set times the depth of water in the swimming pool was lowered for the younger children. Mrs. Jones has been at sea 5 years.

Children's hostess surrounded by toys onboard *Chusan*. P&O Heritage

Magic lantern shows were a highlight of many Victorian and early twentieth-century sea crossings. Magic lanterns — an early slide projector entertainment — could show 3D and even moving images (much like today's GIFs) to entertain captive audiences. The presentations usually came in series, including many that were specifically for children. *Puss In Boots, Jack And The Bean-Stalk* and other fairy tales were favourites. Series on Biblical stories like *Jonah and The Whale* were supplied by Christian societies and used for onboard Sunday School. There was even a series depicting *The Emigrant's Voyage*, which has passengers boarding, the ship's life, crossing the Equator, a disastrous fire at sea and the rescue of the passengers. Dramatic stuff for those who had never set foot on a ship before!

The Emigrant's Voyage to Australia. Theobold & Co. 1900

Emigrants boarding/Crossing the Line. *Theobold & Co.*

Children's afternoon tea or, better still, birthday parties during the voyage were exciting events. It was usual for the Captain to pop in to say hello.

Ship's Captain Playing Deck Game with Child. Sam Hood Collection. *Australian National Maritime Museum.*

Children's Fun at Sea.

A novel feature on the post-WW2 *New Himalaya* will be amusement facilities for children.[20]

In that section will be a slide, roundabout, and "whirl gig," gramophone with special records, library, and, perhaps most unusual of all, a model of the navigating bridge, complete with a movable steering wheel. Colour drawings on the walls are by Elaine Haxton, an Australian artist.

A Hop, a Skip and a Jump

Birthday party onboard ship. *A.F.U.*

IN THE 1960S, Italian ships transported thousands of assisted migrant families. According to diaries, the crew on these ships were experienced in amusing passengers.[21]

> The Italian crew were experts at organising people to entertain themselves. They had heaps of theatrical costumes and endless ideas about improvising. As a result, we had some memorable evenings, including Wild West night, Arabian night. Everyone got into the swing of it because the days were so boring.

Dressing up at sea. Alison Parsons. *Achilie Lauro. Museums Victoria*

In the nineteen-thirties, shipping lines began to open up most of the ship to all travellers... first, second and steerage. Entertainment was mainly directed at adults with singalongs, dances, lectures, magic lantern shows and talks to stimulate the mind. Children were expected to be 'seen but not heard'.

Sporting events like horse racing, cricket, boxing matches, and animal fights entertained children on later voyages. They also participated in popular activities like dancing, swimming, and boat racing.

A good old fashioned catch me race onboard *Canberra*. 1960s. ©
P&O Heritage Collection www.poheritage.com

Even today, some adults look back on their junior fascination with ship life. In a 2018 conversation[22] with pianist and musical arranger Bernard Waltz and company director Michael Hughes, both recounted how, as young children, they were fascinated by all things maritime, especially cruise ships and ship life. Their interest had been akin to a passion for stamp or coin collecting, except they collected deck plans for all the famous cruise ships from the White Star, Cunard, French Line, etc. Forty years later, they could still reminisce about deck plan oddities, the charm of certain rooms and hulk and funnel colours. As child passengers, they were 'entertained well' when they cruised to Europe or around the Pacific. They both had fond memories of the Matrons assigned to look after the child passengers. Some ships had separate dining rooms for the children; throughout the day and week, there was an endless program of activities and entertainment. Birthdays were always an occasion for a special party with hats, games and a cake. Some of the activities included plaster of Paris moulds, which, when ready, were painted. Hughes recalled making and painting a Humpty Dumpty figurine. Fancy dress parties were a popular pastime. Afternoon teas sometimes included a visiting uniformed officer. The pool was also full of action with races and games.

What better place to play 'Hide and Seek' than a tender. *A.W.W.* 1907

Crossing the line on the *Oriana*. *Museums Victoria*

KING NEPTUNE'S GARDEN. For most ships, the final leg of the journey to Australia included a celebration when crossing the Equator. Everyone was involved, as it alleviated the boredom of life on board. By this stage, passengers had come to know each other quite well, and some of the initial shyness and inhibitions had been broken down.

The origins of this ceremony go back to ancient Roman times when sailors made obsequious pleas to the god *Neptune*, the ruler of the seas, to bring them home safely.

'*Neptune's* Journey' or 'Crossing the Equator' has been a feature of immigrant voyages since the 1800s. However, it became increasingly elaborate in the twentieth century as shipping companies sought to attract more passengers.

Initially, the celebration largely recognised that the equator had been crossed safely and a significant part of the long journey was over. However, as the journey became safer, the ceremony became more entertaining and took on the flavour of the period. Thomas Park migrated from England in 1852 and recalled:

> Presently, old Father Neptune made his appearance dressed in full regalia. The crown on his head was dazzling, and the trident he carried was formidable.

Crossing the Line on *The Sobroan*. National Library of Australia

In one 'Crossing the Equator' ceremony, the crew were dressed in flowing robes or grass skirts and had painted faces. Passengers who volunteered were covered in shaving cream, shaved with mock razors and then thrown into the pool. Everyone, including children, received a certificate to mark the occasion.

School at Sea. 'Jean', writing in a New South Wales regional newspaper in 1914, wrote:[23]

> There were four hundred children aboard our ship, and it was proposed early in the voyage to give them a schooling similar to the schooling they would be having ashore. Twenty ladies volunteered their services as teachers, and a round number of three hundred responded cheerily to the first roll call. Every morning, as regularly as the meal gong came the call of the school bell, and away they went, happy little troops of youngsters, to their school on the upper deck. This kept them out of mischief and gave the mothers a rest. There was lots of musical talent aboard, which helped pass the nights.

In 1928, another newspaper reported on the large number of very young children on a particular voyage, dubbing it a 'baby' ship.[24]

> Children on the *Benalla*.
>
> A Baby Ship. That was how a ship's officer on the *Benalla*, which arrived this week from London, described the vessel. It was an apt description. Arriving at Fremantle the *Benalla* had onboard 880 passengers for Australian ports. Out of that total 171 were children under 12, and 67 were infants in arms. On the long trip out, the *Benalla* has been seven weeks at sea, experiencing rough weather practically from Capetown to Fremantle, but there was no sickness of any description.
>
> The *Benalla's* youthful passengers came from all parts of the United Kingdom. Scotland predominated, with England a good second. The children are going to the inland portions of the Commonwealth, and the majority are leaving the ship at Sydney. There were many families of five, six and seven children, but the

record was held by Mr and Mrs William Fraser, who will increase the New South Wales population by nine. Mr and Mrs Fraser came from Shortts, Lanarkshire, Scotland, and the ages of their children are Richard 11, Jean 9, May 8. Jessie G, Don and Jim (twins) 5, Ian 3, Robert 2 (he had his birthday on the ship yesterday), and Margaret six months old. Mrs Fraser's father and mother are already in Sydney. On the voyage a boy was born, and was christened James Benalla O'Hara.

~

Father Christmas at sea.
Illustrated Sydney News

SPECIAL DAYS like Easter and Christmas were a cause for additional fun for children. At Easter, eggs, sweets and small toys were hidden around the ship, and a hunt was announced. Father Christmas appeared on Christmas Day and gave children sweets and presents. [25] A concert typically followed.

Children Flee From Ship's Santa

Young children of displaced persons in the migrant ship *Nelly* fled in terror when they saw Santa Claus on Christmas Day. Ship's officers said this when *Nelly* berthed at Sydney yesterday morning. Chief steward Willy Ernst said the Caribbean Land and Shipping Company of Panama City, owners of *Nelly*, had provided presents for the children. Santa Claus was the ship's linen-keeper, full-faced, smiling Birger Scheen. "On Christmas Day, we made Santa a robe out of two red flags, gave him a mask and a beard, and presented him to the children at their Christmas tree," said Ernst.

"As he came up to the Christmas tree on deck the little ones who had never seen Santa Claus before ran away crying. Birger didn't know what to do until the first assistant in the engine-room brought out a life-size doll and gave it to him. "Santa Claus took the doll in his arms and walked around the deck, showing it to the children. They weren't afraid of him then and soon caught on when he started handing out the gifts."

L: B deck nursery on *Rangitang*, 1937. R: Playroom on *Orcades* (Orient Line) 1948. *State Library Victoria*

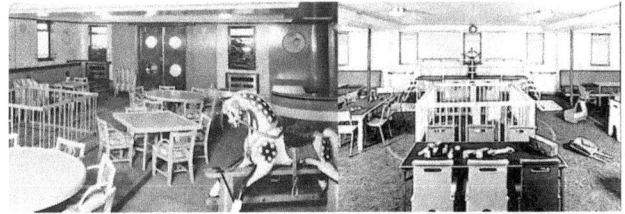

L: *P&O Himalaya* 1st Class nursery, 1960. R: 1st Class Nursery *Orcades* (Orient Line) 1948. *P&O Heritage Collection*

By the late 1930s, many sea cruise holidays were usually marketed as family affairs. Local lines typically cruised around the Pacific going up to Vanuatu, Tonga, Fiji, Samoa and New Zealand. Post WW2, for those who could afford it, and preferred sea over air, saw an increasing market for more exotic outbound itineraries, including the Middle East, en route to England. In the late 1950s and early 60s, cruise prices out of Australia were inexpensive as lines tried to balance their books and fill the many arriving migrant ships on their return journeys.

June and Brian Foster at Port Said, Egypt, on the *MV Georhic*, 1955. *Museums Victoria*

Shipboard Life "Great Fun" - Happy Children.[26]

'Great fun' was how the party of British children who reached Melbourne on Sunday morning described their voyage from England. The children were divided into six sections, and there was keen rivalry among them to secure for their respective sections the greatest number of marks each week when the winning section received as a trophy a beautiful Dutch doll. Marks were given for all kinds of competitions, games for spelling bees, and essays. One small lad with a particularly merry twinkle in his eye volunteered the information that naughty pranks meant the loss of marks and added with a disarming smile that his section had received the booby prize, which was a toy pig, four times.

For the younger children, however, the trip was not all play, as all those under 12 had to attend school two mornings a week. During the voyage, the children gave several concert performances, including a play entitled *The Tale of Wiggle Woggle*, written by Leonard Ellis, one of the party.

Several families were on board, the largest of which were the MacLagans. Sheila aged 14, has acted as 'mother' to Brenda, aged 12, Ian, aged 11, and John who turned 10 the day of the arrival in Melbourne. The Child Welfare Organisation has tried where possible to keep families together, in the case of the MacLagans, Sheila and John will live with a family in Brighton, while Brenda and Ian will be with relatives of this family who live at Croydon. Thus the children will be able to keep in touch with each other and often see one another.

The ship's captain was so popular among the children that they took up a collection among themselves and gave him a present - a mulga wood tobacco holder. "He was so nice to us, and let us do all sorts of things, and gave us parties," they said. The children also gave a mulga wood inkstand to the chief escort.

Joy For Children In Modern Shipboard Life. 1937[27]

In this age of thoughtful planning and luxurious accommodation for travellers, children have not been forgotten in the design of modern passenger liners. Facilities are provided for the comfort, entertainment, and above all, the safety of children. Seas, beaches, and islands are represented on the nursery floor of one large passenger vessel, where a miniature ship, with steering wheels and cabins under its 'decks.' holds pride of place among the novelties to entertain the children. There is even a boat-shaped mattress as tender to the ship.

In another liner, a slide with platforms of different levels caters for the climbing ambitions of the young 'sailors.' Closely wired railings surround the edges of the deck nursery where a novel note is introduced by a long seat resting between the trunks of two wooden elephants, a drawing room suite, an exact replica of the real one on board, gives that feeling of 'grown-up importance,' and side by side in the playground area stand two rocking horses.

There are always stewardesses to take care of the children on board, and they are, generally, trained nurses. Then, at the end of a long but exciting day. comes the dinner hour. The tiny travellers sit side by side in their own specially equipped dining saloon to eat food suited to their ages.

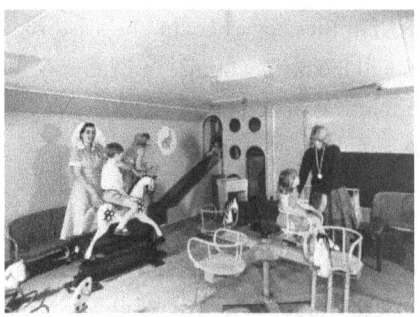

1st class nursery *P & O Himalaya*. 1960. *State Library of Victoria*

MODERN AUSTRALIA IS OFTEN CALLED the world's most successful multicultural country. We have more cultural groups than any other nation, including the United Kingdom, Canada, and the United States of America. The majority of our migrants arrived by ship.

After World War 2, Australia believed that it must increase its population to avoid invasion and launched an immigration program whose goal was to increase Australia's population with the slogan "populate or perish". Hundreds of displaced Europeans came to Australia after the war, and altogether more than three million people immigrated from Europe from the late 1940s until the 1960s. Our migration programs concentrated on young people from the United Kingdom were particularly favoured and many brought young families. It was a successful program; however, the availability of ships limited the flow. The government looked to other European countries and flows from Italy, Greece, Estonia, and Latvia to continue the program. Local shipping lines were enlisted. After the White Australia Policy was eased by Prime Minister Holt in 1966 and officially disbanded by Prime Minister Whitlam in 1973, Australia saw much more Asian immigration.

Many migrant ships were at capacity and, travel was sometimes arduous, especially for non-English speaking young families. Shipping lines, carrying a mini United Nations, did their best to keep passengers safe and amused. Programs about what to expect in

Australia were particularly important. Some ships conducted English classes, and Australian information newsreels were also screened. There were also occasions for the entertainment of the children. Marianna Mazzarino, who travelled on the *TN Rome* in 1961, is shown in the following image at Christmas Day celebrations, with an unusual Santa Claus who looks like he had climbed down the ship's sooty funnel to spread cheer.

Mazzarino family on the *TN Roma* 1961. *Museums Victoria*

Young passengers on the P&O *Canberra* in 1962 were invited to a Sport's Day program that included a potato race, egg and spoon race, sack race, obstacle race, tug-of-war, and a special race for mothers and fathers. The highlight must have been the 'babies crawling race'.

IN 1972, young passengers aboard the P&O *Canberra* were invited to a Tea Party with an exhaustive and somewhat exotic menu offering: cream soup, sausages on sticks, grilled filet steak with mushrooms, baked beans, noodles in tomato sauce, minced lamb followed by ice cream, assorted jellies, strawberry milkshakes, fancy pastries, peanut butter, party cake and cocoa. Milk puddings were available on request!

Promotional leaflet from Australian Government 'Australia's offer to the British boy'. *Australian National Archive*

A BETTER LIFE. More than 130,000 children were sent to a 'better life' in former colonies, mainly Australia and Canada, from the 1920s to 1970s under the child migrant program.

Fairbridge Children onboard and ready to travel. *A.F.U.*

Fairbridge Farm School, Molong NSW arriving ex SS *Oronsay* 23 April 1938

Aged between 3 and 14, these children were almost invariably from deprived backgrounds and already in some form of social or charitable care. Many of the children were on record as 'orphans'; however, recent investigations show that, although some were genuine orphans, many were from single parents forced by economic and social circumstances to surrender their children to care facilities. The belief being they would lead healthier and better lives. Most parents had no idea where their children would be sent.

Charities such as Barnardo's and the Fairbridge Farm School, the Anglican and Catholic churches and local authorities helped organise emigration. Kingsley and Ruby Fairbridge established the world's first Fairbridge Farm School in Albany, West Australia, in 1912, expressing, "little children shedding the bondage of bitter circumstances and stretching their legs and minds amid the thousand interests of the farm." The program eventually brought 3580 children to Australia. Much of the playtime focussed on competitive sports, including the school's own 'Olympics'.

It would not be cynical to say some of these organisations had ulterior motives. Some children found they were expected to provide free labour, and some church-run orphanages and foster homes have much to be ashamed of. Children were often ill-treated, separated from their siblings and too often were subjected to physical and sexual abuse.

2

INDIGENOUS PLAY

Kids poking fun. 1908. H. D. Bulmer, Lake Tyers, Victoria. *A.F.U.*

T*he area of Indigenous play is a specialist study and far beyond my competence. This chapter is included simply as an introduction and acknowledgement of the fruitful world of Indigenous children's play culture.*

The available evidence - explorers' and settlers' accounts, official records etc., makes clear that pre-European childhood was fairly idyllic. There were obvious challenges for the mainland hunter-gatherer people, but overall, family life was well-structured and favoured children. Young children were essentially the responsibility of female extended family members with men keeping an eye on developing skills that would be useful in later life. Initiation marked a rite of passage from childhood to adulthood. Play was (and in some areas still is) directly related to the skills and knowledge that would be essential to survival. In play, they engaged in activities that stimulated their imagination, developed muscle coordination and strengthened their powers of observation.

Surveying Aboriginal and Islander children's amusements understandably needs to reflect the diverse territorial and cultural spread of the Aboriginal and Torres Strait Islander people and the fact that before European settlement, there were between 250 and 600 different nations inhabiting the continent and surrounding islands. Tribal community life encouraged children to enjoy games, dance, music, and toys. Most mainland people were hunter-gatherers, and to some extent, nomads, and this meant that material possessions were limited. Many of the games used improvised balls and other artefacts and few toys were retained. New balls and toys could be made. Children were also expected to help gather food by picking berries, collecting firewood, checking fish traps, and helping the women prepare food. Games and songs were used on such occasions.

When I started visiting Aboriginal and islander communities in the late nineteen sixties, very little was known about Indigenous play. Yet, all the early anthropologists noted the important role of children and how they were incorporated into society. Some Indigenous children's songs were recorded, and some 'observations' were made. Today, museums, libraries and the Australian Institute of Aboriginal and Torres Strait Islander Studies actively document all aspects of traditional and contemporary life. Studies have examined and compared Indigenous playmaking in other countries. At first glance, much of Indigenous playmaking appears to mimic adult behaviour and the tools used in general community life such as warfare and hunting. Miniature tools and weapons are fashioned out of wood or reeds and shaped to resemble totem animals or reptiles such as tortoises, stingrays and snakes. Dances and songs were adapted to suit children.

Lake Tyers, Victoria, 1908. H. D. Bulmer

The most knowledgeable person in the area of Indigenous children's games, Ken Edwards, noted:[1]

> The accounts of traditional games often need to be placed in the cultural context for a particular group even if they can no longer be meaningfully interpreted by that continuing group. For many of the hunter-gatherer and some other types of societies, once present, there was a relatively large amount of leisure time available for cultural practices, which included traditional games. Based on accounts available there were a limited number of games in some cultural groups while other groups had a much larger number of traditional games recorded. Where food-gathering for survival in small family groups was required there were fewer games and less time available for traditional games. Although the Aboriginal and Torres Strait Islander peoples sought to amuse themselves, they appreciated the benefits of relaxing or 'doing nothing' as opposed to the need always to be doing something. The concept or idea of boredom may have had different meanings and interpretations in various Aboriginal and Torres Strait Islander cultures.

Improvised play Alice Springs, 1927. Photographed by Theodor Bray.
SLSA B64383/109

Indigenous play changed with the times. Mission schools, sanctioned by Government policy, replaced traditional games with competitive European games. Corroboree dances were replaced with hopscotch and rounders. Traditional string making and reed weaving were replaced by sewing and knitting. Physical sport was encouraged and seen as a 'clean and healthy' activity, especially where teamwork was involved, and competition between external groups especially so. Edwards suggests that this was an exertion of power to some extent, and games like cricket were an example of British 'civilisation'.

Bobbing for apples at Nepabunna Mission, 1936. SLSA B48970

'Father Christmas' visited the missions every December and distributed gifts to the children. The 'Easter Bunny' also made an annual visit. It is difficult to imagine what the children and their parents thought of all this change. Considering the anguish and confusion created by the Stolen Generation programs, they likely surrendered, adding to their misery and diminished view of their new world. As the mission schools retreated and the communities returned to a more normal way of life, albeit still with much interference and confusion, the children, like all children, improvised in their play. Toys were made from available junk, much of it the remnants of old buildings, cars, etc. They also invented new games, many incorporating indigenous traditional games with the newer ones. In some ways, these communities had one saving grace - the absence of television.

In 1983, Robyn Howell wrote about the Kwiambul people of the Ashford district, north-west New South Wales.[2]

> Children were taught all through their lives. Much of their childhood was spent in learning, but they had time for games, singing and dancing. Discipline with the children was rarely needed. They had so much to do they would have found it difficult to get into mischief. There was always someone around to help them, play with them, tell them stories, sing to them, and teach them what they had to learn. They copied many of the things they saw the older people doing. They learned to swim when they were very young, and loved to play in the water.
>
> Children were taught from an early age to be perceptive. For instance, the following is one of their training games. They were shown an area, then objects were added to or taken away from this area. The children had to be able to say what was added or what was missing, even to the smallest stone or stick. Another method was to have them pick out an ant from a group of ants, then follow the movement of that ant, no matter how many ants were there.
>
> Endurance and ability were tested constantly in many ways. There were often competitions to see who could club the quickest, throw a spear most accurately over a distance, or retrieve an object from a branch.

In 1934, a Sydney newspaper mentioned a list of tests given by

Aboriginal people to their children[3]. For each test, there was a certain time allowed for them to train, and then they had their test. One test was to find a small bird's eye that had been buried. Another was to track frogs that had been set free by a stream. The children had not seen where the frogs had been released, and their test was to track their prints across pebbles and find the frogs. If nothing else, these fascinating examples show how far Europeans have been removed from the environment.

Australian literary legend Dame Mary Gilmore grew up in the Wagga Wagga region and observed local Aboriginal children at play.[4]

> The training of the very young children is the women's work. I have seen a mother take a small twig, break it till only about three inches of wood and a knot were left. A toddler of two years taught first to recognise it among others held in the hand, and then to find it when thrown a distance, the child being given only a general idea of the direction in which it had been thrown, sometimes it would be a small piece of grass-stem that would be used.

One of the leaders of the women from the Wiradjuri clan started to teach young Mary Gilmore to count through play in the Aboriginal way of group counting:

> She began as she would with her own children, showing me two fingers, two sticks laid together, two eyes, two ears, two elbows, two feet. She did not show me two thumbs then, as thumbs had a group meaning, and she did not want to confuse me. Later, she used tiny sticks, bark fragments and little clods of earth. This was to show through differing shapes or differing places, two remained two, and it was also to make the child quick in perception. As soon as I grasped two, I went to threes... I have not seen the Guaranis (from Paraguay) count the stars, but as a child, I saw the Aborigines do it many a time, and the smallest of them could beat me at it. I used to number by our arithmetical progression, and being small, I would lose my count and my place in the heavens at about three or four hundred, but the little

Aboriginal children of the same age still kept on.... Aboriginal stockmen could quickly count the number of cattle in a mob of about four or five hundred in no time at all by using group counting...

Basic warfare and hunting games started with male children when they were young. Both were means of survival in an often hostile environment. Whilst the idea was to have fun, the learning was serious. Boys needed to know which reeds and trees provided the best materials to fashion toy spears, shields and boomeramgs, how to creep noiselessly through bushland, accurately throw spears or boomerangs, patiently stand in the sea and rivers to catch fish and turtles and to respect nature. Girls needed to make string, which reeds to use to make fish traps, baskets, etc, and how to prepare food and natural medicines.

It was important for boys to know which reeds and trees provided the best materials to fashion toy spears, shields and boomerangs. Girls needed to know about native fibres and how to make string for nets, baskets, etc.

Anthropologist Herbert Basedow described using toy spears made from bulrushes and reeds.[5]

> With these "weapons," the lads have both mock fights and mock hunts. In the latter case, one or two of them act the part of either a hopping kangaroo or a strutting emu and, by clever body movements, endeavour to evade the weapons of the hunting gang.

Adults or children fashioned toy spears from reeds, spear grass, native bamboo, or wood. They also made toy boomerangs and bullroarers.

Alan Marshall described spear play that took place in Milingimbi, in the Northern Territory.[6]

> The children rushed to a lump of rushes where they gather bundles of the stiff straight stems for use as spears. They took sides and commenced throwing them at each other... They went swiftly

through the grass in a crouching run, they leapt from behind trees and yelled in mock ferocity. They circled each other warily, vibrating their knees, dancing from foot to foot... They were very accurate in their throwing and experts were recognised as in all children's games

Playing a game called 'animal tracks' encouraged and demanded particular skills. The players, mainly young boys, reproduced the tracks of animals scored, dabbed, or scratched into surfaces like sand, rock, or tree. These tracks were also interpreted with dance steps. In Central Australia, children would inspect sandhills in the early morning to see what specific animal tracks had been made during the night, identify them, and then practice imitating them.

For example, the player would produce tracks for a kangaroo that was grazing, for one that was running, and a different one again for a female carrying a joey. Where camel tracks were known, a camel track would be made by momentarily sitting a baby on a smooth patch of sand - the imprint of its buttocks supplying the outline!

In a coastal area, children would leave turtle tracks in the sand by kneeling and thrusting out the sides of their legs. Imitating an animal's gait and the animal and bird calls were practised with great enjoyment.

WESTERN SOCIETY HAS a long history of keeping pet animals. The Aboriginal people semi-domesticated wild dogs, and children would make pets of the young of various species - baby magpies, koalas, wallabies, frogs, goannas, cassowaries, turtles, brush turkeys, carpet snakes (having first had their teeth removed), and possums. It has been observed that pet cockatoos would learn to speak phrases of the Aboriginal language. Pet animals would usually be tethered to a tree with string. A baby wallaby might be carried around on the head, claws clinging to its owner's hair. A hunting party often brought home a young animal for the children's amusement.

Indigenous relationships with animals reflected the role of game in their diet. Other than dogs, pet animals were viewed as disposable and often consumed.

Anthropologist Dr Walter Edmund Roth observed boys and girls playing at hunting and preparing food. The boys playing with toy boomerangs, spears, woomeras and shields while the girls played with dolls, baskets and digging sticks. He also observed them enacting family situations in Cape York:[7]

> Playing at "Houses", "Grown-up", "Marriage", etc, is in one form or another as common among black children as it is among white ones. On the Upper Normanby, the youngsters pretending to be married will build an impromptu hut, and sit contentedly within its shade; suddenly a boy rushes forward to steal a [girl], over whose possession he and the husband now make-believe to have a fight. On the Lower Tully, the boys and girls will make miniature huts... and finally go away in couples into the scrub. It is a game often being played, but whenever the parents catch them at it they generally give them both a good smacking.

Such playing 'house' or 'family' included building windbreaks placed in the correct positions relative to one another according to the inhabitants' relationships. They learned to build with the right materials and in the correct way.

Doll 'children' of the family were simple but effective representations. The most popular was a forked stick placed over the shoulders or a 'baby' made from grass tied together to make it compact.

Indigenous doll from Mapoon, Cape York, Queensland. Collected in 1903 by Dr. Walter Roth. *Australian Museum.*

String Games

Australian Aboriginal and Islander people were highly skilled in making native string and creating string games where the string is looped across hands and fingers to create a picture, often a moving picture like a wallaby hopping. Dame Mary Gilmore recalled the young girls and women playing the game we know as 'Cat's Cradle', and that there were at least seventy variations of the game. [8]

> "They were played mostly around the fire and taught to children." She added, "I once knew the 'Flying Possum running up a tree and out on a branch', 'The kookaburra laughing' and one or two others."

Teaching string games.

String was made from natural bark or fibre typically 'spun' by looping the fibre around the toes and twisting until the 'string' develops. Later, where tufts of wool or fur might be available, they were spun into the string. The string was used for everyday binding and playmaking, especially string games. Hundreds of indigenous string games have been collected, many extremely complicated. Coupled with storytelling, they are extremely effective. Howells observed a string game called 'Lightning' where the continuous string was placed around the necks of two little girls facing one another, and a small piece of wood twisted in it. When they bent their heads back, the wood would be catapulted out.[9]

Ken Edwards put the string game tradition in perspective as:[10]

> String games are almost universally part of traditional Aboriginal and Torres Strait Islander play and movement expressions. Playing string games, either singly or with groups of players, was a commonly recorded activity within Australia as it was in other cultures around the world. The string games had different levels of meaning and forms in different cultures and were associated with the opportunity to exchange ideas/knowledge or communicate and have fun with others. Usually, string games were played by the girls and women, sometimes at special times and for special purposes, such as during the first pregnancy or as part of storytelling. In some areas, men also played string games. String figure designs often represented animals and people or abstract ideas such as the forces of nature. As people played the string game, designs would change quickly from one thing to another.

It stands to reason that a culture highly skilled in making string dilly bags and fish traps would have a wider use for string, including playtime.

G. A.V. Stanley, a science research scholar from the University of Sydney, writing to the *Gundagai Independent and Pastoral, Agricultural and Mining Advocate* in 1926, mentioned having:[11]

> I collected over sixty patterns, chiefly from children at Yarrabah Mission Station, near Cairns, and several more from natives of Darnley Island, in Torres Straits, near Darwin. Although essentially a game played by children, many women and men remember the

patterns and delight in teaching them to anyone patient enough to learn.

An earlier newspaper article, from *The Australasian*, 1902, under 'Science Notes by 'Physics' described some of the Aboriginal string games:[12]

> Perhaps the most remarkable of all the children's games is Cat's Cradle, so well known to our children. Dr. A. R. Wallace, in his book on the Malay Islands, tells us that one wet day when time hung heavily, he thought he would amuse his native servants by teaching them some of the points of the game. They looked on politely till he had finished, and then borrowed the string and showed him that the European was a mere novice in the act. In the same way the North Queensland aborigine is an expert, and Dr. Roth has been at an immense amount of trouble to draw the complicated figures that they make, and a series of nearly eighty pictures is the result. . We understand that Dr. Roth vouches for the fact that all his drawings will work out. It requires a good deal of imagination, often, on the part of the players to see any resemblance between the loops of string and the objects they are supposed to delineate. Still we have vague recollections of being satisfied in our childhood that a series of loops did very closely resemble "a bunch of candles"- whatever that was. Amongst the figures given of this method of representing objects by hoops of string, as given by the author are women in various occupations; animals such as kangaroos, bandicoots, cranes, emu, bats, snakes, crabs, and other. The representation of a palm tree is particularly good, and others are decidedly suggestive. The game seems to widely spread in Australia, for Bunce, in 1857, describes it as played by children in the Westernport Ranges. It is not confined to children, for both men and women occasionally play at it. During the progress of manufacture of some of the figures, hands, feet, mouth, and knees may all be employed, and as sometimes two loops of string are used, a couple of assistants may be pressed into the service.

A contributor to *The World's News* in June 1934 described indigenous string making.

> Even the youngest members of the tribe are taught string-making, and any Aboriginal can generally supply his own wants. They use mainly animal fur, hair (even their own), wool, and the bark of many native trees and shrubs. The medium is generally teased and thinned out by hand. Then, sufficient to make the desired thickness is worked and rubbed, often for hours, against the naked thigh. It is incredible how strong the string gets, and the joins stand any amount of strain.

Roth also mentions other games played with hands. One, similar to charades, involved acting out the structure of a tree from which native beans were plucked or honey was gathered. Questions and answers were part of the game.[13]

Eleanor Adams studied indigenous children's games for her Graduate Diploma in Child Development at I.E.C.D. in 1984. She describes the 'Honey' game as played in North Queensland. The game is imitation of the search for bush honey.[14]

> Played by two or more young children of both sexes. The children squat on the ground, each placing the tips of the fingers over another child's hand below. These six hands represent the trunk of a tree. The tree is symbolically felled by a side cut, knocked from above down. Before knocking off the lowest hand, its owner puts her finger into each digital interspace to see if any honey has dropped. She pretends to find a snake there and tells her mates. All three children hold their hands behind their backs, and the following dialogue ensues:
> A: "Have you a tomahawk?"
> B: "No."
> A: "Are you sure you haven't one?"
> B: "I have a very little one."
> A: "Well then, give me the little one."

B then proceeds to hand over the imaginary tomahawk. B's arm, the wrist of which is held by A. next represents the trunk or limbs in which the honeycomb is found. A. then makes a chop at the elbow to cut off the limb encircling as far as she can the joint with her fingers and, from here, rubs the limb once upwards and once downwards to indicate complete discontinuity. (it is interesting to note that the upper portion of the tree where the comb lies is 'taboo' to the women. But the lower portion where the dirt and drippings are is 'free' to them.)

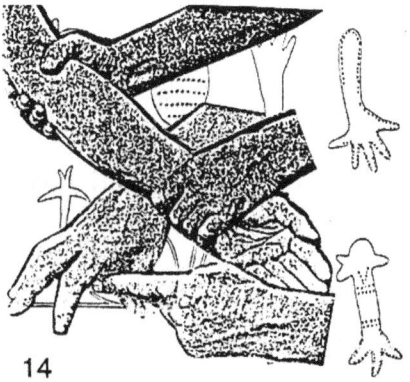

The Honey Game. A.F.U.

A. now does exactly the same to B's other arm, then goes over the same process with C's arms and finally does the same with her own. The honey is now supposed to have been collected from the removed limbs and mixed with water, placed in a bark, though represented by all the cupped hands resting upon one another.

Each bends down her head in turn to get a taste. "Too sweet!" is the verdict. They pretend to add more water and make a show of eating it when satisfied with the consistency.

ADAMS DESCRIBED a memory training game of the Walbri people of the Northern Territory.[15]

> The children make a large circle on the ground and around this are placed pieces of sticks, stones and odd bits of things to represent objects in that area. Should the children live near a highway, the sticks represent bridges, stone houses, bits of earth, motor trucks etc. As many as fifty objects are placed around the circle at any one time. The leader of the game places the articles along the circle line and arranges them. He calls the others to examine the positions, when they are satisfied they have memorised them, they turn their backs.
>
> The first player calls an object at a given point and continues to call each article on the line until he/she calls wrongly, then another player takes up the call. When all fail, they go away once more while the leader arranges the pieces for the next game.

Storytelling has always been a favourite pastime and, in some areas, has also involved music, dance, and puppetry. Certainly, in the Muni Muni tradition of Central Australia, the storytellers used leaves as representative puppets as part of the telling. Other storytellers would draw images in sand or use pebbles to illustrate their tales.

SKIPPING, that perennial favourite, was played using native string or vines swung to and fro like a pendulum. Ken Edwards explains:[16]

> A favourite game of the Juwalarai people of New South Wales was brambahl or skipping. As a long rope was turned by two players the player in the middle performed a number of actions such as jumping like a frog or taking thorns out of their feet. The winner was the player who could vary their performance the most. A skipping game played called jirrakayi-ku (which means jumping in the Panyima dialect) was played in northern Victoria. In playing this game as many as 12 players at a time skipped.

The campfire as play-central.

The campfire was an essential element of Indigenous life, and while Aboriginal people were skilled at lighting fires, they often carried burning cinders from one camp to another for convenience. Children were raised respecting fire and learned about it from an early age. C. P. Mountford writes about this early relationship.[17]

> Children would sit around the fires, chanting their childish songs. They would play with fire-sticks to set alight shrubs and tufts of grass, driving out lizards and small game. They also enjoyed pinning two long leaves together with a thorn, which, when thrown on a large smokey fire, would whirl upward on a hot current of air.

According to Edwards, numerous fire games were played, and the campfire was also a natural place for related activities.[18]

> The kal boming (fire hitting) game was played in the Southern districts of Western Australia and called for both agility and strength. A fire was lit either on the ground or the top of a Xanthorrhoea ("grass tree") and the players divided themselves into teams. One side tried to put the fire out with short branches of trees while the other side defended it. A wrestling game of the Ngungar people of the south-west of Western Australia was called meetcha kambong. A meetcha (nut) was buried about 20cms underground. Four or five players guarded it while an equal number attempted to dig it up. Only pushing and pulling was allowed. Each year teams from far and wide gathered at a "place of wrestling" (at Dingulami) in Kabi Kabi territory in Southern Queensland for a wrestling competition. Each pair in the competition attempted to push each other back over a line. Various forms of wrestling for a bunch of emu feathers or similar held by a player were played in different areas of the southern parts of Australia. Tur-dur-er-rin was a wrestling game from Victoria. Wrestlers placed their hands on each other's upper arms near the shoulders, and holding on tight, moved around, pushing and pulling in an attempt to knock the other to the ground.

Girls also played games around the fire. In her memoirs, Daisy Bates recalled how the young girls would play 'firesticks'.[19]

Girls have also a game played with a lighted firestick, similar to the European game. A firestick is taken and twirled round and round, the player calling out the names of all the fish she can think of until the light goes out.

Above all, the campfire was the central place for childhood pastimes. Certainly, singing and dancing were the favourite amusements. This is not surprising when one considers the central role of the campfire for nourishment, warmth and ceremony. Kids would compete in jumping over the flames and devising fire games. Guessing games were extremely popular. One might be staged around the result of a day's hunt - guessing what the men saw or what the women saw when gathering reeds and food. The campfire was also the place to dance, sing and play music.

Anthropologist T. Hernandez, writing in 1941, says of the Drysdale River children:[20]

> The most favourite entertainment for native children is dancing and singing. No sooner is a dance invented than they are practising it for themselves...They dance as if their lives depend on it.

The corroboree was always the standout event of the adult world, and the children took immense interest in learning the dances. They held their children's corroborees to practise the steps, inevitably trying to outdo each other in improvisation and mimicry.

Toys.

Indigenous children did not have or appear to need many toys. Necessity and reality are the parents of invention and play creativity. Just as today's toddlers will find fun and adventure in old cardboard boxes, Aboriginal and Islander kids made fun of what was available; they could make play toys out of just about anything. Robyn Howell continues:[21]

They played with what was known in some areas as a 'weet weet' which was a small knob of wood attached to a flexible stick, up to or over a half a metre long. This could be twirled around rapidly. Toy spears, boomerangs and other implements were made from wood by the fathers for their sons, and for the girls they made toy digging sticks. Girls learned to make woven baskets and net bags. When they were very young, their mothers, aunts or grandmothers would weave little bags so they could carry their 'babies' just like their mothers. These were made from wood, grass or mud, whatever was handy at the time... Balls were made from various things such as rolled-up possum skins, tightly laced into a round shape; wet mud made a quick, ready-to-use ball for an instant game. These, or a disc of bark, made a rolling target for their toy spears.

Lyn Love, writing in 1983, observed 'wit wits' in Queensland.[22]

> Wit Wit - is described as something with a spindle shaped head made from wood) or, again, as a club-shaped playing stick of mulga. It had many names (including Wik Wik, Weet Weet, kukerra etc) and was played with in widely distributed areas of Australia and the Torres Strait islands. It was thrown by the men, especially at an ant hill or tussock, from which it would ricochet and hop like a kangaroo rat or slide like a snake - to the amusement of the children. It was played with by children in Queensland where it was described as being 'like a tadpole' and called a Tirra.

Lyn Love tells of a game called 'Tipcat'—played by sharpening both ends of a short wooden peg, making it jump by striking one end with a somewhat longer stick, and batting it as far as possible while it is in the air. This is not far removed from the common game known as 'aerial cricket' or 'aerial baseball', where an object is thrown in the air and belted with any form of bat.

Games of physical prowess were extremely popular, especially for those boys nearing initiation age. Early photographic images show young children as very healthy-looking with taut bodies and keen eyes. Their natural diet and physical activities kept them agile and healthy. Unsurprisingly, games like wrestling, mock fights, dodging and tug-of-war were popular. In coastal areas with rivers and billabongs, aquatic games were similar to any child's visit to water: diving, water fights, underwater swimming, swings and sliding on bark across the slippery sand or mud.

They were also highly skilled in making models with clay and bark. A separate, more contemporary tradition has evolved for making wire figures. They can be of a stockman or horse and are found in many regional communities where the men work as stockmen or drovers.

Sue Thomas, an Institute of Early Development graduate, spent 1988 and 1989 in Hall's Creek, West Australia, where she observed local children making tow truck toys out of old Sunshine powdered milk tins (billies were also used for similar tow toys).[23]

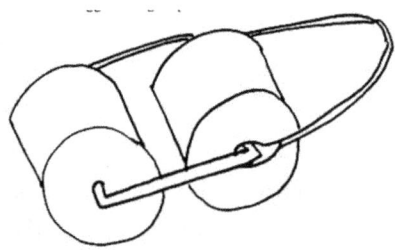

Sunshine Powdered Milk Can toy truck. 1989/90

They put two holes in the tins and thread wire through - wire as thick as coat hangers - so that the tins can be dragged along or pushed in front.

Much has been written about the universal popularity of the traditional 'Hide and Seek game. Lyn Love highlights two variations played by Indigenous children.[24]

Hide and Seek. The seekers would hide their eyes by placing their heads on the ground or looking into the sun.

Hide the object. The object being the lens from the eye of a cooked fish hidden in a patch of sand, or a goanna claw hidden in the bark of a tree.

One game, similar to 'I'm the king of the castle', possibly called the 'sand game', involved building a sand mound where the 'king' sat, and others tried to topple him or her from the royal seat.

Sport

Indigenous sportsmen and women are now considered among the world's best, especially in the various sorts of football. Many different ball games were played in traditional society. Balls were made from available materials, including kangaroo bladders stuffed with fur and grass and then sewn with sinew, plaited bandanas, wild melon, or even wood. Later, footballs were made from wet newspaper and rags tightly bound with string.

Howells observed football.[25]

> Children and adults played ball games which sometimes could last for hours. In one of these each side had a leader and the idea of the game was to keep the ball away from the other side by throwing it around the team, or by kicking it. The feather game was also enjoyed by both children and adults. A stick with a feather attached was placed on the ground. One side defended the stick, while the other side tried to get it. A great amount of wrestling and struggling went on to protect the feather stick. Wrestling was popular (including team wrestling).

Edwards talks about hunt-related skill games.[26]

> Spearing the disc of bark or disc rolling was a favourite game in most parts of Australia and there were different versions. In one area it was called gorri and a player would call gool-gool before rolling the disc in front of a line of throwers. Sometimes the disc would be bounced along the ground or thrown into the air. A spear dodging game called

tambil tambil was played by the Jagara people of southern Queensland. One player stood 10-15 metres out in front of the rest of the group and hopped around as the other player tried to hit them. In another version played elsewhere the player being used as a target could use a small shield to protect themselves. In the Wembawemba language of western Victoria the word ngalembert referred to an expert at dodging spears.

Edwards also mentions games of stone rolling. One, 'Turlurlu', from the Great Sandy Desert of Central Australia, has each player holding a mukurro, or fighting stick, as a bat. Each team takes turns to underarm bowl a wild ball (colloquially known as a 'kamikaze') at the opposing team, aiming to make it pass through the line without being hit. Another game was more like tag bowling, where a player threw a marker stone, and others tried to hit that stone.

A telling feature of play within indigenous society is the fact that participation and skill were more important than winning. Admirably, there was no keeping score or awarding of prizes.[27]

> Feats of skill received admiration and respect: while ridicule and whoops of derision greeted a poor showing. Certainly in some cases, older men would watch a game to assess the potential skills of the young hunters.

Eleanor Adams discussed how the Djinghali people of the Northern Territory played ball.[28]

> The ball is similar to one used in cricket, but it is made of grass tied up tightly with string, then covered with beeswax. Sides are taken (as in football) and the game is started by kicking the ball into the air. Once kicked off, hands must not touch the ball again, only the feet. The side that has kept it in the air and away from the other is the winner.

A Hop, a Skip and a Jump

Lake Condah Aboriginal Station, Corranderck.: children playing cricket, 1874. A.F.U.

Numerous accounts in the diaries of settlers, explorers, anthropologists as well as artist depictions point to the widespread existence of a ball game not only in South-Eastern Australia but also in the Northern Territory. The game not only served as amusement but also as a means of reinforcing kin relationships.

In a number of these accounts that predate 1858, the date attributed to Tom Wills for the creation of Australian football, extensive descriptions are given that reference the quintessential elements of AFL, that is, keeping the ball in the air, free flowing play and high marking.[29]

The earliest sketch of a 'parndo' or oval football of the Kaurna Adelaide Plains people is found in AW Cawthorne's papers held in the Mitchell Library dating from the 1840s; 'The players stand together in a ring or a line. One of them kicks the ball in the air, sometimes to the height of fifty feet... The merit of the game is to kick the ball perpendicularly and to keep it in the air as long as possible.'

NOTE: *This section is primarily based on material from old newspapers, citing early anthropological works and memoirs and using phrases from earlier times. Many of the words, like 'blackfellows', 'natives' and 'primitives' are not acceptable today but however condescending and insensitive they may appear, they are a matter of public record. Some items come from children's sections in regional and metro newspapers where*

editors, one assumes, were trying their best to explain Indigenous life and play. Hopefully, we learn from history.

The following from 1935 is a very simple boomerang - with instructions on launching it![30]

A Toy Boomerang.

This little toy, which will afford you lots of fun, can easily be made from a piece of fairly heavy cardboard, about three inches square. Cut the cardboard to the shape shown in the corner diagram.

Place the boomerang on the edge of a book with one end projecting over in the way shown. Then, take a pencil and strike the projecting edge of the boomerang. It will spin through the air, curve around, and come back to you.

How the Australian Blackfellow used to play games.[31] Aboriginal Substitutes for Cricket, Golf and Tops. Makers of Ingenious toys.

The discussion about boomerangs which followed the discovery of such a weapon in Utah the other day brought out the fact that the Australian blackfellow is the sole manufacturer of boomerangs that actually return to the thrower. It is not every boomerang that comes back, and these that do are mostly playthings. Our aborigines used to be very fond of playing games. They were light-hearted people once, and some of their toys were very original and ingenious.

The blackfellow's inventive skill was by no means confined to the production of playthings. The fighting boomerang was a very dangerous weapon and is still no joke among the few wild natives who are left to use it. It can be thrown to fly in a wide circle, but that is not its principal purpose. The fighting boomerang is thrown to kill, but it can be warded off with a nulla-nulla or shield — so long as it has not got a hook on the end of it. The inventor of the hooked boomerang was an artful fellow. He saw how the ordinary boomerang would bounce off any stick held up to intercept it; so he added the hook, to catch on the shield, and swing the boomerang round it with such force as to dash a man's brains out.

Throwing Sticks

The come-back boomerang is a very different article, although one of the games in which it used to figure is what civilised people would call rather rough. No one ever studied the sports and pastimes of the Australian blackfellow more intelligently than Walter E. Roth, the author of a rare little book called *Ethnological Studies Among the North-West Central Queensland Aborigines*. The play boomerang seems to have been evolved from the fighting boomerang and from a highly ingenious toy throwing stick and Roth saw both throwing stick and play boomerang in use. He has left us an interesting description of the games in which they were employed. The throwing stick, he says, is a thin straight stick with a knob on the end of it, which, if cleverly thrown up against some thick foliage, or down at a tussock, can be made to shoot through the air twice as far as it can be thrown in the ordinary way. There is a curved throwing stick which will bound up and whirl about in an astonishing way if thrown against a log on the ground. Nearly related to this is the comeback boomerang, which is quite an entertaining plaything.

But the Queensland blacks, at all events, were not content just to throw the play boomerang and watch it circle in the air and return. They devised games for it — trying to make it come back in such a way as to hit one another or to fall directly on an agreed spot marked with a peg in the ground— a sort of aboriginal game of quoits. The natives used to have at least three games of ball — catch-ball, stick-and-stone, and spin-ball. Children played with a leather ball, bound with hair-twine, not vastly different in its component parts from the earliest golf balls.

'Stick-and-stone' was remotely suggestive of cricket. There were opposing teams of/from four to six players, armed with sticks and ranged up fifteen or twenty yards apart. 'The game,' says Roth, 'consists in throwing a stone of convenient size from one side to the other, each individual trying to intercept it with his stick as it skips or rolls before him on the ground.'

Blackfellows' Tops

The spin-ball was generally of baked clay, brightly coloured and spun between the fingers on the ground —clearly related to the top of the European boy. Roth's black friends were also fond of skipping and used a rope made from the roots of a tree, which two persons swung backwards and forwards — and not over and over — while a third did the skipping. Then there was 'hunt the eye,' something like 'hunt the slipper'. It was played with a tethered object, often the lens of an opossum's eye, which was hidden in the sand while the players, sitting round in a ring, held their hands before their faces. 'Hide and seek', the aborigines used to play just as our children play it today. Throwing a leaf into a column of hot smoke in such a way as to make it ascent in spiral curves, was another innocent pastime. The Australian savages with whom Roth was acquainted even played a sort of golf, but without clubs. There was only one hole, and that was a pit, guarded by a cross bunker, in the form of a net. The game was to throw a human shinbone from a prodigious distance and to 'hole in one.' Altogether, the passion for sport seems to have been felt in this country even before white settlement.

THE FOLLOWING DETAILED ARTICLE, from 1924, observes the play of Queensland indigenous people.

Native Games. By 'Castlebar'[32]

The Australian blacks have impressed many observers as being simply big children, cheerful, irresponsible, and with no care for tomorrow, and there is no doubt that their lives before the advent of the white man were, in the main, very happy.

The blacks are natural optimists and love fun, and they had no terrifying doctrines of a future world, few diseases, and no natural enemies save themselves. There was practically no bickering in the camps of the tribesmen but endless frolic and laughter. With them time was no object, and, especially in seasons of plenty, every day was a holiday. The blacks had numerous games, many athletic, and ball games of skill and everyone, even fine old men and women, joined in the games, which never failed to cause tremendous excitement and emulation. The various corroborees were, of course, the national games or ceremonies, but apart from these unique performances, the many and often clever pastimes of the blacks have never received the attention they deserved.

The favourite sport was tug-of-war, which was carried out on a different plan from that of the white men. A pole, cut from, the bush and trimmed with the stone axe heads, was used instead of a rope, and the contestants pushed instead of pulled, while the onlookers sat in rows and shrieked encouragement to their favourite side. Wrestling bouts, were for men only, and these were looked forward to and well prepared for before the great gathering of the tribes for the Priodle Boorah, or initiation ceremonies. They had also several ball games, the ball being made from portion of the skin of an old man kangaroo, stuffed with gins' hair. Two opposing sides or teams had each a captain, and totem played against totem, such as White Cockatoos versus Pelicans. The game was for each side to keep the ball away from the other, and there the men and women took part, but it was considered too strenuous for the children. Another popular game was spearing the kangaroo. A piece of bark was stripped from a tree, shaped into a circle and then bowled along the ground, while the players from given positions, had to pierce it. It was an excellent practice for their hunting.

The blacks, wherever water was plentiful, spent much time in swimming, and they had numerous water games. Besides ordinary swimming and diving for objects, and the imitation of swans, turtles, etc. Tremendous laughter invariably accompanied the grown-ups, both sexes participating. They were also fond of holding sham fights, excellent practice for their extreme quickness of eye, for real spears were thrown, and only the watchfulness of the attacked one prevented real injury. Much time was spent in teaching the children thoroughly to fight, swim, hunt, track, etc. In these mock battles, a black was upon his honour not to move off the ground when dodging a spear, and to avoid the hissing missiles by only the slightest possible movement of his body. The children's games, of course, were imitations of these of the adults. The boomerang was used in several games, usually the returning boomerang, which was largely a toy, and seldom used in fights. Contestants each lighted a small fire, at which the boomerangs were prepared and rubbed with fat. They were then thrown, and the game was to make them return as near as possible to a given spot. At night the blacks were fond of sending thousands of boomerangs tipped with fire circling through the air together.

Another species of native fireworks was that known as "poolooloomee." They peeled off great sheets of green bark from white gum trees, and shaped hundreds of "poolooloomees," which resembled bark spoons with long handles. These were put into the campfires till they glowed red and then the display began. Each black had a long stick stuck firmly into the ground, and when one lent against this the glowing head was broken off and sent whirling through the air. Hundreds were sent up at once, the lubras rushing backwards and forwards to the fires to keep the men supplied, while the night rang with wild yells of revelry. Skipping was another accomplishment well known to the blacks, and much indulged in, and they had developed the art far in advance of the white man's methods.

A vine was often used for a rope, and the two turners tried by every means to catch the performer, man or woman, off his or her guard. At first the skipper went through the ordinary steps but this was soon followed by amazing variations, such as taking turns of feet, digging for yams, grinding seed, imitating a frog, or other, creatures.

Playing at snatching up a child, or lying flat on the ground, measuring the full length in that position, and recovering in time to jump the rope, which was kept going constantly during the whole pantomime. Many of the oldest warriors and gins were excellent performers. The blacks also spent much time in carving implements and even whole trees, in decorating with differently coloured ochres, and in painting figures in caves. The famous gigantic painting of' "hell-fire" at Nardoo Creek, in which hundreds of human hands appear to be lifted out of a sea of flames, is well known. They were also fond of fireside stories, mostly tales of wonder and magic, and were adept in merit of oratory, in which their eloquence was wonderful. Singing or chanting took up much of their time, and, according to the first of all authorities on the aborigines, Mr J Mathew, almost every blackfellow is a maker of lyric verse, and whiles away the hour in expressing the poetry and music that is in him. The special bards or song-makers of each tribe were held in great esteem, and they were overeager to learn new songs. They had songs to the dawn, and to the kookaburra; songs for various occasions, and many humorous chants or action-songs. Whenever the successful game they came in chanting the emu or the kangaroo song, as the case might be. Some were magic or ceremonial songs for the corroboree. Whether in far off times, the blacks, with their genius for mimicry, evolved the corroboree from the marvellous dawn-dance of the brolgas, or native companions, cannot be known; but they declare that the brolgas learnt their quaint quadrilles from the corroborees, and for that reason these birds were never molested. Apart from the way the ceremonial dances of the boorah, and other semi-religious functions, the blacks had an unlimited repertoire of corroborees, which were the native plays or operas. Most of these were humorous and imitative of some bird, animal, or event. The dancing grounds were lit by great armfuls of dead timber, placed in forks of surrounding trees, and fired, and the gins sat in rows and did the singing, keeping time on their 'possum rug "drums." It was always a wild and impressive spectacle and seemed express all the weirdness and mystery of the Australian bush. Among the favourite performance were the sick baby dance, startled birds, the poisoned dingo, cattle raided by the blacks, the coming of the first steamer, and the imitation of different birds and their cries, and were in reality dramas, and each had its appropriate music. Numerous riddles were also acted in pantomime. One was called "the wild dog dance," and began by the life-like howling of hidden dingoes in the darkness answering each other, and then they finally came to the fire, running about, snarling and snapping, etc. Another was the "imitation of a stormy shore," in which the performers imitated to perfection the long rhythmic sweep of the waves and their recoil, together with the hiss of spray and the boom of breakers. In the canoe dance also there was the same perfect- rhythm of the swaying bodies. Among the humorous pieces were "an old man tormented by 'possums," and "crossing a river in a leaky canoe."

3

PLAYTIME IN THE BUSH AND CITY

Drawings to set the imagination in motion

Whoever first said "Easy as child's play" knew little about children. Play is one of the most important aspects of the life cycle and although it looks simple, it is complicated. Adults often look in amazement at how children can escape into magical 'play lands'. These play lands can be summoned up instantly and must be the ideal form of escapism. They require nothing more than desire and a Peter Pan attitude that everything is possible in a child's world. Children see magic because they look for it. Adults rarely find such escapism. Even the *'Walter Mitty'* in us is frail compared to the power of a child's imagination.

Children have always invented games. They create them to entertain themselves and their friends. Games are part of their world.

While there are certain rules in children's games, there are no rules as to how games are named. The same game can appear in different localities with different names. The game is the same yet known by a different name. And while the wider rules of the games do change, the central rules tend to remain static. Children generally sweep objections away with a simple "That's not the way I play it" and then explain their version of the game. There are no hard and fast laws for playing games, and children seem ready to accept other versions.

We now have a more informed view of how play works and the benefits it brings to the child, family and community. Considerable research has been done to study childhood behaviour, but some of the most valuable work was carried out by good fortune and near accidents. Family historians documented how games were devised and played in their family, oral historians tape-recorded interviews with adults asking them about their childhood, some active folklore collecting was done in an attempt to collect the sung rhymes of the playground, and academics have scratched and scraped through diaries, newspapers and manuscript collections. Certainly, the most comprehensive collection sits under the banner of Museums Victoria and its Australian Children's Folklore Collection. [1]

> The Australian Children's Folklore Collection (ACFC) brings to Museum Victoria a direct and personal voice from children at play. It is one of the largest and most significant archives of its kind in the world, reflecting Australia's cultural and regional diversity. It is the first Museum Victoria collection and one of the first collections in Australia to have been recognised through listing on the UNESCO Australian Memory of the World Register. It documents children's verbal folkloric traditions from the 1870s to the present. It includes more than 10,000 card files and over 1,000 pages of letters recording

children's games, rhymes, riddles, jokes, superstitions, taunts and chants; over 300 traditional and homemade play artefacts; photographs and audiovisual material; and field and research studies.

The ACFC germinated with research in the 1970s and 1980s by Dr June Factor (then an academic at the Institute of Early Childhood Development) and Dr Gwenda Davey. Armed with a pad and pencil, tape recorder and camera, they conducted field research to document Australian children's play. As their research progressed, they gradually acquired contemporary and historic materials. The Australian Children's Folklore Collection was formally established in 1979. Dr Factor was invited to join the founding members of the Australian Centre at The University of Melbourne in May 1989 as a Senior Research Fellow. She brought the Australian Children's Folklore Collection to the Centre and agreed to have it housed in the University of Melbourne Archives. In 1999, she donated the Collection to Dr June Factor and Museums Victoria.

Dr Dorothy Howard, pioneer Australian children's folklore collector.

Play in an Earlier Time.

There were two sides of life in the early colonies. Those who lived in the coastal cities and towns and those who lived in what was referred to as the 'bush', which, in reality, was often only twenty miles out of town. Because of the 1850s rush for gold, when Australia's population more than tripled in two decades, most Australins lived in the 'bush'. Gold was followed by farming, raising sheep and breeding cattle. Whether in town or in the bush, most people lived simply in modest cottages, most with a small garden. Families were often large. Like the local goats, children often roamed free as parents and guardians did their daily chores. Children were expected to do their 'fair share' of work and entertain themselves. Many outback properties were remote, and station children rarely saw other children. City kids were better catered for but were probably more liable to run amok.

A LAND of Make-Believe

The ability for young children to invent is endless and, like this account by Eliza Chomley of growing up in 1850s Melbourne, even imagining an island was within the realm of possibility[2]. Once designated, such imaginary places, or even worlds, could be returned to and 'grew' with the child or group of children.

> Tom and Will, 'the boys', as we called them, were 15 and 14 respectively; Minnie 10, myself 8, Teddy 6, Little Alice a sweet baby child of 3, very pretty and the pet of all of us.
>
> We were all great chums and companions, and then and for the next two years, the boys joined in all our games, or rather invented them for us - Willy wholeheartedly, Tom with a certain reserve or patronage, but enjoying them all the same.
>
> We had certain 'make believes', 'the Island of Bodan' ... among them, whose map, something like Ireland, I would still recognise. The boys drew and painted a long and excellent panorama of its principal river, and its Capital City, 'Burk'. The boats they cleverly built, rigged, and painted were its navy. We drilled with wooden swords and daggers in its Army, and the weekly paper that the boys edited at home was the *Botanic Gazette*. Minnie, always very clever with her pen, wrote leaders, the most epoch-making being one in which she pleaded for (and obtained) a Saturday holiday for us 'little girls' to be on the same footing as the boys. I wrote for the *Poets' Corner* 'Laments for my lost youth' and other effusions.
>
> Our games and pursuits were mostly out of doors. We went for walks before breakfast every morning, sometimes to the swamp ... where the overflow from the Yarra formed a series of little islands in

wet weather, and broken and boggy ground in dry - at all times eminently suited for daring deeds, duckings and narrow escapes. What is now the Fitzroy Gardens was a favourite happy hunting ground - the pretty Gully with its fern trees was then a sort of drain we called 'the ditch'. I remember jumping into instead of across it one wet morning when it was a flood of yellow clayey water. We played in fallen tree-trunks - sometimes ships; sometimes mountains, or houses, but always productive of scraped shins and bruises. There we used to pick gum and manna, and in the Spring came home with our handkerchiefs full of locusts, in various stages of emergence from the Chrysalis - the ugly formidable-looking beetle, its only sign of life two little red dots of eyes; the limp caterpillar just emerging; the elegant half hardened one all rainbow colours, with gauzy wings; and finally the big strong black locust that flew away with a whiz. We had them all over the breakfast table, I wonder we were allowed to. At William Street we all had our gardens, and when Tom was promoted to the office he made out a beautiful miniature deed of transfer, correct in every detail, of mine of which I was tired, to Willy. Minnie wrote stories, and Tom and Willy had albums of their own drawings - they were very talented in this way.

When the diggings broke out, we would drag my Uncle William's carriage, left in our safekeeping, from the Coach-house, and play at lucky diggers in it. Uncle William's [family] visited England while we were at William Street, leaving various things in our charge, among them a wheeled bath chair, which lived on our verandah. It had a very hard life in their absence, being transformed by Will into a stage coach. If we could safely get in, we had drives round the garden, but as we were loaded up with huge parcels, and not allowed to start till the Coach was in full career, our attempts to hurl ourselves in were seldom successful, usually ending in a general upset of passengers and luggage with the chair on top of them. On one occasion, I remember the accident occurring in a large Prickly-Pear bush.

DOUG KELLY TELLS of frequent childhood visits to Neverland, an imaginary land, no doubt inspired by *Peter Pan*.[3] Like many children, Doug could fly over hills and plains. His favourite game was climbing trees and having a friend in a nearby tree, exchanging messages over a string-tin can walkie-talkie. Robyn Laurie had a "wonderful time imagining I was 'Corporal Rusty' in The *Adventures of Rin Tin Tin*. The handrail of the steps covered by a pillow was my horse and saddle. I spent hours in this imaginary world .... or imagining I was a Mouseketeer in The Mickey Mouse Club."[4] Lilo Blyton entered her imaginary magic world via the sliding doors of her bedroom wardrobe.[5] Elizabeth Hawkes remembered, "I had a willow tree which grew down the slope from the septic tank, so it was huge! I would climb it; each branch was a different room in my imagination. The bedroom had a double branch so I could comfortably lie down. I would pretend to make food on the kitchen branch and watch the view from my living room branch. I occasionally shared it with friends, but they weren't as skilled at climbing as I was. One girl fell out of my home and hurt herself quite badly, so my mother told me not to invite my friends to climb with me anymore. Oh well, I was always happier on my own, in my own head dreaming away."[6] Juditha Mary recalls growing up in Potts Point. "I was a believer in Fairy Land. I visited regularly when I was falling asleep. There was a king and queen of the fairies, and everyone in that land had wings. I was given wings when I went there. Even the animals had wings, like cats and dogs. The sun always shone, everything was really bright and colourful, and there was always an abundance of lush green hills and flowers, and nothing bad ever happened there."[7]

IMAGINATION IS A WONDERFUL THING, and in devising play games, 'monkey sometimes does as monkey sometimes sees', so it is not surprising that children should create games that mimic those around them.

A Hop, a Skip and a Jump 85

Children acting out a fairy tale about a sleeping princess.
State Archive NSW

In the bush, the arrival and departure of the Cobb & Co coach, Afghan traders, or the old bullock dray, was a significant event and, by this account from Mary Fullerton, 1870s Gippsland, in a remote home surrounded by bushland, tells of such mimicry.[8]

> We also had many original pastimes suggested by the material about us. One of these sports was bullock-driving; another I remember was playing at pack-horses. Bullocks and horses in human service were familiar to us, and it would have been strange had the sight of animals in harnesses not given us the imitative impulse. We made of ourselves beasts of burden at these games, bearing willingly the whip of a driver who took his office seriously. The whip was not, however, of a very terrible character, having generally for string a strip of the under-part of stringy-bark tied to a long stick. If the driver were an expert, he could crack it successfully, but more often than not, in the first flourish, the lash would fly off the handle, just as he so jocund drove his team afield. We used to bring a rare lot of light wood for my mother's fires in a wooden cart made by my father out of an old packing case furnished with wheels of small circumference from sawn-off logs. It was a vehicle inelegant enough but serviceable and joy-giving. We used to draw lots, I remember, to decide who should be driver of the team. Dick would hold the lots in his hand, and it is to me still a mystery how it was that the law of chance so frequently favoured the holder of the lots.

When we played at being pack-horses, the wood we carried was in bundles on our backs, as we saw the men load the horses when preparing them for the trips up the mountain track, whither our father's team frequently went in front of the whip of a hunch-shouldered driver. These were certainly games suggested by our environment, as I have since seen the children of miners in an up-country town setting forth with their picks and shovels and 'crib tins' to the play that was their father's work.

'Hide and Seek' can be played just about anywhere. It can be played with two children, an adult and a child, or with groups. The rules are simple - one hides, and the other seeks and finds. This ancient game has been analysed inside-out for lessons that can be learnt: the hider must be creative in the choice of the hiding place, even in predictable places, must be able to stay put in silence (a lesson of being alone) and must be discoverable. Although the game rules that there should be a hider and seeker, hiding where you cannot be found is pointless. Such a hiding place defeats the basis of the game - in, eventually, being found. Once discovered, the hider must accept success and defeat. Such discovery is rarely a disappointment and, in some ways, just as exciting as playing the seeker. It creates a fair atmosphere, a level playing ground for hiders and seekers. Mary Fullerton recalls the game in Gippsland in the 1870s. Mary also has something to say about how restrictive, bulky Victorian clothing put her at an unfair (and unappreciated) disadvantage to the boys.[9]

> The 'hide-and-seek' that Cain and Abel undoubtedly invented was our heritage. Ours was a world specially designed for such games as these, indoors or out. There were barns and sheds everywhere, and haystacks and standing crops, and farther afield the bush about the creek, and the bush itself. I remember once tunnelling into a haystack so deeply to make a good hiding of it, that I was almost smothered, and once Fred hid himself so recklessly among some bags of chaff in a barn that after a time, in response to his involuntary

movements, an avalanche of bags descended upon him, so that all the ambushed ones within hearing of his muffled cries had to emerge from their several hiding-places to render the struggler first-aid.

I make a serious claim to our having if not invented, at least developed in pursuit of this same game of hide-and-seek the art of camouflage so much heard of today. To find 'Red Riding Hood' in our wood, where most objects suggested her, was a pretty puzzle for a searcher. Annie's striped pinafore swishing forth from a scrub clump by no means proclaimed, though it suggested, the immediate presence there of Annie herself. Nor did the crown of Dick's hat peeping above a fallen log necessarily mean that the curly head and mischievous brown face of its owner were reconnoitring below it. I remember to this hour the experience of literally seeing stars where stars were not. The perils of blind man's buff played on a half-cleared landscape where abounded stumps of felled trees as high as one's face are not to be minimised. To come with bandaged eyes hastily into contact with one of these is to bring about the immediate necessity for a bandaged nose. Blind man's buff is more suited to an environment where nothing more solid than chairs and tables is to be encountered. It was a bitter day for my tomboy pride that on which it was borne in upon me that there is a tyranny of garments - that the child of the skirted sex is, becoming subject to the skirt, thereby tamed. Moral lectures from certain aunts used to the more 'correct' ways of little town girls had in their sundry administerings failed to curtail the athletic ventures of Claribel and myself. There was not a tree, dared by the boys, along whose limbs we too had not swung and clung.

A lengthened frock was the real reformer. It was, though, a bitter day when a trammelling skirt reduced me to inferior place in the matter of 'vaulting with the pole'. Tournaments of this diverting exercise Dick and I often had, and for long I could clear a height at which he boggled or brought down the barrier. And then a new skirt of more generous length brought me my Waterloo. Was it, I wonder, symbol and epitome of much in woman's race in life? I rebelled sorely, I know, and smarted at my cousin's derisive and triumphant laughter when my flying sails brought my downfall. It was the same in running. I was no more the peer of the boys, and for a year or so had the further chagrin of seeing Claribel, my yet unfettered junior, surpass me in such sport...

Blindman's Buff - a ancient game with many variations. *A.F.U*

'Blind Man's Buff' has been played in many variants. Like many early games that have continued into popular culture, it smacks of uncomfortableness. In these days it is clearly not acceptable to use a perceived disability as the centre of a game but children, of course, are less judgemental than adults and, hopefully, their innocence allows them such a trespass. Others have suggested such a game, allowing the child to imagine what a disability is like, has a positive effect. We also note that the game is nominated as 'man', although it has no restrictions on girl or boy.

The most common game is for one child to be nominated as the first blind man. A handkerchief or rag is securely tied over the eyes, and the child turns around three or four times for disorientation. The blind man then proceeds to catch any other player. The players tease 'it', pulling at clothes, tickling with a feather and getting as close as possible without being caught. The word 'buff' is Middle English for blow, as in thump or push. Once the blind man has seized a player, he must guess who it is. If the guess is correct, that person will become the new blind man.

Other versions include 'The Bellman', where everyone is blindfolded except one player who carries a small bell, which he rings from time to time. The blind man who catches the bellman changes places with him. Another version, 'Guessing Blind Man,' has the players seated on chairs, forming a circle, with the blindfolded player in the middle. He is turned around three times (during which the players randomly change seats). The blind man sits on the lap of the first person he finds - and then needs to guess who it is.

'I SPY WITH MY LITTLE EYE'. It is difficult to imagine a child who hasn't played 'I Spy With My Little Eye'. Guessing games have a noble history, including riddles incorporated into ancient ballads and epic stories. Children love guessing games because they spark the imagination and make the player think sideways. The game can be simple or complex. 'Charades' is a more complex game where each player takes turns acting out a series of performances to identify, for example, whether the character is from a book, film, music, etc. They next act out a scene to identify an activity associated with that character. The players, in rotation, get one guess until the character is successfully identified. Another version has a person's name taped to the player's forehead so everyone can see who the person is except the wearer. In this game, once again, a sequence leads to the eventual identification - "Am I male or female?" "Am I an actor?" etc. The wearer is only allowed yes or no answers to all questions.

'TAG'. One of the easiest and most popular games is 'tag', yet it has rules. Standard 'tag' has one player selected as the 'chaser', or 'it', and he or she pursues the others, trying to tag them by touching them. Players are free to run wherever they wish. Bolder players allow 'it' to get closer, before being touched. When a runner is tagged, he immediately becomes a chaser and takes up his place without pause. There are many versions of tag; some have complex boundaries chalked on the ground, and some have rules whereby the runners have to skip instead of running. One of the most popular Australian tag games is 'British Bulldog', sometimes called 'Cockylora' or 'Cockylorum', 'Bullrush' or 'Red Rover Cross Over'. Essentially, the runners are in lines; the catcher is in the centre of the playground, and on the signal, the runners all race down to the opposite end - trying to avoid the tag.

Indians! from Farrer School for Deaf Children. *State Archives NSW*

'**Cowboys and Indians**'. For children growing up in the nineteen-forties and fifties, going to the pictures was a big event, and many went weekly to get their dose of cartoons, 'Dead-eye' Dick' mysteries, and Cowboys and Indians serials. One of the most popular series was about a fictional cowboy, 'Hopalong Cassidy', (played by William Boyd), with sixty-six features produced from 1949 onwards.

Bill "Hopalong" Cassidy was usually strikingly clad in black (including his hat, an exception to the Western film stereotype that only villains wore black hats). He was reserved and well-spoken, with a sense of fair play and was often called upon to intercede when baddies tried to take advantage of honest citizens. His white horse, 'Topper', was loyal and clever.

Hopalong Cassidy Bar container featuring William Boyd as the cowboy hero. *Museums Victoria*

Children bought chewy Hopalong Cassidy Bars at the lolly counter, wore Hopalong Cassidy badges and assumed his life in make-believe backyard games. Many of the films saw the cowboy captured by Indians only to talk or shoot his way out to escape.

CHASEY, CHASING - YOU'RE 'IT'.

'Chasing and catching' games have always been popular with

children, often even better if chased by a parent. Once again, there are many variations.

'Moving Statues' calls for one player to stand at the end of the room or outside on the lawn, and the other players have to advance while the 'statue' looks the other way. When the statue turns, all the advancing players must turn into statues; if any make even the slightest move, they must return to the designated starting line and begin again. The first person to get close enough to touch 'it' is the winner, and if the game continues, the winner becomes the new head statue.

Michael Hughes recalled playing 'German Spotlights' when growing up in the bush in the 1970s.[10]

> One of the players, the 'German', had a torch and would hide on the verandah or behind a bush or shed or wherever, and the game was for the players, the Allied soldiers, to sneak up on him, as close as possible, without being caught. The 'German" was then to tag the players and imprison them until the last was caught.

Adults get bored. Children get restless.
Meg Lees talked of never being bored.[11]

> We would also make games out of anything that came to hand. We had one of those tiny music box things that you wound with a tiny handle and used it to create a mini Olympics. Whoever could turn the handle the fastest and get through the whole tune would win. That led to using other toys in a competition like 'Dress the doll', the quickest, billy cart races, longest nose measurement, jump and hit the eaves of the house, and race on tin cans with a string attached.
>
> I was totally addicted to elastics. I used to wrap one end around a fence post and the other around a heavy chair or my poor, long-suffering brother's leg, and I would jump for hours.

In 1992 oral historian Rob Willis recorded an interview with pioneer folklore collector John Meredith and asked him about childhood games he played in the 1920s. Here, Meredith describes the game of 'Bushies and Bobbies', an Australian version of 'Cops and Robbers'.[12]

> **Bushies and Bobbies!** It was always Bushies came first. Well, that was short for Bushrangers and Bobbies (Police), of course, or the old 'Cops and Robbers'. The Bobbies got together in a group, and the Bushies always got a start. I don't know whether they (the Bobbies) counted - they probably counted up to 50 or something or other. The Bushies all raced off and hid behind fences and trees, and the Bobbies came along as a team, and they had to chase them. And I think it was either played with a tennis ball - like 'Brandy' - to hit them with, in which case they were shot and caught, or to touch them. It involved lots of running around the playground, ducking behind trees, and hiding.

Physical Games

Physical games are an essential part of childhood. They allow physical exercise, appropriate body touching, competition and the equally essential lessons of winning and losing. Running wild, following imagination, allows for unbelievable freedoms as participants, solo or in a group, imagine being pursued by a wild beast, a monster or even the dreaded boogeyman. Then there are the structured physical games, some traditional tried and true, and others, one suspects, developed by what was known as physical culture programming. Before 1975 (it is funny how much of the old ways changed with the increased popularity of television), many councils operated play centres during the school holidays. These centres offered weekday programming, mainly for children between 6 and 15. Much of it, one imagined, was to guide the kids on the right path, to avoid the formation of gangs, etc. There were other movements with similar aims of 'building young Australians', including The Young Australia League, Police Boys' Clubs and the Youth Hostel Association.

In retrospect, many of the physical games played seem trivial, almost two-dimensional, but there was much fun to be gained by games like leapfrog, tunnel ball, pass-the-parcel, sack races, and even egg-and-spoon races.

State Electoral Commonwealth Picnic - preparing for the egg and spoon race. 1954

It is not surprising that fun sports like egg and spoon and three-legged races, greasy pole contests and tug-of-wars help assimilate children in multi-cultural schools. If only it were as easy for adults!

The three-legged race. *MV*

A Hop, a Skip and a Jump

The sack race at St George's Terrace 1938.

OUTDOOR and indoor games develop skills in children; as children develop, these skills and efforts help them grow physically and mentally. Very young children need to squeeze, cuddle and hit things as they explore the world around them. At two or three, they grab wooden or plastic rings (or anything else in sight), move on to simple block puzzles and try to fit the proverbial square peg in a round hole. A little older, the three to five group move to participation games, then, later, board games and so on. All the while, they are gathering skills in coordination, execution and assessment. Simple skills like imitating animal noises, usually associated with story time, move on to other sounds like aeroplanes and trains. Around six and onwards is generally the most active time for pretend play.

ROLE-PLAYING, a much-discussed subject in the 21st century, is far different from the previous centuries. Girls were expected to play mothers, nurses, and cooks, and boys were expected to play pirates, postmen, firemen, train drivers, and aeroplane pilots. It was also a time when boys wore blue and girls pink; however, as we now know, not all is as it seems.

Constructing cut-out models from paper and cardboard.
State Archive NSW

Just about anything can be used in play. Yesterday's children, whether in the bush or city, were masters and mistresses of creativity and had a select stock-in-trade of paper, paint, chalk, clay, plaster of Paris, scissors, glue and sewing kit. Disused objects like clothes' pegs, knitting spools, old tobacco tins, car tyres, cigar boxes, cardboard hat boxes, etc became important playthings.

W. P. Thornton, writing in 1953, lamented the disappearance of home-made toys.[13]

> Although even the simplest toys these days are relatively expensive, many of them are manufactured with such skill that parents shirk away from trying to produce homemade substitutes. But around the turn of the century- and even for many years afterwards—things were different in homes in the Australian outback.
>
> In the first place, incomes were small. In the second, families were often large. Third, maybe there was greater pride in original workmanship. As a direct result, many outback dwellers turned their hands to making toys for their children, using raw materials available to them in the bush.
>
> Those home-made toys brought joy to the hearts of the children in those days, just as surely as today's modern child thrills over an

expensive talking doll or a scale model of an aeroplane. Not only did parents embark on large-scale toy-making, but the children made many toys for themselves.

Given a piece of willow wood or any other light timber from the bush, the bush boy could quickly fashion a cricket bat that served its purpose well. Manufactured cricket balls were usually beyond the means of the bush lad, but he made quite a good substitute out of a fungus called Blackfellow's Bread. This fungus was found a foot or so beneath the ground's surface close to the roots of eucalypts. It was soft enough when first unearthed to shape with a pocket knife, but after a few hours' exposure to the sun it was as hard as a rock.

Lads often searched for a small sapling with a knobby root so that it could be used as a nulla-nulla - copied from the aborigines. A bush lad had great fun with one of these nulla-nullas. He could, for example, bowl over a rabbit at anything up to 20 yards distance. A small forked stick and strips of rubber cut from an old motor inner tube were all that was necessary for the bush lad to make a shanghai or catapult. A good catapult and a pocketful of small stones, and a bush lad was happy. He would have hours of fun shooting at rabbits, kangaroo rats, bandicoots, sparrows and other noxious birds. (In those days, anyway, most bush bred boys had commendable respect for the valuable birds of the bush.)

Rabbit-skins were worth little half a century ago, but the handy bush mother made some splendid toys out of them. Families generally kept white, black and yellow rabbit skins for making toys, especially "teddy bears."

White rabbits were very rare, so a "teddy bear" made from white rabbit skins was highly prized by the little girl who found one in her stocking at Christmas or received one as a birthday gift.

Many outback fathers were handy with tools, and from old tins, packing cases and bush timber many dolls' tea-sets, sets of furniture and other toys were fashioned.

If the family meat was killed on the farm or if the family knew a butcher, it did not take long to collect enough jackbones to make a set of "Jacks" - a popular game for girls. To make them more attractive, the jack bones were dyed different colours. Sometimes I think that children have lost the art of enjoying simple homemade toys - or is it that parents no longer have the urge to make them?

A Selection of Other Games

Jigsaw Puzzles. [14] A good deal of quiet fun may be derived from playing with jigsaw puzzles, which can quite well be made at home. Take, for instance, one of the pretty pictures so often shown on postcards, and mount it on thick cardboard, and then cut it into small pieces, and you have a jig-saw ready-made.

'**Bib-bob**' [15] is another amusing game, sometimes called 'Bib-bob' is prepared by fastening a cord across one end of a room, and from this cord, suspended with cotton, are many small presents, sweetmeats, oranges, and apples, all tied in paper. The children stand at the opposite end of the room and are, in turn, blindfolded. They then have to walk across the room and, with one hand, feel for a present, which, when found, may be pulled down and consumed. Here, again, a few dummy gifts will add to the merriment of the game.

Vonnie Boreham recalled playing a game with cotton reels.[16]

Cotton-reel races. An ordinary tack would be driven into one end of the cotton reel, a thick rubber band threaded through, and a matchstick placed at the opposite end to sit flat against the end through the end loop of the rubber band. The matchstick would then wind up the rubber band. The cotton reels would then be placed on the table and walked across the table. Small grooves could be carved around cotton reel edges to provide traction.

I Do Like to be Beside the Seaside

Around the time of in Federation 1901, most Australians lived in coastal cities and towns, reflecting new employment in manufacturing and commerce. Most of them also worked a six-and-a-half day week. No longer tied to the demands of farm life, they discovered leisure time. Families picnicked, went to sporting events and generally sought entertainment. Beaches like Sydney's Manly, Tamarama, Bondi and Coogee or Melbourne's St. Kilda became entertainment destinations. They responded by staging events and building aquariums, water slides, rides and other amusements for all ages. Children could see Punch and Judy shows and tableaus, and ride camels and donkeys. Musicians played concertina, fiddle, whistle, harmonica and pump organs on the boardwalks, and all manner of curious entertainments could be found, from skating cockatoos, jugglers, snake handlers to dancing monkeys. Grand pavilions were built, many modelled on English seaside pavilions. St. Kilda beach had a sea baths pavilion as early as 1860 and a grander structure built in 1910.

St. Kilda Sea Baths and Hotel. 1910.

Down by the seaside at Bondi Beach

Pem's Pools, Ramsgate - pools, zoos and fun

Privately owned swimming pools were constructed in both the city and bush. Pemberton's at Ramsgate, Sydney, combined their pools with a zoo and a hall of novelty machines and distorting mirrors. Opened in 1924, and better known as 'Pem's' or, because of the tendency of youngsters to pee in the warm water, 'Pem's piss pools', it was operated by Arthur 'Pops' Pemberton. His most popular attraction, apart from the potato scallops, chips and performing zoo animals, was his daily 'penny scramble' where he rang a bell and proceeded to throw handfuls of pennies into the children's pool.

Arnott's Biscuits Beachside Buckets limited release 1930s.

In the first quarter of the twentieth century, numerous pleasure gardens and amusement parks were constructed to attract families who wanted a day by the sea. Wonderland City was an extraordinary amusement park located at Tamarama, on the conveniently named Wonderland Avenue. It opened in 1906 and was, at the time, the largest open-air amusement park in the Southern Hemisphere. The 20-acre colossal playground had a balloon ride, which could go up 3,800 feet (1160 metres). An enormous switchback railway snaked around the clifftop, and a steam-driven miniature railway operated over two miles (3 km) of track. Other attractions included a large wooden bridge built over an artificial lake where the Alpine Slide would take you to the 'Rivers of the World' Seal Pond. There was also an open-air roller skating rink, an American Shooting Gallery, and a program of special events, spectaculars, and daring deeds. A visit to Wonderland City must have been amazing for adults and dazzling for young children. Sadly, it closed in 1911.

Sydney's Wonderland City amusement park, Tamarama.

One of Sydney's main attractions from 1913 to 1916 was The White City at Rushcutters Bay. A pleasure park of six acres, it offered a scenic railway (winding around a snow-covered plaster Matterhorn), river cave boat rides, a Japanese Village (with 'real Japanese'), merry-go-round and other rides, plus programs of spectaculars including hire-wire balancing, devil-dare shows and halls of mirrors ('where time stood still'). There was also a dance palace (with the White City Band) and a roller-skating rink. Up to 35,000 people would descend on the site on Saturdays. The entrepreneurial manager, Mr T. H. Eslick, known as the 'P. T. Barnham of Australia' regularly programmed fancy-dress days and treasure hunts. It was a children's paradise. Eslick was also responsible for the design of Melbourne's Luna Park in 1912.

The illuminated gates of The White City, New South Head Road, Rushcutters Bay. *AFU Collection*

White City's Scenic Railway. *AFU Collection*

Bush Picnics. Life in the bush could be lonely for small children. They made fun where they could. The big events of the calendar centred around Christmas and the occasional picnic days. Bush picnics, official and informal, were a welcome diversion for all rural people. The cows still had to be milked, cattle and sheep fed, and a hundred other farm duties attended to - but there was a day, or sometimes a weekend, of fun with picnics, sporting events, games for the children and, usually, music throughout the day and night. Stories were told, poetry recited, and more music played. Sometimes, there were curiosities such as a display of strength by a local strongman, and sometimes, animal novelty acts like a talking cockatoo, camel ride or mysterious flea circus. It would be even better to have a picnic at a local creek.

Up in the Mountains

Recess at Kiandra Public School. *State Records NSW*

A completely different childhood was available to youngsters living in remote areas, including on our mountain ranges. During the winter months, school kids at places like Kiandra, in the NSW snowfields, had to take advantage of playtime as best they could. Ball games like cricket and tunnel ball were impossible. School recess was an opportunity to build snowmen, ride toboggans, or ski the nearby slopes.

Wherever children lived - in snowfields, deserts, endless plains or wild bush, they found their own local adventure and amusement.

. . .

CHILDREN TAKE THE STAGE.

The ability of children to skip into and out of imaginary worlds places them in the ideal position to assume the role of actors in a play. Whether structured, including scripted, or simply an improvisational-themed play, it is a game some children return to regularly. Meredith Fuller recalled,[17]

> I made plays at recess and in the classroom, and then I would get other children to act in them. The teachers were great about allowing me to do this.

Toyshops in the twentieth century had a dazzling range of games for children. Some, like draughts, chess, Monopoly, and Scrabble, have a long history. Many of these games have pieces, which the player moves along a board, game cards, etc. Game tokens often disappear miraculously. Where do they go? Do they travel to the Land of Lost Socks? Missing game pieces is a problem parents learn to live with.

Every Australian city had a favourite toyshop. Sydney's largest was Walther & Stephenson, a two-storey wonderland on George Street. Melbourne had Cole's Book Arcade. Opened in 1873, in Bourke Street, Cole's Book Arcade was something else again - it boasted offering over two million books. It also had a confectionary store and toyshop. If that wasn't enough, customers of all ages were also enticed with a string band, a symphonion powered by a clockwork mechanism, and other mechanical devices such as a hen that clucked and laid tin 'golden' eggs (containing either a sweet or a toy) when a penny was dropped into a slot. The hen and symphonion are part of the Melbourne Museum Collection. Cole's Book Arcade closed as a victim of the Great Depression.

The large department stores also operated expansive toy shops and supplied rural families with mail orders.

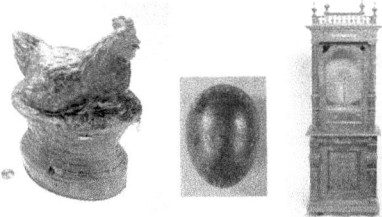

E. W. Cole's mechanical chicken, tin egg and symphonion. All circa 1889. *Melbourne Museum*.

BY THE 1960s, local toy manufacturers and distributors realised the need to rally against importing cheap and sometimes unreliable toys. A Sydney newspaper reported: [18]

> A record range and quantity of Australian-made toys were available in stores in Parramatta and districts, shopkeepers reported yesterday. The wheel toys, they said, were equal to and often better than some of the imported toys. What was more, the prices were at least competitive with prices of toys from overseas. Manufacturers say the western costume and fur soft goods sections enjoy record business, while toy koala bears and kangaroos, made with real kangaroo fur, are being exported to more than 30 overseas countries.
>
> President of the Toy and Games Manufacturers' Association of New South Wales, Mr. Alex Tonkin, said today that parents were once more returning to the notion that children should play with toys and not merely be entertained by them. Most Australian toys, he said, required participation by the child and were therefore much more educational than many mechanical toys, which required no active play by the children. Mr. Tonkin added that there had been a marked swing from the battery operated toy, which wore out its novelty appeal almost as quickly as its batteries. Mr. Tonkin said the other advantages of Australian made toys were: — The knowledge that they were built to certain safety standards, such as lead-free paints, rounded edges and hygienic and non-toxic materials for fillings. (It had been reported recently that some imported soft toys were being filled with used hospital dressings).

Australian manufacturers were in a position to know the right type of toy for the Australian child. Parents had easy recourse to manufacturers, should maintenance or spare parts be required. Because steel was relatively cheap in Australia, manufacturers had no reason to stint on raw materials. Even the small pressed steel toys were the same gauge metal as real motor cars.

∽

DOWN AND DIRTY

Let's face it, kids love to get down and dirty. Considering many of today's children are born and grow up living in apartments, they need to be reminded of the world around them by digging in the dirt, playing with sand, making mud pies, playing with sticks and stones, climbing trees and rocks, rolling on grass and running through the bush. Such activities and places are full of wonder and excitement. One only has to go to a beach and watch how first-time beachgoer children react to the expanse of sand and water. Firstly, along with awe, is trepidation; then, after a water kick and a dig into the sand, pleasure is found. The smiles on faces tell everything about joy. It's the same with other earthly discoveries, and no child should be denied the full spectre of touching, smelling, listening, or manipulating whatever attracts, for it is through such activity they learn size, weight, texture, colour and shape. Mother Nature can beat all the fancy toys, and children know it.

In 1919 the Sydney *Daily Telegraph* reported:

Playtime in Lean and Mean Times[19]

Creativity is a close relative of the old saying 'necessity is the mother of invention' and in Australia's history of lean times, especially evident in economic depressions and wartime rationing, creativity was far from stifled. Toys were made out of whatever was available - orange crates, cigar boxes, cigarette, baking powder and jam tins, string, rope and, of course, the great multi-tasker, the hessian sugar bag.

In today's disposable world of excessive packaging it seems laughable that children once used simple brown paper for fun and games. These suggestions come from the war year of 1915.

Brown Paper Games.

A brown paper party is good fun. The little guests all wear costumes contrived from brown paper, a quantity of which can be bought for a few pence. With a little skill, some really good costumes can be arranged. Red Indians, cowboys, soldiers, Eskimos, Brer Rabbit, prairie girls, and nurses are a few of the most obvious suggestions.

For another brown paper game, two or three reams of medium-quality brown paper are required, as well as numbered badges of brown paper. Safety pins are ready for each guest to wear, and space is left for the scoring of each player.

For an animal competition, have ready on a small table four sets of animals cut from brown paper. Blindfold the competitors, and then let them feel the paper's outline and guess the animal it represents. Three may be given to each, and the judge must note the guesses and mark one point on his card for each correct answer. A kangaroo, native bear, dog, tortoise, cow, pig, or elephant, are all suitable models and can be cut from children's toy books if artistic skill is lacking.

In another brown paper competition suitable for big children, the players are paired, and each is given three sheets of brown paper, strong cotton, needles, pins, and scissors. In half an hour, a head-dress must be provided, cut out of the paper, and worn by one of the pair, together with any accessories that may enhance the costume.

It is surprising how much can be done with these simple materials and what ingenuity is displayed. A Pierrot's sugar-loaf hat and rosettes, the folded fichu and plain cap of a Puritan, Old King Cole with his crown and brown paper twisted pipe-stem and pipe, Queen Elizabeth's crown and outstanding ruff, and the cap with strings and apron of a Red Cross nurse, are a few suggestions.

The children who have no costume vote for the one they think best—3, 2, and 1, respectively. These numbers are added to the cards of the headdress wearers and the assistants with whom they are paired. Prizes are given for the best and worst cards.=

Another standby was the now-threatened cork, which was useful in making enough animals to fill Noah's Ark. Here are some corkers from a 1940 newspaper.[20]

Cork Toys These amusing little models are made from corks of various sizes, pins, matches, paper, a little wool and some glue. The Dachshund comes first. He is made of one large and one small cork. Join his head to his body with a piece of match stalk fixed into a hole. Pin the body and a hole in the head. The legs are made of short pieces of match stick with the match head forming feet. The tail is a piece of rolled-up paper glued into place. The eyes and nose are put in with paint.

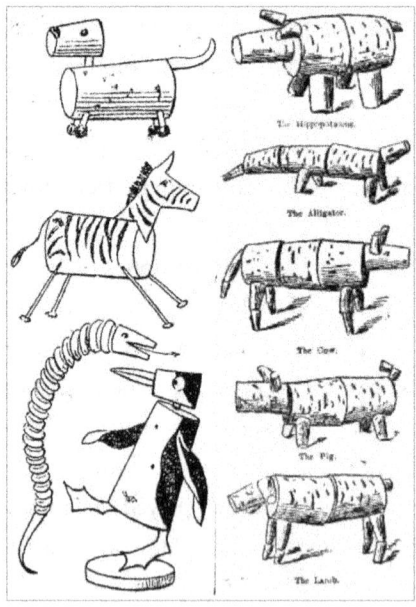

Enough animals to fill Noah's Ark

For the zebra, cut out a cork head as seen in the illustration and stick on a mane of black wool. Make a slit in the cork at the neck and fix the head onto the body as shown. Add four pins for legs and a tail of wool frayed at the tip. Ink, or paint in the eyes and stripes.

The snake is made of graded rings of cork threaded on a wire. The head and tail are also of cork cut, as shown.

A piece of the wire, projecting from the mouth, forms the long tongue. A tiny blob of sealing wax, carefully moulded, makes the forked tip.

The penguin's head and body are made of cork with a match stalk for the neck. The beak, flippers, and feet are made of paper. Paint in the eyes and the black parts of the head, flippers, and body. To allow him to stand, as shown in the picture, glue one of his feet to a firm circle of cork.

AROUND THE FIRST decade of the twentieth century, there was a craze for children to make animals and people from potatoes.[21]

Potato People from Spudsville

Potatoes can be great fun. They are excellent fun and a splendid challenge for a party competition.

Idaho Bess, Potato Puss, Porky Spud and their friends

All you need is some potatoes and a penknife apiece to shape them. When you come to examine potatoes you will find they are of various shapes. The potatoes which are nice, even, and oval are generally the best for this purpose. Peeling the potato is apt to make the surface uneven, so take a scrubbing brush and brush all the brown skin away. This is easily done, and any little eyes can be got out with the penknife.

THE POTATO PEOPLE looked stranger as the spuds got older and older.

SOME HOMEMADE TOYS not only looked good but actually worked. Here is a description of two musical instruments that could be played.[22]

MUSICAL TOYS

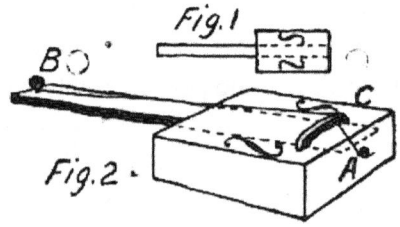

The first illustration shows how to make a simple little one-stringed guitar. Procure a cigar-box, and strip all the paper off it. Then get a strip of wood, measuring two feet long by two inches wide, and sandpaper it to make it smooth. Take the cigar box, and after having cut two S-shaped holes in it, nail it onto one end of the stick, as shown in the picture. Now nail the lid firmly onto the box, and put two screws in—one at the end of the box (A) and the other at the end of the handle (B). Next, get a "D" violin or banjo string and a small banjo bridge. Tie the string to the screws, and put the bridge underneath it towards the end of the box {(D). The toy guitar can be tuned to any key on the piano by tightening or loosening the screw on the handle, and different notes can be made by pressing the fingers of the left hand on different parts of the string and plucking it with the thumb of the other hand.

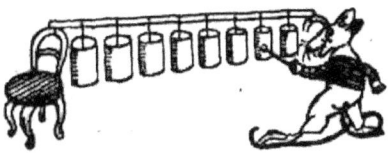

The second toy is equally simple. It is a set of chimes, and eight round tins are required to form a complete scale. One can find its notes by tapping them with a pencil, and no two tins ring exactly alike. Free them of all paper and make a hole in the bottom of each. Cut eight strings, each six inches long, tie a knot at the end of each, and thread them through the holes in the tins.

Procure a long stick or rod and tie the tins to it. Arrange the tins in order of size, smallest to largest. A hammer can be made from a knitting needle, with the end covered in thick felt. With the chimes hanging down tap them with the hammer., A simple little tune can soon be picked out, and it is surprising what a pretty mellow note the chimes have.

A few of these homemade toys, including musical instruments, survive in our national institutions, including the Melbourne Museum, the Museum of Australia in Canberra and Sydney's Powerhouse.

Tin-Plate Toys

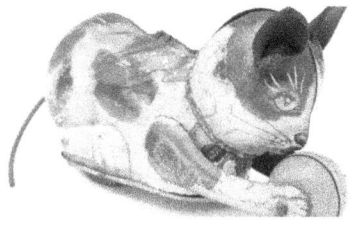

Tin plate pussy. 1895. *Powerhouse*

Tinplate was used in the mass production of toys from the mid-19th century following the invention of sheet metal stamping machines. They were cheap, considerably lighter than cast iron or wood, and therefore cheaper to export. They were manufactured in segments and hand-assembled, then hand-painted with colourful designs. After the 1880s, lithographic printing provided a more detailed finish. The toys, especially the spring-loaded toys, wind-up, and ones that could be propelled, remained popular right up until WW2 when manufacture was discontinued to allow the metals to be used for war production. The major Australian manufacturer was Melbourne-based Leckie & Gray, whose output included some wonderful Australian designs, including a Blinky Bill tea set, Australian trains, Peter's Ice Cream delivery vans and a Minties plane.

Some of the tin-plate vehicles were a work of art.

Tinplate delivery van. Circa 1930. *Luke Jones Collection*

The most popular tin plate toys were cars, trucks, planes, ships, robots, and musical Ferris wheels. Production resumed after the war, particularly in Japan and China. However, in the 1960s, there was a scare that tinplate was dangerous, and many toy makers converted to plastic.

REMEMBERING the Games We Used to Play.

Here is a detailed, passionate and often rambling reminiscence of childhood in the Northern Territory from 1919. Although many will be familiar with it, it is a unique record of the rhymes and games transplanted here. Although attributed to an anonymous 'contributor', such written regional proof is difficult to find.[23]

> What do the children of the Northern Territory play at? Do they know the old games that we played when children? Do they ever play at 'hop-skitch', either with the square or circular diagram? Are 'rounders', or 'prisoner's base', or 'honeypots', or 'egg-cup' known to them?
>
> Do they, ever sing the old songs that we sang in school days? Or our action songs?
>
> HONEYPOTS, HONEYPOTS, ALL IN A ROW,
> *Twenty-five dollars to let one go.*
> *Draw a bucket of water,*
> *For a lady's daughter;*
> *One in a rush, two in a rush,*
> *All creep under a gooseberry bush!*
>
> ORANGES AND LEMONS,
> Say the bells of St. Clements,
> You owe me five farthings,
> Say, the bells of St. Martins,
> When will you pay me?
> Say the bells of Old Bailey,
> As soon as I can,
> Say the bells of St Ann.
> When will that be?
> Say the bells of Old Hackney,
> I'm sure I don't know
> Says the great bell of Bow.
> Chip chop, chip chop, last man's head off.
>
> Who plays "Poor Mary is a weeping" or "See this pretty little girl of mine? Do the Darwin children play "In and out of the window," or

Here comes a duke a-riding

To court your daughter Jane.

Here comes a 'duke a-riding

To court your daughter Jane.

"My daughter Jane is yet too young

To be controlled by such a one;

Go back, go back, you saucy Jack,

And clean your spurs so bright.

"My spurs are bright and richly wrought,

And in this town they were not bought,

And in this town they, were not sold

Neither for silver nor for gold.

Go through! the kitchen, go through the hall

And choose the fairest one of all

The fairest one that I can see

Is little Alice! Come to me.

Who now plays

Here comes an old soldier from Botany Bay,

And what have you got to give him today?

When we played it, we were not allowed to answer any questions with the words "yes, no, nay, black, white, or grey." Doing so put us out.

And our counting games. Who plays them now?

Onery, ooery, ickory, Ann,

Firisty, foresty, ickalum jam

Mickalum, mackalum, mack.

or tongue-twisting nonsense rhymes like

Ena, dena, dina, doe,

Cattlea wena, wina woe,

> Each, peach, pear, plum,
> Out goes old Tom Thumb.

These counting games originated, I believe, among the children of the shepherds of Dartmoor, who still use early English (Anglo-Saxon) words when counting their sheep.

Similarly, "Parley" (a breathing space) has been corrupted to "Barley," and "Here we come gathering knots (i.e. bouquets) of May" is now corrupted to "Here we come gathering nuts and 'may' as if nuts ever ripened at Maying time.

Who now - remembers ."London Bridge is broken down."

And what child now sings:

> GREEN GRAVEL, GREEN GRAVEL, THE GRASS IS SO GREEN,
> The fairest young lady that ever was seen!
> I washed her in milk and I dressed her in silk
> I wrote down her name with gold pen and ink.
> Oh Bessy, oh Bessy, your true love is dead,
> He sent you a letter to turn round your head.

Or do the children ever play and sing 'Drop the handkerchief'?

> I WROTE A LETTER TO MY, LOVE AND ON MY, WAY I DROPPED IT,
> Somebody has picked it up, and put it in his pocket.

We played them all in the old days, boy and girls together - 'Bull in the Ring,' 'Prisoner's base,' 'Eggcup,' 'Rounders,' and hundreds of other games now forgotten. Do the Territory children ever play any of them, I wonder? And who now plays 'A penny to see a poppy-show?'. The little squares of glass, carefully covered from prying eyes, behind which lay pressed flowers, picture scraps, or photos. How proud we were of them? Have they vanished to the limbo of forgotten?

MANY MAGAZINES PUBLISHED material for children. Louisa Lawson, the pioneer feminist, mother of poet Henry Lawson, and erstwhile publisher of *The Dawn Magazine*[24] , often included puzzles and stories for children, such as the following.

'**Forfeits**'. To sit down on the carpet and get up without touching anything.

'**Statues**'. To stand motionless as a statue for three minutes by the watch.

'**Seats**'. For a boy: To repeat the following lines correctly:

Louisa Lawson's magazine, *The Dawn*

> Here I must stand distracted and alone,
> Only just kicking my unhappy feet,
> Until some kind and gentle hand shall come,
> And lead me back to my vacated seat.

He is then to stand until some girl comes and leads him to his seat.

Other games included:[25]

'**Invitation**'. To give some boy or girl an invitation, it must be accepted.

'**Compliments**'. To go around the room giving each boy or girl a compliment

'**Football**'. To tell how a touchdown is made in football without once using the word "and."

'**Donkey**'. Imitate a donkey to the best of your powers.

'**Courtesy**'. To curtsey to everybody in the room without smiling.

'**Backwards**'. To count twenty backwards.

'**Snap**'. To tell instantly, without counting, the fourteenth letter of the alphabet.

'**Spelling**'. Spell Constantinople backwards instantly and without mistake.

ONE RURAL NEWSPAPER columnist bravely suggested some indoor games, adding, 'Try these - if you're game'.[26]

'**Dexterity**'. Lie down on your back full length on the carpet, cross your arms, and try to get up again without using your hands or elbows.

Fold a newspaper so that when you stand up on the floor, it is about a foot high; then, holding the right ear with the left hand and the right foot with the right hand, pick up the newspaper in your teeth.

Place a bottle lengthwise on the floor, sit on it with legs straight out and ankles crossed, and endeavour to pick up a box of matches on your left-hand side and a candle with them on your right-hand side, balancing on the bottle.

Lie on your back on the floor, fold your arms, and, keeping the knees stiff, raise your body to a sitting position. Then, cross your legs, tailor fashion, drawing the feet well in under your body, and, by pressing the sides of the feet onto the ground and straightening the knees, endeavour to gain a standing position.

Kneel on the floor, place the elbow of either arm against one knee, and extend the hand and fingers straight out. With the other hand, place a coin on the floor, just touching the tip of the middle finger. The feat is to pick up the coin with the mouth and thus place it without falling forward, a rather difficult task. (By extending the hands behind the back and drawing the coin towards you with the upper lip, the trick is made rather easier).

Well, that was easy, wasn't it!

For the Children. (By 'Malvina') Outdoor Games.[27]

'**Duck on the rock**'. Each player provides himself with a stone the size of a man's two fists, called a 'duck'. A leader is chosen by "counting out," and he immediately places his duck on a flat-topped rock and stands near it. The other players take positions 8 or 10 yards from the rock, and each in turn tosses his 'duck' at the one on the rock, to knock it off, if possible. As soon as each player has thrown his duck, he runs up to it to watch his chance of securing it. The player who is "it" is on the alert to touch any one trying to secure his duck, and if he succeeds, the one thus touched becomes "it" and at once places his duck on the rock. If one of the players knocks the duck from the rock, the owner of the duck, who is "it," must replace it upon the rock before he can attempt to touch the player, thus allowing the latter to recover his duck in safety. If the leader is skilful, he can often succeed in keeping two or three of the players out of the game by preventing them from picking up their ducks.

'The Sheepfold'.[28] To commence this game, two persons are chosen who are called the wolf and the lamb. All the rest of the players join hands to form a ring, which is called the sheepfold. The lamb stands inside the ring, and the wolf outside; the wolf attempts to enter through the line and capture the lamb. If he seems likely to succeed, the sheepfold opens at the opposite side and lets the lamb out as the wolf enters. The wolf is now imprisoned, but he tries to break out; as he does so, the lamb is again admitted. If the wolf succeeds in catching the lamb, the two players who are responsible for his breaking through become the lamb and the wolf. This is a most fascinating and exciting game. The larger the sheepfold, the longer the wolf can be kept at bay.

And here's an oddity - a game called 'Hissing & Clapping'[29]

Again, this game is useful for soothing things a little when, as they say, the fun has waxed fast and furious. Half the players leave the room, and the rest, having arranged chairs in a row, occupy alternate ones. Each selects which of those outside shall occupy the chair next to his. When this is settled, the outsiders are invited in, one at a time, and told to take the chairs they think have been allotted to them. If the choice is correct, the sitters clap, and the lucky chooser stays in the chair; if not, he is greeted with hisses and sent out again. Another player then comes in, and so on, till all have found their proper seats. It sometimes adds to the interest of this game. Those who are sent out are boys, and those who remain are girls, or vice versa.

So, how do children entertain themselves in the twenty-first century? Firstly, of course, they are involved with all things electronic and the screens offer extraordinary choice. But there are thousands of other options. Many traditional games and activities are still played, and some have been adapted to modern times. As we move closer to the screen, many of the old amusements will disappear. A recent survey of 'what to do with the kids during holidays' came up with some new suggestions: dumpster diving, volunteering as a group for local charity work, hosting a spa party, holding a movie marathon, staging a concert, play or ridiculous fashion parade (with the suggestion of using parent's clothing!), hold an organisational party when the group clean out a room, garage etc; host a junior dinner party or a Masterchef competition (with a specified number of ingredients); have a plastic cup-stacking; photographic contest with smartphones; organise a bedroom makeover party. - Definitely new amusements for new times.

4

SINGING THE BABY TO SLEEP

The first Australian collection of Nursery Rhymes

In his introduction to *Cinderella Dressed In Yella: Australian Children's Play-rhymes*, historian Ian Turner lamented the absence of Australian nursery rhymes.[1]

There is no independent tradition of Australian nursery rhymes, although several writers have ventured into the field - with little success; but this rhyme, contained in a letter from the journalist A. W. Jose to literary critic A. G. Stephens, 28 April 1898, deserves to be remembered:[2]

> JINKY, JUNKY, ROLLICKING JO!
> Fifty maidens all in a row
> Went to a Sunday school picnic,
> Went out walking down by the 'crick':
> Home they went again, all in a row,
> Fifty - maidens? Never no mo'!

The European settlers of this country indeed brought the rhymes, baby games, and nursery rhymes they had within their family circles. These were mostly the well-known examples of England, Ireland, Wales, and Scotland. However, they also changed the words and, very occasionally, the melody to reflect their new environment and, in doing so, contributed to the continuing tradition. They also did this with the old songs and ballads of their homeland. New rhymes would also have been composed, sometimes to stay within the family tradition and sometimes getting a wider distribution. The real point here is that indigenous rhymes would have had a big challenge to usurp the grand canon of nursery rhymes that had already served so well and were embedded in the public mind.

NURSERY RHYMES ARE SPOKEN, and lullabies are sung worldwide to settle infants in the 'Land of Nod' and to banish the fear of the dark in older babies and children. The calming sound of the steady rhythm, simple repetitive words, and melodies, often accompanied by rocking, patting or swaying, help the most fractious child. Gently singing lullabies can also be therapeutic for moms and dads, allowing them to escape to a quieter, calmer place after their day's work. The child also unconsciously learns rhythms and basic speech patterns.

Victorian Wide Awake Book

ROCK-A-BYE BABY ON THE TREE TOP,
When the wind blows, the cradle will rock;
When the bough breaks, the cradle will fall,
Down will come cradle and baby and all.

Hush-a-by-baby[3] is one of the most famous nursery songs and chills when dissected. It is set in the future; it places the baby in a dangerous situation (what the heck is the cradle doing in a tree top?), and we are left with the thought that the cradle and baby will come tumbling down to earth. Many nursery rhymes and lullabies have hidden stories as part of their history. Many are nonsensical but, of course, this doesn't matter one iota if they do their job.

In the first Australian Children's Folklore newsletter issued by the Institute for Early Childhood Development (Kew, Victoria) in 1981, joint editors Gwenda Davey and June Factor reported how the I.E.C.D. students of 1980 had interviewed 90 Anglo-Australian mothers of babies under 12 months about the games, songs rhymes and routines they played with their infants. The top ten nursery rhymes of a total of 124 remembered items were: Peek-a-boo, This Little Piggy Went To Market, Round and Round the Garden, Humpty-Dumpty, Pat-a-cake, Can you keep a Secret?, Rock-a-bye-baby, Clap hands till Daddy (etc) comes home, Baa Baa Black-sheep, and that perennial evening favourite, Twinkle Twinkle Little Star, based on a melody by W.A. Mozart. Almost all of the above are considered nursery standards of the English-speaking world. The other aspect is that most are touchy-feely nursery rhymes. In these overtly politically correct times, it is important to acknowledge the positive role of physical and sight communication between the parent, carer and child.

Today's parents are generally not natural singers, but necessity encourages them to develop a cobbled-together repertoire. They often call upon songs from their youthful days and are just as inclined to croon 'Moon River' or 'Swing Low Sweet Chariot' as singing traditional rhymes.

IT WAS *THE BULLETIN MAGAZINE*, the former champion of all things Australian, including national poets like Henry Lawson, Henry Kendall and A. B. Paterson, who first campaigned for more Australian-sounding nursery rhymes. Prompted by a letter from an obviously flag-waving republican correspondent, "Ah Gee", who fervently argued:[4]

> In our Australian literature, there is a considerable gap that I propose the Red Pages should fill. I mean nursery rimes. Surely Australian nursery songs are as important (nearly) as Australian drama or fiction. This field has been almost neglected, despite a large and expectant public... At present, we have to give our youngsters 'Banbury Cross' and 'Dick Whittington' and 'I've been to London to see the Queen' - which are quite out of place in this land of kangaroos, rabbits and politicians.

The magazine's editor of the famous Red Pages, Arthur Adams, took up the challenge and, in October 1917, announced that around a thousand rhymes had arrived. The contest offered

> One guinea for the best nursery rhyme written by an Australian - for Australian kiddies - no parodies will be accepted… Competitors need not deliberately drag in Australian references or Australian colour - an Australian kid has an outlook different from that of an English kid: the sort of songs he wants to sing will not be those that the English kid sings.

It is obvious from many of the contributions that people had different ideas of what a nursery rhyme should sound like. Jean Macpherson's 'The Moral Tale' had elements children liked, including scary characters and simple rhyme, but it is in poem form, not nursery rhyme, and certainly not intended to be sung. Nevertheless, the editor must have liked the poem, and it certainly celebrates our native Bunyip, our very own boogeyman, and, strangely, the recent arrival of the aeroplane.

THE FIERCE AND FRIGHTFUL BUNYIP

Lives in a lonely scrub,
And catches all the dirty boys
Who do not like their tub.

He has a rapid aeroplane
Steered by a flying-fox,
To grab the naughty little girls
Who never darn their socks.

And many a boy who played the wag
The fearsome Bunyip caught,
And girls who would not do their task
Back to his den he brought.

> There in a dark and horrid pool
> He soaks the dirty boys,
> and feeds small bunyips on the girls
> In spite of all their noise.

The Bulletin's gold guinea was divided between two writers, D. H. Souter for 'The Man from Mungindi' and Walter E Perroux[5] for 'Old Bob's Canter'.

> **THE MAN FROM MUNGINDI WAS COUNTING SHEEP;**
> He counted so many he went to sleep.
> He counted by threes and counted by twos,
> The rams and the lambs and the wethers and ewes;
> He counted a thousand, a hundred and ten -
> And when he woke up, he'd count them again.

> **OLD BOB'S CANTER**
> **THREE HA'PENCE FOR TUPPENCE,**
> Three ha'pence for tuppence,
> That's what the hoof beats do say.
> Daddy rode off to the township
> To buy me a dolly today.
> Soon, I will hear him returning,
> Three a'pence to tuppence,
> Three a'pence for tuppence,
> Oh, daddy, I do so love you

In comparing traditional rhymes to Australian originals, a writer in the *Brisbane Telegraph*, 1931, was extremely generous, saying: "How near to perfection, on the other hand, does our own Louis Esson come in this fascinating Australian lullaby":

> **BABY, O BABY.**[6]
> Baby, O baby, fain you are for bed,
> Magpie to mopoke busy as the bee;

The little red calf's in the snug cow- shed.

And the little brown bird's in the tree.

Daddy's gone a shearing, down the Castlereagh,

So we're all alone now, only you and me,

All among the wool-o, keep your wide blades full-o!

Daddy thinks o' baby, wherever he may be.

Baby, my baby, rest your drowsy head,

The one man that works here, tired you must be;

The little red calf's in the snug cow- shed,

And the little brown bird's in the tree.

The following lullaby, written by the Australian poet Maurice Furnley and first published in 1918, has an appealing nursery rhyme feel.

SLEEP SONG

Half past bunny time,

'Possums by the moon;

Tea and bread-and-honey time,

Sleep-time soon.

WRAPT IN A MOONBEAM[7]

Wrapt in a moonbeam,

Sealed with a star,

Something came o'er the mountain

So blue and so far.

A cobweb here caught it,

But Eola swept along,

And wafted it on with

The breath of his song.

The wallabies are watching:

With bright eyes agleam,

And the breezes are bringing

The wee one — a dream!

The very rhythm of some of the lullabies makes you sleepy - which, of course, is why they remain popular and memorable.

DAY IS OVER 8

By, baby, day is over,

Bees are drowsing in the clover,

By, baby, by;

Now the sun to earth is sinking,

While the cow-bells tinkle, tinkle,

By, baby, by.

MATTHEW, MARK, LUKE AND JOHN 9

Matthew, Mark, Luke and John

Guard the bed that I lie on

Four corners to my bed.

Four angels round my head;

One to watch, one to pray,

And two to bear my soul away.

ANOTHER VERSION.

Matthew, Mark, Luke and John,

Bless the bed that I lie on,

The are four corners to my bed,

Four angels round my head,

One to watch, and one to pray,

And two to bear my soul away.

Now I lay me down to sleep,

I pray the Lord my soul to keep.

If I should die before I wake,

I pray the Lord my soul to take.

In 1959, *The Bulletin Magazine*, in an article on nursery rhymes, cited a parody:[10]

> Matthew, Mark, Luke and John,
> Guard the bed that I lie on.
> One to watch and one to pray,
> And one to keep the fleas away.

ROCK-A-BYE [11]

Oh, rock-a-by, rock-a-by, baby, my darling,
The whispering gum leaves will hush you to rest;
When the little bright eyes of the possums are peeping
'Tis time for my baby to creep to his nest.

Oh, lull-a-by, lull-a-by, wattles are bending,
And singing their songs of the day that is dead;
The cry of the curlew comes weird in the darkness,
So 'tis time for my baby to go to his bed,

Then hush-a-by, hush-a-by, baby is sleeping!
The night songs that bush babies only can hear
Have lulled him to sleep, and the gumtrees will guard him,
And the bright stars are watching to drive away fear.

It is probably unsurprising that a government department publication would tend towards safer rhymes like the following. The truth is that such inclusion shows a certain ignorance of the role of lullabies.... they are not primarily for adults to admire the poetic setting, but rather about catching the child's imagination.[12]

BABYLAND

How many miles to Baby-land ?
Anyone can tell;
Up one flight
To your right—

Please to ring the bell!

What can you see in Baby-land?

Little folks in white;

Downy heads.

Cradled beds,

Faces pure and bright.

What do they do in Baby-land?

Dream and wake and play,

Laugh and crow,

Shout and grow—

Jolly times have they.

What do they say in Baby-land?

Why, the oddest things!

Might as well

Try to tell

What the baby sings!

Who is the queen of Baby-land?

Mother, kind and sweet;

And her love.

Born above,

Guides the little feet.

WYNKEN, BLYKEN & NOD *13*

Wynken, Blynken, and Nod one night

Sailed off in a wooden shoe—

Sailed on a river of misty light into a sea of dew.

The old moon laughed and sang a song

As they rocked in the wooden shoe,

And the wind that sped them all night long

Ruffled the waves of dew.

All night long their nets they threw

For the fish in the twinkling foam,

Then down from the sky came the wooden shoe,

Bringing the fishermen home.

Wynken and Blynken are two little eyes,
And Nod is a little head,
And the wooden shoe that sailed the skies
Is a wee one's trundle bed.

So shut your eyes while mother sings
Of wonderful sights that be,
And you shall see the beautiful things
As you rock in the misty sea,
Where the old shoe rocked the fishermen three
Wynken, Blynken and Nod.

The following poem counts fingers. This was published in numerous Australian newspapers.

The Fingers

This is little Tommy Thumb,
Round and smooth as any plum.
This is busy Peter Pointer;
Surely, he's a double-jointer.
This is mighty Toby Tall,
He's the biggest one of all.
This is dainty Reuben Ring;
He's too fine for anything.
And this little wee one, maybe,
Is the pretty Finger Baby.
All the five we've counted now,
Busy fingers in a row.
Every finger knows the way.
How to work and how to play;
Yet together, they work best,
Everyone helps all the rest.

A Hop, a Skip and a Jump

The man from Meninche was counting sheep;
He counted so many he went to sleep.
He counted by threes and he counted by twos,
The rams and the lambs and the wethers and ewes;
He counted a thousand, a hundred and ten—
And when he woke up he'd to count them again.
—D. H. S.

Parents as Singers.

Not every parent or carer is comfortable as a singer; however, babies and young children never mind. They enjoy the fact that the big person is singing a pattern of words to them, which is comforting. One of the reasons standard, age-old nursery rhymes have survived so long is that they are memorable and so easy to sing; even a bad singer can string the words and tune along. Songs with inflections, especially surprise endings, such as 'Pop Go the Weasel', can usually produce a giggle from babies and young children and, combined with a facial expression when the 'pop' appears, only adds to the fun. We know these small brains, ever curious, ever being conditioned to what's around them, soon get used to particular rhymes, and their eyes tell you they are waiting for the strange bit - like when where the 'pop!' comes in.

Very Australian Nursery Rhymes

The search for Australian nursery rhymes became a minor obsession, especially in the first quarter of the twentieth century - indeed, if the number of articles and reader submissions can be taken as a guide. Perhaps the interest was spurred by the mass population shift in the 1890s when so many people relocated from the bush to the coasts and cities. There certainly was a nostalgia for the old ways of bush life, and we know part of the popularity of Henry Lawson and A. B. Paterson was attributable to a certain reflective romancing of bush life, a simpler life. It also has to be taken into account that the first decade of city life, from Federation in 1901, was a time of topsy-turvy for many who lived in cramped urban accommodation, often shared with other families in areas often described as slums. Influenza was also rife, especially amongst children, resulting in more bedtime and, understandably, more reflection. Add to this mix the ongoing feeling that Australians, as a people, were feeling isolated from Britain. Feelings of nationalism ran high post-Federation, and possibly, part of this started with the rhymes sung to small children. Wombats, kangaroos, waratahs and wattle were more real than dairy maids, fairy kingdoms and flowery dells.

Here are three nursery rhymes published in the *Northern Territory Times* in 1930.

BAA BAA YOU BOSHTER 14 SHEEP, HAVE YOU ANY WOOL?
Too right, you bet your life I have - bonzer bales quite full.
Some they'll ship across the seas to keep the people warm

A Hop, a Skip and a Jump

But some we'll keep at home, mate, for our mills to spin and form,

Baa away you boshter sheep make haste and grow your wool.

Keep well away from dingoes so the bales may be packed full.

THERE WAS A LITTLE AUSSIE BOY WHO MET A KANGAROO,

She put him in her pocket and off with him she fled,

Hop skip and jump through trees and scrub

And then across the plain

Oh, what a tale he had to tell when he got home again.

THEY SAY THE LITTLE BLACKBOYS CLIMB UP THE TREES

And eat the lovely honey - they steal it from the bees.

But I wouldn't be a blackbody for while he eats and clings

His mouth may get the honey but his legs get all the stings.

Australian Nursery Rhymes. In the 1930s, Australia was feeling cocky - we had fought well in WWI, and we had done well in the 'roaring twenties'. We had also seen our cultural flag waving in London when Arthur Benjamin's opera 'The Devil Take Her' was staged at Covent Garden in 1931, conducted by Sir Thomas Beecham. It made us more determined to find the elusive Australian nursery rhyme.[15]

Australians seem so far to have failed to develop an indigenous set of nursery rhymes with as universal an acceptance as these which the ancestors of the present generation brought from a colder climate. Excellent as are the verses in *The Children's Treasury of Australian Verse*, and the larger *Oxford Book of Australian Verse for Children*, none of these poems has achieved the universal popularity of the older nursery rhymes. While Ethel Turner and May Gibbs and many another have produced most appealing sets of verses for children, few of these can be said to have reached the heights of fame or the depths of popularity of the traditional nursery rhymes. For just as, despite all climatic obstacles, the cold country Christmas of tradition has perpetuated itself in this tropical region, so the old traditional favourites still remain the traditional favourites, and children in a country, that may be crying out for rain, early learn to chant:

'Rain, rain go away - Come again some other day.'*

The power of tradition is very strong in children's games and verses. Australia was founded too recently to have established many traditions of its own, and, in any case, it was founded at a time when such traditions as these had become well set, and however popular the native singers have become, they have failed to displace the old nursery rhymes which have been handed down for many generations. Perhaps it is because in the present age of sophistication when Australia began to reach cultural maturity, genuine inspiration capable of producing Indigenous nursery rhymes was lacking. *The Sydney Bulletin,* it is true, some years ago, in one of its campaigns on behalf of a thoroughgoing native literature, unearthed a wealth of material that it accepted as the basis for a collection of Australian nursery rhymes. These it divided into several classes. There were Aboriginal rhymes built upon the language of the Australian blacks; there were rhymes of station life, rhymes of city life, nonsense rhymes, rhymes based upon nature life in Australia and war rhymes. But as admirable as the gems of this collection appeared, there is no evidence that they have secured an enduring hold upon the minds of Australian children. One contributor to *The Bulletin* research, upon this occasion, recorded that she had heard Australian children singing:

> *Captain Cook*
> *Wrote his book*
> *Looking for Australia.*
> *Captain Cook*
> *Wrote a book*
> *All about Australia.*

Then there was this parody of 'Ten Little Black Boys', which gave this idea an Australian setting:

> **TEN LITTLE RABBITS.**
>
> *Ten little Rabbits playing around a mine,*
> *One slipped down a shaft, then there were nine.*
> *Nine little Rabbits, hopping through a gate,*
> *One caught in a snare, and then there were eight*
> *Eight little Rabbits, gazing up to Heaven,*
> *An eagle-hawk swooped down on one; then there were seven.*
> *Seven little Rabbits, up to their tricks. -*
> *When a, red fox grabbed one, then there were six.*
> *Six little Rabbits, hunted in a drive,*
> *One got a dose of shot, then there were five.*
> *Five little Rabbits, drinking round a bore,*
> *One got squirted up, then there were four.*
> *Four little Rabbits, scratching round a tree.*
> *One ate a quince-jam bait, then there were three.*
> *Three little Rabbits saw a jackaroo,*
> *One got asphyxiated, then there were two.*
> *Two little Rabbits, flirting in the sun,*
> *A goanna swallowed one, then there was one.*
> *One little Rabbit, feeling lonely, when*
> *She had a family, and again there were ten.*

Several others of the rhymes, for which contributors claimed some degree of local acceptance, certainly conformed to the requirements of a perfect nursery rhyme. This one —

> **WALLABY, WALLABY, WHY DO YOU JUMP,**
> And never fall down on your head with a bump
> And why is your tail so thick and so strong,
> And your front legs so short and hind legs so long?

— possesses the simplicity and charming in consequence of the best models. And, amongst the nonsense rhymes were to be found qualities that should appeal to the most discriminating sense of nonsense —

> **JUMPITY, JUMPITY, KANGAROO,**
> Tell me where you are jumping to?
> Over the grass-trees all the day long,
> Till my hands grow short and my tail grows long.

Altogether, *The Bulletin* investigation seemed to indicate that, considerable local material existed, but the impulse to popularise the indigenous product seems to have been lacking. In this particular sphere, the child is the final arbiter, and if he/she continues to prefer the old rhymes, then the old rhymes will retain their popularity.

IN THE LATE nineteenth and early part of the twentieth century, there was a continuing interest in encouraging Australian nursery rhymes, either new ones or remodelling of the old. Several newspapers ran competitions to encourage readers to contribute. *The Arrow*, a Sydney newspaper, launched such a competition in 1889, suggesting the first line: 'He told them he came from Bourke', and that they intended to 'get up a list of rhymes for Australian towns'. They offered a 5/- prize. Most submissions were limerick-style verse.

HE TOLD THEM HE CAME FROM THE BARWON.
To be a clown In a circus— a 'star' one.
Thus, the manager spoke.
When he tried his little joke,
'You can't act the fool, for you are one.

From Windsor Town, he made his way,
And went to see the English play.
He strongly backed the parson gent,
And wandered home without a cent.

In 1924, *The Advocate*, Burnie, Tasmania, announced a nursery rhyme competition specifying native animals, trees, or flowers. L. P. Gilham, East Marrawah, won first prize.

WALLABY, WALLABY, HOPPING ALONG,
With his front legs so short and back legs so strong,
He hopped into the paddock to dine off the grain,
But when he saw me, he hopped out again,
I called, "Wally, Wally, I want you to stop,
And I'll give you some feed if you'll teach me to hop,"
But he only went faster, he was frightened, you see,
Because I look pretty big, and today I turned three.

Here is a selection from the competition shortlist:

COCKATOO, COCKATOO, WILL YOU TELL ME WHAT YOU DO,
When you come in flocks and settle on the plain,
The people all about shake their heads and say, "No doubt
We are going to have a lot of wind and rain."

LITTLE GREY COTTONTAIL, WHERE ARE YOU GOING?
Over the hill where the green grass is growing.
If you go there, you're sure to be shot
Baked in an oven or stewed in a pot.

LITTLE MISS POSSUM

Sat eating some blossom

Under a big wattle tree.

"I think," said a 'skeeter',

"For lunch, I shall eat her,

But what'll I have for my tea?"

EARLY IN THE MORNING WHILST WE'RE STILL IN BED.

Oh! My goodness, gracious! What was that I said?

Sitting on a wattle bough, hear him sing so far,

Mister Jackass laughing, Ha! Ha! Ha!

THE EMU RACED WITH THE KANGAROO.

Across bare paddocks and through the bush, too;

The emu ran, but he kept on stopping

So the kangaroo won - for he kept on hopping.

ONCE A LITTLE JACKASS

Sat upon a tree.

He laughed and talked and chattered,

And didn't think of me.

But one day I wandered closer,

and asked him what he said,

And then he straightway answered me

By jumping on my head!

THE LITTLE GREY POSSUM

Climbed up a gum tree;

The foolish old jackass

Laughed loud with glee.

The naughty young dingo

Came out of the bush,

And gave the old wombat

A very big push.

In the search for Australian nursery rhymes an article in *The Bulletin* magazine, 1910, reported a local Sydney chant:[16]

JOHNNY AND JANE AND JACK AND LOU,
Butler's Stairs through Woolloomooloo,
Woolloomooloo and 'cross the Domain,
Round the Block and home again.
Heigh ho, tipsy toe,
Give us a kiss and away we go.

Northern Territory Times September 1930

"COME INTO MY POCKET," SAID BIG MRS ROO
"There's plenty of room for a kiddy like you".
But I said, "No thank you, your pouch is too small -
There's no room for a girlie at all
Why when your own baby hops into his bed
He has got to sleep there with heels over his head?"

In 1919, *The Farmer's Advocate, Melbourne, decided that* Nurseryland was out of control - enough was enough!

WE HATE THOSE SILLY NURSERY RHYMES
You teach your son and daughter -
"Jack and Jill went up the hill
To fetch a pail of water."

If any young Australian went
To look for nature's fountain,
We rather think he'd seek the creek,
And not go up the mountain.

"Mary, Mary, quite contrary,
How does your garden grow?"
Now, there's a silly thing to ask,

> For how could Mary know?
> But ask a young Australian,
> And she'll tell you in a minute -
> "The garden doesn't grow at all,
> You mean the things that are in it."

Nursery rhymes stereotyping farmers as yokels. [17]

Nursery rhymes were blamed for the popular picture of a farmer as a 'hayseed' by Mr J. Wain, President of the National Farmers' Union, in a speech to farmers.

> "Complaining that whenever in a nursery rhyme it was desired to set out something that was ridiculous, it was always done in rural terms, he said: 'Little Bo-Peep, with its rhyme about sheep — leave them alone and they'll come home — tends to give the impression that farmers are a Macawber sort of people who have a blind trust in Providence. 'In 'Three Blind Mice,' when they selected someone for the mice to run after — 'They all ran after the farmer's wife'— though it would be the last woman they would run after. Then, what was the moral of Simple Simon, 'Going to the Fair,' which was a well-known rural custom? It was that he was trying to get possession of something of which he was not in a position to pay, a principle flouted much oftener in towns than in the country".

In 1923, a Queensland newspaper offered a 20th-century lullaby reflecting on technological change.[18]

> **FATHER'S IN HIS MONOPLANE, SAILING ROUND THE MOON,**
> *Mother's in the taxicab, won't be home til noon,*
> *Brother's in his motor boat, on the silent sea,*
> *Rock we motor-cradle in the nursery.*
>
> *See the silver dream balloon down the Milky Way,*
> *Floating through the starry drift to bear you far away,*
> *Aeronauts with poppies crowned at the helm I see,*

Rock we motor-cradle in the nursery.

And another Queensland newspaper in the twenties took a more rural approach.[19]

> I HEAR THE CATTLE LOWING
> *Above the bleat of sheep,*
> *My arms will be your cradle*
> *While shadows 'round you creep.*
> *The koala is crying*
> *Where creek and river meet,*
> *And tall blue gums are crooning*
> *This lullaby so sweet.*

Even the *Australian Women's Weekly* joined in the cry for Australian nursery rhymes when, in 1938, Colin Wills wrote:[20]

'Wally Wallaby' Means More Than 'Miss Muffet'

Nursery rhymes are more than the earliest entertainment of children. They develop the sense of rhythm, the sense of humour, and the imagination.

Traditional English nursery rhymes are, in their way, perfect works of art. But it seems to me that they must eventually be supplemented by new rhymes and, in the case of Australian children, by Australian rhymes.

This is not an absurd piece of petty patriotism; I do not suggest that Australian rhymes would be superior, or that we ought to prefer them. But the old rhymes are gradually losing some of their value to our children not through any fault in them, but because we are growing away from them. They are based in a tradition that becomes, every year, more remote from anything Australian children know or understand the tradition of pastoral England. It is true that they can be explained to our children in so far as they can be explained at all. Some of them are so old that their significance is completely lost;

they are merely rhythmic sound patterns. But while you can explain to a child that 'Little Miss Muffet's' tuffet was a little hassock, and that curds and whey is junket, you cannot make these things link up with the familiar environment. You are translating from a foreign language.

Ding Dong Dell, Pussy's in the well...

It is still a delightful ballad, but its significance is not immediate. The church-bell as the village signal of alarm is unknown here; the well is a rarity, not a universal, familiar thing I don't suggest that the rhyme should be modernised like this:

Phone the cops again - Pussy's down the drain.

Any attempt to amend the old nursery rhymes, however artistically, would be ridiculous as well as outrageous. But you see that much of the sense of the rhymes is lost to the young child, this doesn't matter at all. A pleasing rhythm and a few familiar words are enough for him, but older children must get the feeling that these rhymes belong to a world they don't know, and that not merely because it's antique. Unconsciously, the lack of a familiar tradition, the lack of a native folklore bound up with the surroundings of one's own childhood is bound to produce a sense of detachment and exile.

This may sound far-fetched, but consider the state of mind of most Australian adolescents; they are restless, sceptical, and susceptible to any foreign influence because they have no homeland influence to inspire them. America long ago realised this danger - a danger inevitable when people move to a new world. So, an American tradition has been built up, not only in the crude sentimentality of "the old hometown," but also in little local customs, American folk stories, and even American nursery rhymes.

These don't replace "Mother Goose" - they supplement her. And that's what we must do here.

For the nursery rhymes of children, they are the beginning of the art and culture that make a country a home land, not merely a place in which we happen to live. There have been several attempts to produce Australian nursery rhymes, and some of them have been charming.

But what is needed is a steady flow of children's rhymes, from which time and the unerring taste of children will select a few to endure I've written a few little rhymes which appear on this page, not with any idea of trying to set a standard, but just to start the ball rolling.

OLD WALLY WALLABY, BLUEY ON HIS BACK -
Hop along, hop along, hop along the track.
Give him tea and 'bacca, and tucker for his pack,
But don't give him yakka - or he won't come back.

The following verse—'Sent by Annie W. Scott, Port Kenny, was published in a newspaper's children's column in 1927[21]

LITTLE JIKA JIKA!
All the darkies like her
In her dainty Sunday dress and pinny.
Give her wattle blossom
And a joey 'possum.
She's a good Australian picaninny.
She lives outside Benalla

With her father Doutta Galla,

Who eats snakes for breakfast till he's pale

He kills them with a waddy,

And devours the head and body,

And little Jika Jika eats the tail.

Events in Australia's history produced nursery rhymes. The discovery of gold in 1851 spun the world, and even the simple nursery rhyme couldn't escape the lust for gold.

Nursery Rhymes For the Diggings.[22]

(Air"—Hush-a-by Baby.")

Rock away, cradle, at the pit top;

When the stream flows, the cradle must rock;

When the gold fails, the digging's a bore,

And away go the diggers to look for some more.

(Air—"Sing a Song of Sixpence.")

Sing a Song of Sixpence, a pocket full of gold,

In four and twenty hours, you've a fortune there, I'm told;

When you've staid a fortnight, you're rich as any king,

Isn't that to contemplate, a very pleasant thing?

In *The Bulletin Magazine* 1917, one contribution fit well into the tickle and body identification tradition.[23]

My little bush humpy

Of wattle and daub (touches baby's head)

With bark on the roof (touches baby's hair)

And chimney of slab (touches baby's nose)

The door's in the middle (touches baby's mouth)

The windows are two (touches baby's eyes)

So pull down the blinds. (touches baby's eyelids)

Scaring the Baby. The Boogeyman.

Enjoying being scared is a reaction to things we usually shun. Spooky stories have been part of storytelling for centuries. As a society, because of films, we may have become conditioned to being scared by horror as enjoyment. Indeed, in the early twentieth century, some of the most popular Hollywood films were in the shock (and shlock) horror genre. Films starring Bela Lugosi and Boris Karloff attracted large followings. Horror books, especially Bram Stoker's *Dracula* were extremely popular. Horror films and grisly urban myths are still popular with teens.

Is it acceptable to scare young children? One of the earliest play games is Peek-a-boo, a strange game to play on very young children considering our general use of the word "Boo!" to scare people.

Few would doubt most children enjoy being scared by a parent or carer. Perhaps they willingly enter an unconscious agreement, accepting that they will not be harmed. This, of course, doesn't stop them wanting to be scared. There is a line between play scared and being terrified. After all, so many of the traditional fairytales are extremely bloodthirsty and very very scary. The threatening giant that makes the ground rumble, the wicked witch in her gingerbread house, the capricious elf and so on have lately joined the cast of trolls, dragons, slithering snakes and other terrifying creatures featured in books and films like *Lord of the Rings* and the Harry Potter series.

Of course, parents and carers have been using these monsters to scare, cajole and generally bully children into obedience and bed for centuries.

The 'Sandman' is one of the most notorious night visitors used to scare children into sleep. If they don't sleep, the Sandman slips in through the window and throws his sand into the eyes of any child awake during the night.

> THE SANDMAN COMES ON TIPTOE,
> Will through the window peep,
> And look at the little children

> Who ought to be asleep.
>
> And when a sleepless child he spies,
>
> Throws sand into its eyes.
>
> Lullaby, lullaby, O sleep, my little child.

"The bushrangers will get you!" was a common 'scare' told to nineteenth-century Australian children who would not go to sleep or generally misbehave. It's hard to imagine a scary Ben Hall or Ned Kelly, and none of the bushranger history points to any harm done to children. The terrifying 'Banksiaman' out of *Snugglepot and Cuddlepie* is a different matter altogether. Many will recall May Gibb's frightening drawings of the 'Banksiaman' carrying off small children by the feet as if they were newly caught chickens.

Some parents use the 'Boogieman' to scare children into eating meals by tapping under the kitchen table with a loud knock - knock - knock and then pointing out to the alarmed child - "It must be the 'boogieman' looking for the child who doesn't eat its supper". Others have the 'Boogieman' hiding under the bed to try and catch children who do not go to sleep.

∼

THE TOOTH FAIRY. One of the most traumatic experiences for a child is the process of losing baby teeth. In comes the 'Tooth Fairy' bearing gifts. Belief in the 'Tooth Fairy' is a relatively recent myth, although exchanging gifts for baby teeth is ancient. In some cultures, the tiny teeth were retained for good luck; in others, it was disposed of in fire or water for additional luck. In Australia, the Tooth Fairy appeared early in the twentieth century, and a child who lost a tooth was advised to place the tooth under their pillow, and, with luck, the Tooth Fairy would collect it while they slept and exchange it for either money or a gift.

. . .

BELIEF IN THE 'TOOTH FAIRY' is an example of the trusting nature of childhood.

Rosemary Wells, in *The Making of an Icon: The Tooth Fairy in North American Folklore and Popular Culture* [24] pointed out:

> While parents are often unsure of themselves when promoting the fiction of the Tooth Fairy, most children report positive outcomes. Upon learning that the Tooth Fairy is not real, 75% of children reported liking the custom; 20% were neutral, and 3% were not in favour and said they did not intend to continue the practice when they became parents.

Children often discover the 'Tooth Fairy' is imaginary as part of the 5- to 7-year shift, often connecting this to other gift-bearing imaginary figures such as 'Santa Claus' and the 'Easter Bunny'.

The author meets Father Christmas at Anthony Hordern's Department Store in the 1940s. *A.F.U.*

Counting **Rhymes** are an important part of nursery lore. They teach children simple mathematical progressions.

One, Two, Buckle My Shoe

One, two buckle my shoe (pretend to tie shoe)

Three, four knock on the door (pretend to knock on the door)

Five, six pick up sticks (pretend to pick up sticks)

Seven, eight lay them straight (pretend to lay sticks down)

Nine, ten, a big fat hen!

Here is the Beehive

Here is the beehive (make a fist)

Where are the bees?

Hiding inside where nobody sees

Watch them come creeping out of the hive

One, two, three, four, five (release one finger at a time from the fist
    (hive)

…BUZZ-ZZZ (wiggle fingers)

Five Green, Speckled Frogs

Five green and speckled frogs (hold up five fingers)

Sat on a speckled log,

Eating the most delicious bugs,

Yum, yum! (rub tummy with other hand)

One jumped into the pool (tuck one finger down)

Where it was nice and cool,

Then there were four green-speckled frogs,

Glub, glub!

Four green and speckled frogs…

(Continue until there are no speckled frogs on the log).

Five Little Ducks

Five little ducks went swimming one day (hold up five fingers)

Over the hills and far away (hold arm across the body and tuck fingers behind the shoulder on the opposite side of the body)

Mother duck said, "Quack, quack, quack, quack" (use your other hand to make a mother duck beak and open and close your hand to quack)

But only four little ducks came back (bring the first hand back to the front with four fingers showing

Continue until no little ducks came back, then;

Old Mother Duck went out one day,

Over the hills and far away,

Mother Duck said, "Quack, quack, quack, quack"

And all of those five little ducks came back.

THE ANTS GO MARCHING 25

The ants go marching one by one (hold up one finger)

Hoorah! Hoorah!

The ants go marching one by one,

Hoorah! Hoorah!

The ants go marching one by one,

The little one stops to suck his thumb (suck thumb)

And they all go marching down to the ground to get out of the rain.

The ants go marching two by two (hold up two fingers)

Hoorah! Hoorah!

The ants go marching two by two,

The little one stops to tie his shoe (pretend to tie shoe)

The ants go marching three by three (hold up three fingers) etc.

The little one stops to climb a tree (climb a tree)

The ants go marching four by four (hold up four fingers)

A little one stops to shut the door (shut a door)

The ants go marching five by five (hold up five fingers)

The little one stops to take a dive (pretend to dive)

The ants go marching six by six (hold up six fingers)

The little one stops to pick up sticks (pick up sticks)

The ants go marching seven by seven (seven fingers)

The little one stops to pray to heaven (pretend to pray)

The ants go marching eight by eight (eight fingers)

The little one stops to shut the gate (shut a gate)

The ants go marching nine by nine (nine fingers)

The little one stops to check the time (check watch)

The ants go marching ten by ten (hold up ten fingers)

The little one stops to shout

"THE END!!"

Spuds

One Potato, Two Potato

Three potato, four,

Five potato, six potato,

Seven potato, more!

This Old Man

This old man, he played one,

He played knick-knack on my thumb;

With a knick-knack paddywhack,

Give the dog a bone,

This old man came rolling home.

This old man, he played two,

He played knick-knack on my shoe;

This old man, he played three,

He played knick-knack on my knee;

This old man, he played four,

He played knick-knack on my door;

This old man, he played five,

He played knick-knack on my hive;

This old man, he played six,

He played knick-knack on my sticks;

This old man, he played seven,

He played knick-knack up in heaven;

.This old man, he played eight,

He played knick-knack on my gate;

This old man, he played nine,

He played knick-knack on my spine;

This old man, he played ten,

He played knick-knack once again;

IN NURSERY RHYMES, children encounter new words they would not hear in everyday language (like *fetch* and *pail* in "Jack and Jill went up the hill to fetch a pail of water").

Nursery rhymes are short and easy to repeat, becoming some of a child's first sentences. Since nursery rhymes are patterns, they help children learn easy recall and memorisation.

Nursery rhymes help develop language. When children hear nursery rhymes, they hear the sounds vowels and consonants make. They learn how to combine these sounds to make words. They also practice pitch, volume, voice inflection, and the rhythm of language.

Nursery rhymes usually tell a story with a beginning, a middle, and an end. This teaches children that events happen in sequence, and they begin to learn how to understand stories and follow along.

Nursery rhymes also introduce alliteration ('Goosey, Goosey Gander'), onomatopoeia ('Baa Baa Black Sheep'), and imagery. Children hear these rhymes and act out what they imagine the characters are doing.

The classic collection *Mother Goose, stories and rhymes from tradition,* was first published in 1695. The English version, *Tales of Past Times, told by Mother Goose,* was published in 1729 and introduced 'Sleeping Beauty', 'Little Red Riding Hood', 'Cinderella', and 'Puss in Boots'. Over the years, there have been claims of a 'real' Mother Goose, including a Mrs Isaac Goose, in Boston in the 17th century.

Many Mother Goose rhymes were political statements. 'Baa Baa Black Sheep' criticises Edward 6th's taxation policy. 'Sing a Song of Sixpence' criticises Henry the 7th's transformation of European politics that led to the Reformation. The fall of Richard the Third, the last of the York Kings, is satirised in 'Humpty Dumpty'. One theory is that the original "Humpty Dumpty" was a cannon used by royalists at the 1648 Siege of Colchester, which was finally brought down by Parliamentarian fire.

Generations of Australian children have been brought up with counting rhymes like 'This Little Piggy Went To Market'. Such nursery rhymes use patterns and sequences, so children begin to learn simple math skills as they recite them. Many rhymes also use numbers, counting, and other math words that children need to learn, such as size and weight.

Sharing nursery rhymes provides a safe and secure bond between parents and children. Positive physical touch between a parent and a child or between children, for example, during clapping rhymes, is important for social development. Funny nursery rhymes, especially with a touch tickle, allow children to develop a sense of anticipated humour.

Nursery rhyme characters experience many different emotions. This can help children identify their own emotions and understand the real emotions of others.

When they act out the nursery rhyme stories they hear, children learn to imagine, be creative, and express themselves.

AND IN THE final comment in the search for the Australian nursery rhyme - what could be more Australian than Marion Sinclair's 'Kookaburra sits in the Old Gumtree'?

This simple rhyme has had its fair share of notoriety. It even ended up in a significant legal stoush after the rock band, Men At Work, innocently used part of the tune in their song 'Land Down Under' and the international copyright owner, Music Sales, chased them through the courts. Before the legal case, most Australians assumed the rhyme was anonymous and in the public domain.[26] It was neither. Legalities aside, the simple rhyme has stood the test of time and deserves to be at the top of our Australian list. The major downside of the case is that people are now reluctant to use the rhyme.

· · ·

MULTICULTURAL AUSTRALIA.

Gwenda Davey, writing in the Australian Children's Folklore Newsletter 1998, made the valid point that one day, the nursery rhyme collection might include material representing our multicultural population rather than just the Anglo-Celtic tradition. [27]

> Perhaps one day, a popular Australian nursery rhyme will derive from a language other than English. It might also be from one of the many Aboriginal languages in Australia, particularly since there is a rich Aboriginal tradition of games and songs for children.

5

WORD GAMES

Silence in the court!

Monkey wants to talk!

Speak up monkey, speak!

(and the next one to speak is 'the monkey')

Speak no evil, see no evil, hear no evil.

No doubt children growing up before the age of television and other passive entertainment had a better appreciation of words, because they read more and, in many cases, valued words. It has been proven that reading for a minimum of fifteen minutes a day can greatly increase vocabulary, yet most Australian children read less than the minimum. Yesterday's child also valued word games ranging from the simple 'I Spy With My Little Eye' to complex brain-scratching conundrums. Many were brought up by parents insisting they learn at least one new word daily. Dictionaries and encyclopaedias were popular in most homes, including the ubiquitous *Webster's Dictionary* and *Encyclopaedia Britannica*.

During the first few years of life, babies usually start gurgling their first words - mama, dada, doggie, bottle, no, and *more*. There is so much going on in their tiny heads, and, like computers, they continually add to their vocabulary. They typically know far more words than they use. By toddlers are two years old, their vocabulary is around 200-300 words, and after another twelve months, around 1,000 words. Storytelling and repeated use of words, usually in tandem with pointing, quickly adds words until the acceleration of pre-school and kindergarten, when the average child has around 2000 words. Six-year-olds typically have a 2,600 word vocabulary and around 20,000 - 24,000 words understood but not used. By the time a child is twelve years old, the receptive vocabulary will be around 50,000 words. And, as we know, some children become veritable 'motor mouths' when they get the power.

Vocabulary is inherited. We learn a stock of words from our family. In previous centuries, children put their vocabulary to work with numerous word games. It is a far cry from youngsters using computers and devices, mostly with autocorrect facilities, which has led to a general loss of words in most young vocabularies. Why learn a word when the machine autocorrects?

This chapter celebrates how children have and continue to use words in play. Most children are fascinated by how words sound and quickly get their favourites. They mingle and mangle them and, as parents and teachers know, will use their favourites regularly, often to the point of annoyance. Children are at their most creative when participating in the oral tradition of rhymes and chants, and the book's last two chapters offer some of the most unusual and popular in this tradition.

Harold Gaze's *Chewg-um-blewg-um* book first published 1919

I Spy With My Little Eye

Imagine living in the back of 'Woop-Woop' in the late nineteenth century. In some cases, it was a one-room cabin with an open fire, kitchen table and sleeping quarters separated by hanging blankets. Newspapers and magazines arrived once a month and were devoured by young and old alike. Most newspapers offered a children's section with conundrums, comics, songs to sing, puzzles, connect-the-dots drawings and 'how-to-make' everything from a boomerang to billycarts.

After the pages had been read and re-read they were used as wallpaper. A big pot of flour and water paste was prepared and the pages neatly assembled on the walls as a change of decor. They also provided an opportunity for one of their favourite games - 'I Spy With My Little Eye', something beginning with ... and the used newspapers and magazines inspired many the word game. Some children call it 'Spotto'.

One advantage of word games is they can be played anytime and anywhere and require no equipment or preparation. One of the most popular early word games was Crambo (its meaning has been lost in time). The game calls for one player to leave the room while the rest of the group chooses a word. The guesser is then called back in and told a word that rhymes with the chosen word. For example, the selected word is 'train', and the clue word given to the guesser is 'main'. The guesser could ask, "Is it a plane?" - and this is where it gets tricky because the players cannot say yes or no; they have to use a linked rhyming word in their reply like "No, it doesn't use high-octane." The guesser could then ask, "Is it something in a house?" to which a response could be, "No, not even a window pane." and so on.

Before the popularity of automatic dishwashing machines, children were often expected to wash and dry up, especially after the evening meal. Melanie Ryan tells of a family game, 'Free Associations'[1],

> We played Free Associations when washing up. Someone said a word, and you responded with the first word that came into your head without a pause or thought. Then the next person did the same, bouncing off the new word. You were eliminated if you took too long or used a word that had already been used.

CHILDREN'S PAGES

Children's pages in newspapers and magazines played a vital role in connecting children. These pages, or 'corners,' were unbelievably popular. They sold newspapers and, along with comics, sparked the imagination of Australian children for decades.

Daily Standard, Brisbane, 1922

The Worker, Brisbane

Children's page banner from the *Sydney Mail*.

The weekly children's sections were fronted by a variety of individuals and were, in the children's minds, celebrities and confidants. Letter writing was encouraged, and this must have been such a welcome window into a wider world for so many rural children. While adults were contributing their 300 words to magazines like *The Bulletin*[2] their children were sending letters, and seeing their name in print, in their favourite weekly section, the children's page. They wrote to 'Cinderella' (*Sydney Mail*), 'Pal Connie' (*Australian Women's Weekly*), 'Uncle Ben' (*Johnstone River & Innisfail Advocate*), 'Aunt Betty' (*Maryborough Chronicle*), 'Uncle Sam' (*Morning Bulletin*, Rockhampton), 'Uncle Bob' (*Euroa News*), 'Captain Andy' (*Kalgoorlie Miner*), 'Uncle Toby' (*The Worker*, Brisbane), 'Wattle Blossom' (*Southern Cross*, Adelaide), 'Aunty Mary' (*Western Mail*, Perth) and 'Charlie Chuckles' (*Sunday Telegraph*, Sydney). The children were addressed as Dear Cobbers, Chums, Cornerites, Clubmates, Dear Nieces and Nephews, Dear Little Friends and Dear Shipmates.

Replying to letters must have proved challenging for the journalists assigned to the children's page. The following are all from *The Smiler News* and the Letters section of Victoria's most popular regional newspaper. One wonders how other children viewed these cryptic replies.[3,4]

Yvonne Grady. '*It was very good of you to spare the time to write us this short note*'.

Ivy Oliver. '*Did the grubs do much damage, Ivy?*'

Alfred Nice. *'We are kept busy attending to our 'Page' each week. How sad your dog died like that, Alfred; we do hope you will soon get another puppy to take his place.'*

Games for Indoors

Imagine it is 1904 in a very different Australia. After outbreaks of the bubonic plague in 1900, many parents were concerned about sending their children off to school. Children were often restricted to home and boredom at the sign of a sniffle. Certain relief came in the Sunday papers with suggestions on how to amuse bored children. 'Patience', writing in *The Australasian,* [5] had some good ideas and is typical of games in the children's section. Although the game called 'gossip' sounds rather odd!

> Children's Amusements by 'Patience'.
>
> Very often it falls upon the elder girls in the family to provide amusement for their younger brothers and sisters, and sometimes it is difficult to know how to entertain these little people.
>
> Children soon weary of one occupation. They like variety and activity and are always ready for something new.
>
> Wet days are often a trial when they can't go to school, and it is then that they get into mischief, which very often ends in trouble for the poor little mites. This might not have happened if some amusement had been provided for them. Children are very fond of scribbling on the walls and doors with chalk and lead pencils, and even jammy fingers have been used for the purpose. For little ones who are inclined to that kind of amusement, the following will provide hours of delight:
>
> '**Flowers**'. Take a large sheet of brown wrapping paper, iron it smooth, and cut it into pieces about six by nine inches. In the florists' seed catalogues, a picture of a large rose can usually be found, which may easily be traced off by laying a piece of thin tissue paper over the picture and following the principal lines of the flower with a soft lead

pencil. This done, it is an easy matter to lay the tissue over one of the brown-paper pages, and after being sure that the pencilled side is toward the paper, again trace over the lines previously made with the pencil. After removing the tissue, a dim outline is seen, which may be lined in a little heavier. Now the picture is ready to paint. If you wish a red rose, colour the blossoms and buds red, and by mixing blue and yellow you can get any shade of green for the stems and foliage. Paint very carefully, and take plenty of time. Other pages may be made from this same rose pattern, colouring the roses pink or yellow. Daisies, lilies, pansies, asters, and many other flowers may be found and used; the greater the variety and colouring the prettier the book.

Storytime. A source of never-failing delight to a number of small children is to have a story told, no matter how old it may be, and have each thing mentioned in the story pictured on paper. For example, take the sentence: "A little girl one day started out with a basket of apples for her grandmother"; in this a little girl, a basket of fruit, and a house will convey the ideas. Tell only one sentence at a time, and let the children hunt for pictures to illustrate. As soon as found and cut out, paste the pictures in a line on a long strip of brown paper. At the close of the story you will find that the children not only like to see the pictures come one after another, but that they will be able to repeat the story quite correctly with the aid of the picture.

'**Gossip**' is a new game, full of fun, and is played like this: The children are seated in a room. One of the girls stands outside, and knocks at the door. She asks for Molly to come outside and tells her a story - something like this: "As Mary stepped into the train today, she dropped her books. A gentleman picked them up and gave them to her," Now it is Molly's turn to knock at the door and ask for another little girl, to whom she tells the story, and so it goes on until all the children have been told. The last one to hear it writes the story down, and it will read something like this:-"'As Mary was stepping into the train today, she dropped her books. The train started, and she fell onto the platform and was very nearly killed. A gentleman who tried to save her had his arm broken and was taken to the hospital to have it set." Any short story may be told so that the little ones can remember something about it. You can see that the fun lies in the extraordinary story that arises from a few simple words, just like gossip!

THESE TWO-WORD GAMES were published in a Sydney newspaper column in 1911.[6]

> '**Given Words**'. Every player whispers to his right-hand neighbour a single word. When everybody knows his word, one player begins by asking a question of his neighbour at the left, who is obliged in his reply to introduce the word previously received, as adroitly as possible, to avoid its detection by his interrogator. If the latter cannot discover the word, he pays a forfeit.
>
> '**Shadow Portraits**'. One of the party is appointed an artist. Each, in turn, is seated near the wall to have the outline of his head, which is cast by a lamp, traced by the artist upon a piece of white paper and pinned to the wall. An assistant cuts out these outlines, and the name of the player is put on the back. These papers are fastened to a dark object, and the players are called upon to guess the names of the originals.

Vonnie Boreham described a word game played at her school:[7]

> We played a game at school where one person stood up the front with their back turned and called out a letter and an action, and the others - that were in the starting line had to do that action - e.g. take 10 little steps, take 1 umbrella (where you turned around and took a step forward), 1 giant step etc. The first one to the caller then became the caller - we played it in the large shelter shed.

Melanie Ryan played 'Categories'.[8]

> 'Categories'. I'm unsure what its real name was, but you'd agree on some categories, like girl's name, boy's name, country, city, animal,

colour, etc. Then, pick a letter and write down as many answers under each category as possible.

Cole's Funny Picture Books

Cole's Funny Picture Book, Melbourne 1879.

Cole's Funny Picture Book is uniquely located in the Australian children's world. Originally published in Melbourne in 1879, it has sold well over one million copies, and it has four different book editions. It has given Australian children both delight and nightmares. Devised and published by E. W. Cole, it is a strange mixture of 'lands' where readers find picture puzzles, lists, and peculiar images that pre-date Photoshop and, in its way, strives for Cole's idea of a better world, including acceptance of racial difference, a daring move at the time. Some of the images were indeed frightening to young readers. 'The Patent Steam Whipping Machine for Flogging Naughty Boys' must have set impressionable young minds whirling. Then there was 'The man with a very long beard that had birds nesting in it', and, if that wasn't enough, there was a completely ridiculous, yet nonetheless scary, drawing of a 'selfish brother who became a screw'.

Quirky advertisement for Cole's Funny Picture Book 1.
Guttenberg

A Hop, a Skip and a Jump

The man with a very long beard.

Our selfish bother who became a screw.

Picture puzzle: find the wolf.

World's longest donkey.

The Cole's Funny Picture Book was one of those books which children returned to time and time again.

'FOLLOW ME' word games usually try to trick the opponent into making a mistake and, consequentially, being made the fool. 'Just like me' is one of the most common trick games, and no matter if the player is wise to the outcome, they are supposed to go along for the ride.

One child invites another to repeat "Just like me." after each statement made.

> *I went up the stairs* (Just like me)
> I opened the door (Just like me)
> I went into a room (Just like me)
> I looked in the mirror (Just like me)
> There was a monkey (Just like me)

'**Lock and key**'. A similar word snares game involved the first player making a statement and the second having to substitute the very last word 'lock' with 'key'.

First player Second player

I am a gold lock (I am a gold key)
I am a tin lock (I am a tin key)
I am a brass lock (I am a brass key)
I am a monk lock (I am a monkey)

'A was an Apple Pie'. This game requires the players to name verbs in alphabetical order. The first player begins, "A was an apple pie. A *ate* it." The second player substitutes a verb that begins with B; the third, a verb that begins with C, and so on. The statement "A was an apple pie." cannot be repeated. So, the game would proceed: "A was an apple pie. "A ate it". "B baked it", "C cut it", "D decorated it", "E enjoyed it", and so on.

'The laughing game'. The players sit around in a circle, and the first player says "Ha" and turns to the person on the left, who must then say "Ha ha", and so it goes on with each player adding a 'Ha' until someone breaks the circle by laughing - which is difficult not to do after a while.

'Acting Out Nursery Rhymes'. Players are divided into two groups. Group one goes outside and decides on a nursery rhyme, then returns and acts out that story, with or without any words. When answered correctly, the other team presented their nursery rhyme.

'Written word games'. It would be easy to say children from the earlier age of copperplate writing and concentrated reading had a better understanding of words. They indeed found time to enjoy complicated written word games. Today's child is still encouraged to read, but most of their written word games are available on computer devices. It could be said they miss out on 'family time' and group competition, but the popularity of word games, however delivered, is still with us. Today's players of computer games like 'Scrabble', 'Chess' and 'Backgammon' are tomorrow's champions of the cryptic crossword.

See if you can find the buried birds in the following lines.

. . .

'BURIED BIRDS'.

1. This wireless sends out microwaves. 2. I feel a distinct throb in my leg. 3. The pigs wallowed in the mud behind the shed. 4. Now, let me see about that. 5. It was not the particular kind I like.

Answers: crow, robin, swallow, owl, lark.

CREATING **and posing riddles** has been part of childhood folklore for eons. Although posed as a question, most riddles become quickly apparent, and part of the fun is for the players to go along with the joke, including wisecrack responses. Like all word games, they make the players think. Riddles were often asked in families, groups of riddles on the same theme, for example, the Bible, the alphabet, or farm life.

Q: Who was the fastest runner in history? A: *Adam - he was first in the human race.*

Clever alphabet riddles would ask:

Q: Why is O the noisiest vowel? A: *Because all the others are inaudible.*

Q: What occurs once in a minute, twice in a moment, and not once in a hundred years? A: *The letter M*

Q: What is it that you can take away the whole and still have some left? A: *The word 'wholesome'.*

Some riddles are silly, and their silliness is part of their appeal, especially to younger riddlers who might not necessarily get pun riddles.

Q: Four women walked under one umbrella, and none got wet; why not? A: *It wasn't raining.*

Q: Would you prefer a lion attacked you or a gorilla? A: *I'd rather he attacked the gorilla.*

Q: What does a hippopotamus have that no other animal has? A: *Baby hippopotamuses*

To show the perennial flavour of riddles, here is a collection from the nineteenth century that includes a couple from a very Australian perspective.[9]

Q: Why is the Governor or NSW like a medical student?
A: Because he's a Sir John (refers to Sir William Denison)
Q: Which is the most dissipated – cake or wine?
A: Cake is often seedy and sometimes tipsy, but wine is always drunk
Q: What do you eat every day that nobody else eats?
A: Your dinner
Q: Why does lightning turn milk and beer sour?
A: Because it doesn't know how to conduct itself
Q: Why is Sydney like a piano?
A: Because it's full of flats and sharps ('flats' refers to apartments and 'sharps' a youth tribe of the 1950s.)
Q: What makes more of a mess than a pig in a stye?
A: Two pigs
Q: When are bakers hard up?
A: When they knead bread
Q: Who is a greater dandy than the butcher?
A: No one, for he is always dressed to kill.

SOLVING **conundrums** was a popular pastime for many Australians, especially older children. Although newspapers and magazines often carried them, children also made up their own. A conundrum is a more complex form of a riddle typically based on a pun; the pun may be either the answer or the question. Here's a conundrum which brings in Ned Kelly

> I'm seen in the streets, I'm seen in the lanes,
> I'm seen in the valleys and also on the plains
> I rest under waters and also on land
> I've encountered Ned Kelly and felt his foul hand
> I traverse steep hills and descend into dales
> No matter to me though a tempest prevails
> I'm impervious to heat and likewise to rain
> And to guess what I am you must cudgel your brain
> *(Answer – Telegraph Wire)*

'**Conundrums**' are designed to be brain-stretching and have a long history in play and folklore. Children's pages in the popular press regularly tormented readers with this type of conundrum.

Brothers and sisters, I have none,
But this man's father is my father's son.
Who is it?

Have you seen Tony Chestnut?
(Response): No!
(trickster then points to toe, knee, chest, nut (head).

If Ting-Tong went to Hong Kong to
play ping-pong with Ding-Dong, and died of
influenza, what did they put on his grave?
Answer: a stone

I saw Esau
Sitting on a seesaw.
How many Esau's in that?
Answer: none

Two O's, two N's, an L and a D,
Put it together and spell it to me.
Answer; London

Shake (extending hand)
Spear! (jabbing victim in belly)
and a clip on the ear!
(hits ears).

ABCD goldfish
MNO goldfish
OSAR

A tongue-twisting game[10]

A good memory-testing game is 'One, Two, Three, Four, Five, Six, Seven, Eight, Nine, Ten'.

The players sit in a circle and repeat, each in turn, the line: One old Oxford ox opening oysters.

When it has gone the round of the circle, it has to be repeated with line two added, thus: One old Oxford ox opening oysters, Two toads totally tired, trying to trot to Tetbury,

On the next round, there are three lines to repeat: One old Oxford ox opening oysters, Two toads totally tired, trying to trot to Tetbury, and Three thin tigers tasting three shilling tea.

A fourth line is added to the three: Four fat friars, fanning fainting fleas.

Line five runs: Five fastidious Frenchmen flying to France for fashions.

You must remember it must be repeated in addition to the first four, and not alone.

So it goes on:

Six successful sportsmen shooting a September snipe.
'Seven saucy schoolboys sucking sugar sticks.
Eight elegant elephants elevating elastic eyebrows.
Nine Newcastle noblemen nibbling nonpareils.

And finally, the tenth, in addition to the other nine (if any of the children are still in the game)

Ten tipsy, tired, tumbling tailors trying to thrust tenpenny thread through their thimbles.

Tongue twisters were used for elocution lessons so children would learn speech patterns. Children saw them as an opportunity to trick other players by making them swear, as in the first example, where it is virtually impossible to recite six times without slipping into a particular word.

The sixth sheik's sixty-sixth sheep is sick.

Peter Piper picked a peck of pickled peppers.
How many pickled peppers did Peter Piper pick?
Peter Piper picked a peck of pickled peppers,
A peck of pickled peppers Peter Piper picked.
If Peter Piper picked a peck of pickled peppers,
Where's the peck of pickled peppers Peter Piper picked?

Betty Botter bought a bit of butter.
"But," she said, "this butter's bitter!
If I put it in my batter,
It will make my batter bitter!"
So she bought a bit of butter
Better than her bitter butter,
And she put it in her batter,
And her batter was not bitter.
So 'twas better Betty Botter
Bought a bit of better butter.

A flea and a fly flew up in a flue.
Said the flea, "Let us fly!"
Said the fly, "Let us flee!"
So they flew through a flaw in the flue.

She sells sea shells by the seashore
She sea-shells that she sells are surely seashells
So if she sells sea-shells on the seashore,
I'm sure she sells seashore shells.

If one doctor doctors another doctor, does the doctor who doctors the doctor doctor the doctor the way the doctor he is doctoring doctors? Or does he doctor the doctor the way the doctor who doctors doctors?

Susie, Susie, sitting in the Chinese shop,
The more she sits, the more she knits,
Susie, Susie, sitting in the Chinese shop.

One-one was a racehorse.
Two-two was one too.
One-one won one race.
Two-two won one too.

Black background, brown background.

Can you can a can as a canner can can a can?

How can a clam cram in a clean cream can?

Action games like 'There Was An Old Soldier Of Botany Bay' are a form of 'charades' in which the trade is mimed out, and the players attempt to guess in conjunction with the rhyme.

>Here comes an old soldier from Botany Bay
>Have you got anything to give him today?
>I'll give him a hat. I'll give him a coat.
>I'll give him a meat pie.... etc

In 1987, a caller to ABC Radio's 'Talking History' discussed playing 'Here Comes An Old Woman From Botany Bay'.[11]

There was a lovely game we used to play inside about 'Here Comes An Old Woman From Botany Bay'. We would sit in a circle, and one was the old woman, and she went outside, and she would come back in with a basket and say:
>Here comes an old woman from Botany Bay
>And what do you have to give her today?

She would stand in front of one person in the ring, and that person would give a forfeit, a shoe, a hair ribbon, or whatever they had, and it went into the basket. Then she would stand in front of someone else and say:

Here comes an old woman from Botany Bay And what have you got to give her today?

Until she had collected forfeits all around. And then she would sit in the middle of the ring with her hands over her eyes, and somebody would take a forfeit out one-by-one and say, holding a forfeit over her head:

Here's a thing and a very pretty thing,
And what's to be done with this pretty thing?

Then the old woman would say what she wanted such as "kiss the doorknob three times," "sing a song", "recite", "do a dance", all those sort of things, and everybody would get something to do. The shy ones would be embarrassed no end when they had to sing a song. I can remember that.

Finger Games. Adults usually teach finger games to young children. There are many such games. In the following, the fingers follow the spoken lines of the rhyme: on the first line, interlace fingers and bring palms together; on the second line, point the first fingers together; on the third and fourth lines, turn hands over to reveal fingertips. Progressively, the church is built, showing the steeple, doors, and parishioners.

> Here's the church
> And here's the steeple,
> Open the door
> And there's the people.

Another finger and face game, as usual without an actual name, involved naming the fingers Chicken, Rooster, Hen and Pullet. On Chicken, the player touches the other person on the forehead; on Rooster, touches the mouth; on Hen, touches the chin; and on Pullet, touches the nose and gently pulls it on Pull-et.

In **'Ipsy wispy spider'** (or Incy Wincy), in lines one and two, two hands imitate a spider's crawl; in lines three and four, hands clapped together in lines five and six, arms flung up and back to represent the sun; lines seven and eight, repeat lines one and two. In many cases, the parent or carer gets the 'spider' to chase the child.

> Ipsy wispy spider climbing up the spout,
> Down came the rain & washed the spider out;
> Out came the sun and dried up all the rain,
> Ipsy wispy spider climbs the spout again.

A facial game based on a rhyme is used to designate the features of the face. The speaker, in turn, knocks on the forehead, touches the eyes, lifts up the nose, and puts a knuckle in the mouth.

> Knock on the door,
> Peep in,
> Lift up the latch,
> Walk in.

The weather rhyme has the player drawing a circle on the child's palm, creeping the fingers up the arm, and tickling under the arms.

> Round and round the circle
> Like a Teddy Bear,
> One step, two step,
> Tickly under there.

'The Baby's Cradle'. On the first line, the fingers are interlaced, palms upward; on the second, the hands are turned over so that the interlaced fingers present a flat surface; on the third, the index fingers are pointed, and the pads are rocked.[12]

> There are mother's knives and forks,
> There's mother's table,
> There's mother's looking glass,
> There's the baby's cradle

Name play. Children enjoy puns and funny names. Here are some of the improbable names that can send them into Giggleland: Miles A. Head, Poppy Cox, Drew Peacock, Earl E. Bird, Lori Driver, Gilda Lily, Warren Peace, Hedda Hare, and Mike Rotch. Theresa Green (trees are green), Isabella (is a bell a necessaity on a bike?)

OTHER NAME PLAYS use book or film titles like *The Yellow River* by I.P.Daly (co-written by Ivana Tinkle), *Over the Mountaintop* by Hugo First, *Supporting Athletics* by Jock Strap, *The Future of Robotics* by Anne Droid & Cy Borg, *Why Should I Walk?* by Iona Carr, *Bubbles in the Bath* by Ivor Windybottom, *A Ride On a Camel* by Major Bumsore and *I Was Prepared* by Justin Case.

ANOTHER GROUP of pun games use answers in response to commonplace questions, especially in teaching children not to use "what?" as a question/statement. In this case, "What?" is "Watt invented the steam engine". The inevitable response to "Why?" is - "Y's a crooked letter, and you can't make it straight!". Another is a response to the lazy use of 'Hey' - "horses eat hay". Another answers the use of "she" (especially referring to a female in the room) with "she's the cat's mother."

The continual use of "I see" usually resulted in a response of "I see", said the blind man, when he couldn't see at all.

If something was black, it was always "black as a black man's bottom".

A fit of coughing was followed by the following: "It's not the cough that carries you off; it's the coffin they carry you off in."

How many full faces can you see? From *Australian Town & Country Journal 20 December 1884*.

SECRET LANGUAGES. Children love the idea of secret languages. They love communicating without the wide world, especially family understanding. In earlier Australia, local butchers usually had a secret language—they would invert words; in other words, they would talk backwards. 'Butchers talk' would be spoken as 'rechtub klat'. Many children were fascinated to hear such weird talk when asking for knucklebones!

Another secret formula language needs some explanation. Ian Mudie, writing in *The Bulletin* in 1959, explains.[13]

> Imagine the old secret language, 'icky-way, oz-way, omen-spay, ike-lay, its-that" (i.e., "which was spoken like this") has gone, and the other day I found a juvenile audience none of whom knew the formula.
>
> YYUR
>
> YYUB
>
> ICUR
>
> YY4ME

......which is decoded:

Too wise you are,

To wise you be,

I see you are

Too wise for me

Another secret language, possibly the most widely distributed, was called 'pig Latin'. S. McKerchar, in her *Reminiscences of Fremantle, West Australia, 1933 - 1938*, recalled this secret language.[14]

> One common speech code was the use of 'Pig Latin'. My sister and I became quite proficient at speaking this and our parents were mystified until Mum worked it out. It simply consists of putting the first letter of a word last and adding 'ay' on the end, this 'pig latin' became 'Igpay Atinlay'. If the word started with a vowel just the 'ay' was added, although there were one or two exceptions such as 'early' became 'earlylay'. Where are you going?" translates phonetically as 'Airwhay array ooyay oingay?" Once the speech is mastered and normal speaking speed is achieved, it is completely unintelligible to the uninitiated.

Rhyming Alphabets have a long history in Australia and date back at least to the 1860s. Certainly many Cockneys came (or were transported) and such alphabets were part of their street trade lingo.

> A for 'orses *(hay for horses)*
> B for mutton *(beef or mutton)*
> C for 'th highlanders *(Seaforth Highlanders)*
> D for dog. (or deferential)
> E for Adam *(Eve or Adam)*
> F for 'vescence *(effervescence)*
> G for police *(chief of police)*
> H for respect *(age for respect)*
> I for Novello *(Ivor Novello)*
> J for oranges *(Jaffa oranges)*

K for 'ancis, *(Kay Francis)*
L for leather *(Hell for leather)*
M for 'sis *(emphasis)*
N for 'adig *(in for a dig)*
O for the garden wall *(over the garden wall)*
P for a penny *(pee for a penny)*
Q for a song *(cue for a song)*,
R for mo' *(half a mo')*
S for you *(it's for you)*
T for two *(tea for two)*
U for films *(for me.)*
V for La France *(vive la France)*
W for a bob *(double you for a bob)*
X for breakfast *(eggs for breakfast)*
Y for Gawd's sake *(why, for God's sake)*
Z for breezes *(zephyr breezes)*

And another, obviously dated by its first-letter reference to the actress Ava Gardner. Denis Tracey recalled his mother calling a version of this The Crazy Telephone Alphabet[15]. It is interesting to contemplate whether there are any contemporary versions of this word game.

A for gardner *(Ave Gardner)*
B for you go *(before you go)*
C for yourself *(see for yourself)*
D for 'cate *(defecate)*
E for brick *(heave a brick)*
F for lump *(elephant)*
G for crying out loud *(gee, for crying out loud)*
H for it *(hate you for it)*
I for lootin *(high-falutin')*
J for cakes (Jaffa Cakes)
K for 'teria *(cafeteria)*
L for 'bet *(alphabet)*

N for a penny *(in for a penny)*
O for the rainbow *(over the rainbow)*
P for relief *(pee for relief)*
Q for chips *(queue for chips*
R for pint *(half a pint)*
S for instance *(as for instance)*
T for hurtin *(teeth are hurting)*
U for me *(you for me)*
W for a match? *(trouble you for a match?)*
Y for crying out loud *(why, for crying out loud)*
Z for a joke *(said for a joke)*

Here's some very Aussie questions.[16]

What do you get when you cross a kangaroo with sheep? (a woolly jumper)
What do you call a boomerang that won't come back? (a stick)
Why did the cockatoo sit on the clock? (so he would be on time)
Why do kangaroo mums hate bad weather? (because the kids have to play inside)
What animal can jump higher than the Sydney Harbour Bridge? (all animals. bridges can't jump!)
What do you call a zipper on a banana? (a fruit fly)
What do you get when you cross a kangaroo with an elephant? (big holes all over Australia)
What do you get if you pour hot water down a rabbit hole? (a hot cross bunny)
Why do crocodiles eat raw meat? (because they can't cook)
Why did the tomato blush? (because he saw the salad dressing)
What did the sand at Bondi Beach say when the tide came in? (long time no sea)

Uniquely Australian Board Games

Who's up for a game of 'Monopoly', 'Checkers', 'Cluedo' or 'Scrabble'? Board games have a long history and, essentially, involve a board, dice and individual moveable board pieces for players. Some games are based on strategy but can involve an element of chance, and some are purely chance, with no element of strategy. The earliest games represented a battle between two armies with moves, counter-moves and the accrual of points. Some games, like 'Monopoly' use a specially-designed deck of cards associated with the dice, dictating the moves.

The *'Snakes and Ladders'* of 1901 provided an old-fashioned moral view. Players slid down the snakes of anger, pride, depravity and vanity and climbed the ladders of forgiveness, penitence, pity and faith if they rolled the right dice.

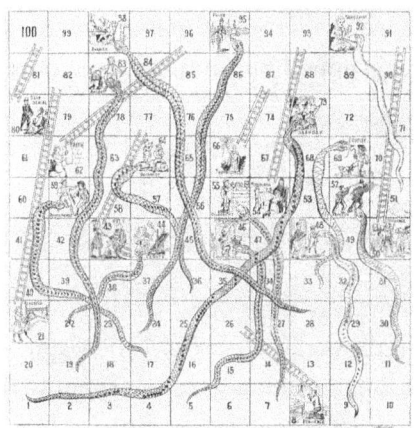

1901 Snakes & Ladders. *NAA*

SHEEP DOG TRIAL. What could be more Australian than a board game about a sheepdog guarding the farm and flock? Interestingly, like many board games, a version of this game has migrated to become a video game on the Internet. It's the same story of the feisty and reliable sheepdog protecting the flock from the ever-present danger of wild dogs and straying into harm.

'Gold Fields of Australia'.[17] The discovery of gold in Australia in 1851 turned the world upside-down, instilling 'gold fever' in over a million would-be-millionaires. The following fold-out board game was published by Darton & Sons circa the mid-1850s. The illustrations detail the progress of the newly arrived immigrants to the colony, their journey across the Blue Mountains, their adventures on the way to the diggings and life on the gold fields. 'Gold Fields of Australia' was played in the same manner as modern board games but with moves determined by spinning a teetotum[18] rather than by throwing dice.

DURING THE REIGN of Queen Victoria, dice throwing was associated with gambling and was considered an unsuitable pastime for children. A teetotum was a six-sided cardboard or ivory disc with a horizontal spindle through its centre. When spun, the number that finished uppermost determined the player's move. Unfortunately, we do not have the game's rule sheet, but it combines the spectacle of daily life on the gold fields with the element of luck to produce a game where the player or 'miner' can make a fortune. This theme would have greatly appealed to British children whose relatives had journeyed to the gold fields to try their luck. The appeal of 'hidden treasure' was enhanced by the newness of Australia as a settlement and its peculiar flora and fauna.

A Hop, a Skip and a Jump

Gold Fields of Australia. Powerhouse.

'**Race to the Goldfields of Australia**'. [19]Published circa 1855 and consisting of a hand-coloured, lithographed sheet mounted on linen, printed rule card and five ship pieces, the illustrated lid of the wooden container shows the ship's 'Passing the Cape of Good Hope'.

Race to the Goldfields of Australia. NLA.

'ADVENTURES OF A MAILMAN'. [20] By the 1880s, the European settlement of Australia was firmly established. Despite a substantial rail network servicing the high postage demand, the trusty mailman still had to traverse considerable distances to deliver the mail. This lively game allows players to join the mailman's adventures as he encounters bushrangers, loses his horse in rapids, and battles bushfires.

Adventures of a Mailman. NLA.

'The Australian Bushman Game'. [21] An Australian children's game produced around the Second Anglo-Boer War (October 1899 - May 1902). Probably published just after Federation, the game celebrates Australia's new nationhood and its participation in the South African conflict, in which the various Australian Bushmen's Contingents played a significant part. It follows the path of a typical Bushman, proceeding from his enlistment to training, embarkation, arrival in South Africa, and engagements with the enemy." Players move around the 60 squares by dice throws, progressing through enlisting in the Bushmen, training, embarkation, promotion, battles, capture, etc. The game includes coloured illustrations of bushmen rounding up cattle in the Australian outback before enlistment, a street parade of one of the Bushmen's Contingents, transport and hospital ships, field hospital, field prison, troop ship *S.S. Medic*, and battle scenes showing Australian prisoners guarded by Boers, and Australian troops attacking a Boer position.

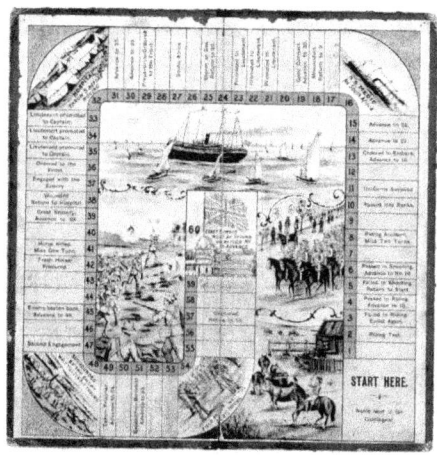

Australian Bushman Game. NLA.

'**The Motor Game**'. [22] The introduction of popular motoring produced poems, songs, comedy skits, and board games. The Motor Game was printed on thin cardboard and used icons and dice to move the motor cars across dangers like loose gravel roads and sheep blocking access. It was produced in Victoria circa the late nineteen-forties.

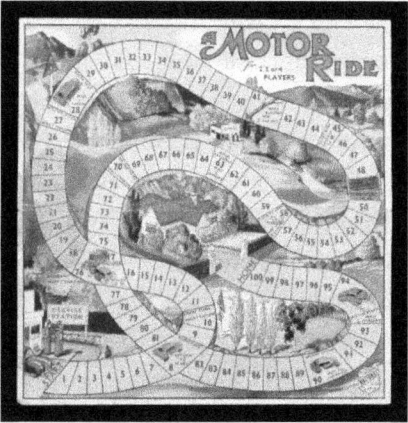

'**The Yacht Race**' [23] board game was produced in the 1940s and coincided with the launch of the Sydney to Hobart race. National

Game Company, Melbourne. It had 16 maritime icons in red, white and blue.

The Yacht Race boardgames circa 1940s.

'Corroboree'. [24] Surely one of the strangest board games was 'Corroboree'. Devised by Jessie Mackintosh and published circa 1940, it coincides with that awkward time in our history where a lack of understanding and appreciation of our indigenous people resulted in what we would now call racism and tokenism. Its creator probably thought she was doing a service with the folding board game based on Aboriginal activities and implements and Australian fauna. Being a roll and move game, there are plenty of special spaces, and you must obey them if you end your move on one. Special spaces include No. 5 Dig for honey ants — miss a turn? No. 13 Throw boomerang — run to the emu space; No. 45 Pointing bone — you are knocked out of the game; No. 87 Lost churinga (shield), go back to No. 71'. And so on. The explanatory notes accompanying the game attempt to broaden the players' knowledge about indigenous culture.

Corroboree. ANMA

Over the past decade, computer games, many digitised versions of old board games, have gained popularity among children and adults. Board games like Scrabble, backgammon, and chess can be played against the computer at varying skill levels, with friends on their devices, or with random strangers worldwide. These games have become very sophisticated, and, for the record, the computer doesn't always win. Card players are also catered for, and for a small purchase of around $2.95, a card pack can be downloaded, offering almost 100 different card games, all playable against the computer.

Board games played with family or friends around a *real* board offer *real* social interaction and remain popular despite the growth of computer versions. New games are continually introduced to the market, including a steady flow of Australian-devised and designed board games. The major drawback is still the mysterious disappearance of the player tokens.

TRICK QUESTIONS. There are word games that aim to surprise the player with a physical move—a pinch, soft punch, or whatever. The following example poses a question: when the victim answers "Pinch me," the trickster pinches them. In the second example, the trickster recites the verse simultaneously as they pinch and punch the victim (unless the victim beats them by saying "No hold barred" or similar).

ADAM AND EVE AND PINCH ME

Went down to the river to bathe;

Adam and Eve got drowned -

Who do you think was saved?

A pinch and a punch for the first of the month

(and the response)

A kick and a lick for being so slick.

The written word

Australians have a long history of writing beautiful and successful books for children. Many of the early books evoked the spirit of the bush with blossom babies, gum nut kids and curious but friendly snakes, lizards, wombats and kangaroos. Children's books also attracted some of our most inspired illustrators, including May Gibbs, Norman Lindsay, Dorothy Wall, Ida Rentoul and Julie Vivas. Our writers have also excelled as storytellers, and the most successful Australian children's books have all had a relationship with the bush; *Possum Magic, Diary of a Wombat, Wombat Stew* and *Edward the Emu* are in fine company with *Blinky Bill, The Magic Pudding* and the much-loved 'Bib and Bub' *Gumnut Babies.*

Two of Australia's most loved children's books, *The Magic Pudding* (1918) and *Blinky Bill* (1939)

The Magic Kangaroo: the adventures of Dicky and Nodroo, written by Mavis Mallinson, was published by John Sands in 1944 and was an early attempt to unite black and white children.

Another Antipodean oddity was Tarella Quin's *Gumtree Brownie: Faerie Folk of the Never-Never*, published by George Robertson in 1910. Although we didn't have a European tradition of the supernatural faerie world, other than those stories transported with family memories, the late nineteenth and early twentieth centuries saw a general rise in the popularity of  spiritualism, revealing itself in public 'wonder' displays like the Davidson Brothers 'public singing seance case'[25] and a general interest in spiritualism, and even those proposing the existence of fairies. Such social comment must have fired up the imagination of many children.

Comic strips. One of Australia's most-loved, homegrown cartoon characters was a mischievous, freckly, red-haired kid named Ginger Meggs. It remains Australia's most popular and longest-running syndicated comic strip, created in the early 1920s by Jimmy Bancks. In 1985, Australia Post issued a stamp honouring Ginger Meggs and four Australian children's books.

1926/7 'Ginger Meggs' books published by Sun Books

Storytelling is worth mentioning as a final word on the value of words. Stories have a beginning, a middle and an end and can be serious or sheer nonsense. Children love stories, for they fire up the imagination as they picture the scenario, the characters and the thread of the story. How many children have pleaded for a story before venturing off to the Land of Nod? Whether the story is incomplete or repeated, they know that stories evolve. Of course, much of the joy is in listening, especially if told by a family member.

TRADITIONAL SOCIETIES VALUE THEIR STORYTELLERS; of course, it's not just the children who are the audience. Most traditional storytellers have large repertoires, much of it passed on over countless years. Western society has seen its storytellers lost in a sea of mediocrity like much of popular entertainment. Although there are professional storytellers, primarily for young children, we seem to have become conditioned to stories produced by the popular entertainment machinery of television, radio and film. Thankfully, the book remains a bastion of storytelling, so we should always celebrate the art of writing. If a fraction of the good stories in books take flight into the oral tradition, we should thank the writers and those who elected to render the stories to memory. Rather than reading aloud, passing on stories from memory still has a certain magic.

6
THE PLAYGROUND

The playground is a wonderland of discover, physically and socially. *State Archive NSW*

For most of the nineteenth century, most Australians worked and lived in what was referred to as the *bush*. The country was opened up by the 1850s gold rushes and, for most of the second half of that century, work was to be found in the wool, beef, wheat, timber and mining industries. From the mid-1890s, the population drifted to the coast and the cities for the 'new work' in manufacturing and commerce. City and coastal town life brought new challenges, including dramatically increased leisure time. Rural life, even for children, was essentially seven days a week; however, in the 'big smoke', the average person worked a six or six-and-a-half work-day week. As the century progressed, leisure time continued to increase, largely due to the growing power of trade unions. By 1925, many industry employees worked less than 48 hours, averaging around 44 hours for clerical, building, boot trades, waterside workers, shearing, clothing trades, flour millers, storemen and packers and shop assistants. In 1947, the Arbitration Court reduced the average weekly working hours across the economy from 44 to 40. In 1983, it was further reduced to 38 hours with increased flexibility. Paid annual leave was a bonus for families who had previously worked every day, often including Christmas Day and other holidays.

Throughout the 20th Centuryn icreased leisure time meant more family fun. Around the coasts swimming pools and waterside amusement parks became extremely popular for a day's outing 'for the kids'. These parks offered animal rides, aquariums, giant slippery dips and water slides, musical shows, clowns and various wonders. Council and private pools opened to teach swimming. Sporting events attracted unbelievably large crowds. Leisure became a new industry.

From around 1910, there were calls for establishing dedicated playgrounds for children. Linked to this development of designated playgrounds is the history of the motor car. Before the popularity of motor vehicles, children played on the street; however, as cars rattled their way into Australian life, demands for safe areas for children to play became a political issue.

Attitudes to play also changed over the decades. The following stern appraisal comes from 1910.[1]

Children's Games. In these days of keen analysis and scientific methods, even children's games are studied with a view to turning them to profit from moulding the character. It might seem that the gambolings of children must be spontaneous to be real play, and that any regulated interference would inevitably spoil the game, and make it, in the child's eyes, partake of the nature of a lesson. Yet experience shows that each interference, when skilfully applied, is undoubtedly beneficial, and Mr Fraser, the school inspector at Gundagai, struck a very true note when he insisted recently on its importance. The natural instinct of a child is to "make believe", but it is not always also an instinct to play fairly or even healthily— from the ethical point of view. For instance, it is known that among some children in vicious surroundings, games will take the form of pretending to thieve, or similar unedifying pretence. This is, of course, an extreme case, nor need one take too seriously the fact of small boys pretending to be highwaymen, or smugglers, though without a shadow of doubt many boys have begun thieving partly as a game. A wise teacher or parent can unobtrusively direct the play of children into a healthy channel and also see that they 'play the game squarely' without mean advantages or grumbling. The latter is, indeed, a very important part of a child's training and the youngster who is allowed, unchecked, to harbour a fancied grievance is not likely to grow up a very agreeable sort of a man. Children's games certainly require supervision, the same as their lessons, but we must beware of attaching too much importance to play and not enough to work. Easy-going parents may run a risk of believing that because certain great men were idle boys, therefore idle boys will be great men.'

In a similar rant, readers of 1917 were advised to guide playtime.[2]

'Mothers should train their children to play games which teach them to be useful in the afterlife. The parent would then be glad later on when the little boy or girl could be a great help. A very good plan is to turn a wooden box into a doll's house and teach your little boys and girls how to make furniture out of used matches, lay down scraps of linoleum, make little curtains, and paper the walls. Let your little girl spring-clean their doll's house and teach her the right way. Making the doll's house will be pleasant work during the evenings. Children are allowed to play far too much without guidance.'

Little people love climbing. *State Archive NSW*

State Archive NSW

In Australia, a playground is designed to enable children to play there. It is typically outdoors. Early playgrounds generally offered a merry-go-round, a seesaw, swings and a slide. Modern playgrounds often have additional equipment such as a jungle gym, chin-up bars, sandbox, spring rider, trapeze rings, playhouses, and mazes, many of which help children develop physical coordination, strength, and flexibility, as well as providing recreation and enjoyment and, at the same time, supporting social and emotional development. Common in modern playgrounds are play structures that link many different pieces of equipment.

Playgrounds often also have associated facilities for playing informal games, especially ball games like basketball and netball.

It is hard to argue with the commonly-held view that Australians are 'sports crazy'. Maybe it has something to do with our relatively young history and the fact that our first recognition internationally was through sport - especially sculling. Or maybe it stems from our colonial male-dominated past where football and cricket were seen as the height of manly competition. Sport is no longer a man's domain, and if media coverage of sports and government funding equates to popularity, then we seem to have an obsession. Oh, that we had a cultural obsession! With sport, the mantra is 'catch 'em young'.

Old style wooden roundabout razzle-dazzle. It is difficult to imagine what danger the authorities thought this wheel posed... *State Archive NSW*

THE PLAYGROUND Movement.³

> After some years of agitation, Sydney is finally to have its first trial playground on modern lines. This is due to the generosity of the Sydney Harbour Trust. A block of land has been given for this purpose near the high-level road at Miller's Point, overlooking the harbour. A shelter shed is being built, and a sand pit is being filled. Blocks and toys are to be provided, and a kindergarten superintendent is to be engaged.
>
> When everything is in working order, it is to be handed over to the Sydney Playground Association. A paper advocating such playgrounds for young children was read in Brisbane last year at the annual meetings of the National Council of Women.'

Maybanke Anderson, a founding member of the Kindergarten Union, was a keen advocate for children's playgrounds and secretary of the Playgrounds Association. For many years, the Kindergarten Union described itself as "administering Kindergartens, Nursery Schools and Playgrounds". Providing older children with a safe environment for outdoor play fell within the Union's remit "to make Children's Playgrounds places of health, occupation and interest..."

> The first children's playground ⁴ was instituted as a result of the cooperation between the Education Department and the municipal authorities, and it was opened by the Minister for Education (Mr. Carmichael) last Friday afternoon. It is a happy announcement that the first of these playgrounds was established right under the shadow of the university. A trained kindergartener has been appointed to take charge of the little ones, and all the delights dear to the juvenile mind, such as swings, see-saws, slides, and sand pits, have been provided. The authorities of the City Council are co-operating with the Education Department, and it will not be long before the teachers' playground in Victoria Park will be among the show places of the city.
>
> The department has received a number of offers from suburban

municipalities to set apart playing areas for children within the parks, and as soon as the first has been established long enough to prove it a success, arrangements will be made to extend the movement into the suburbs.'

The first Playground opened was Lance Playground, Millers Point, Sydney, in 1912. The first government-supported public playground in the City of Sydney opened a year later on land provided by the Sydney Harbour Trust in Victoria Park "assisted, in sympathy and good advice at least, by the committee of the Playgrounds Association".

Maybanke Anderson, writing in 1913: [5]

"For as soon as I realised, as every teacher does, that the way of the child's natural development lies through play, I began to think methodically of playgrounds..."

The Kindergarten Union, in close cooperation with the Sydney City Council, operated four supervised playgrounds at Pyrmont, Moore Park, Chippendale, and Woolloomooloo.

Sydney's first official playground, Moore Park, Sydney. k.u.

Cleanliness next to Godliness in Brisbane [6]

'The Playground Movement. In too many parts of Brisbane, the children's playgrounds were the gutters of the streets, and when one noticed them playing in the green turbid water, sailing leaf boats and dabbling both hands and feet in it, they could not wonder that diphtheria and other epidemics spread so rapidly. In the municipal playgrounds, the child was taught to play in a clean and healthy way. The wading pool and the sand heap were kept clean and fresh and free from the disease breeding elements of the gutter slime, and so the child was led to love and observe cleanliness in all things.

In the public playground, under proper supervision, the child was taught the virtues of comradeship, courage, chivalry, reverence, and discipline, so they entered life fully equipped to play the game worthily. It was natural for children to play, it being Nature's method of development, and it was their duty to guide and control the tireless energy of child life, for never were truer words spoken than these of Jane Addams. a well-known American sociologist that "vice was simply the love of pleasure gone wrong."

Lance Playground Millers Point. *State Archive NSW*

Playground Movement in Melbourne.[7]

The idea behind the playground movement was greater than merely to amuse children. It was to conserve the leisure time of the whole population so that the people's amusements would be constructive, not destructive. If wealthy men would use their money to provide healthy recreation for the people, they would find their benevolence the surest safeguard against national strife and discontent. It was time Melbourne began to lay the foundation of a great recreational system.

Flying High on the swings. The Argus Dec 1923

In *Play & Friendships in a Multi-cultural Playground,* Heather Russell with Gwenda Davey and June Factor, 1986, observed:[8]

"Playground life is an important factor in children's school life, but teachers are more often than not too busy struggling with the immediate issues of curriculum and classroom procedures to observe life in the playground. Yet the playground is the place where friendships are made or broken, games of skill refined and perfected, rituals devised, and taunts, insults and punishments melted out. In the world of games performers are envied and emulated, leaders created, and rules, traditions and terminology are adapted and passed on to the next generation. Playtime is crucial for children's socialisation and important for their physical development. In the playground, children are forced to spend time together; they learn to cooperate and compete with their peers, devise their own codes of conduct, teach others and then practise according to well-established rules for hours and hours, often perfecting physical skills to quit an extraordinary degree."

The slippery dip adventure and fun.

Whether in the city or bush, the playground has proven to be a fertile ground for folklore collectors and remains evidence that children have extraordinarily creative minds. Sadly, many city school playgrounds have been swallowed up by more classrooms and amenities, and the play area has diminished. Even sadder are these schools where asphalt and bitumen have replaced grass.

'Elastics' is still one of the most popular playground activities.
MV

Even today, a playground full of children is a delight to behold. Kids are running everywhere, and squeals of joy and creative play are everywhere. Several play scenarios will be enacted simultaneously in most play areas, each seemingly oblivious to the other games. Some will play in pairs or large groups; some prefer to be solo, yet happily as part of the overall group. Although trees, swings, etc., are preferable, they are unnecessary, as children can imagine stairs, buildings, and whatever are part of their game.

Children love to explore, and playgrounds that offer a variety of closed and open play areas are preferable. Walls to bounce balls off or to use as a home base for tagging games are important, as are spaces where friends can hang out with territorial rights of "that's our spot". In the 1970s and 80s, there was a move to level school playgrounds, with bitumen and concrete being seen as better for ball sports. Expanded classrooms also saw schoolrooms encroach on play areas. It was an alarming trend that was corrected in later school designs. Trees, grass, gravel, dirt mounds and irregular fencing are all preferable to completely flat hard surfaces. The ideal playground should be varied and part of the overall learning experience, allowing pupils to create play within its borders.

'Statues' a new form of 'tableau', Melbourne, Dorothy Howard/June Factor MV

Today's children's parks tend to be more creative in terms of playing with crawling tunnels, musical gongs, jumping castles, swings, and slides. The roundabout and see-saw seem to have been deemed too dangerous and have all but disappeared. Depending on how you look at it, many playgrounds have also been fenced off or fenced in. Landscaping is also a feature; where possible, mounds, trees, and scrubs replace asphalt and flatness. In recent years, the playground has also become more accommodating to the needs of mentally and physically disabled children. With the sharp increase in apartment living, especially in the larger cities, the local playground has become a precious green space and a vital sanctuary for children and parents.

In 2018, the television morning program *Today* set off a national discussion by responding to a call to ban monkey bars from playgrounds.

Child healthcare experts claim that monkey bars are one of the leading causes of injuries in young children. A survey suggested a 41% increase in hospital presentations due to injuries sustained on monkey bars, prompting the push to ban them.

Despite efforts to improve monkey bar safety, including reducing the equipment's height to 2.2m and softening the surface beneath, Professor David Eager from UTS, chairperson of the committee investigating the ban, still believes they will need to be phased out in favour of space nets and spider webs.

Speaking to *The Age*, Melbourne, Mr Eager said:[9]

> "Monkey bars were okay when I was a kid 60 years ago, but they're not an appropriate form of play equipment in 2018. Most councils and schools have been pulling them out and replacing them with spatial nets, but not as quickly as we would like."

One could argue that bars have been part of playground equipment for a very long time and that we have all become a tad too precious. That other dangerous playground staple, the merry-go-round, disappeared because of similar claims. Do we really want our kids bubble-wrapped and protected from all such adventure equipment?

Homemade see-saw, Balmoral, Victoria, 1925. Museums Victoria

Clive James left us a colourful account of schoolyard crazes in the 1940s. [10]

> There was a craze for dongers. Crazes came one after the other. There was a craze for a game of marbles called 'followings'. There was a craze for cigarette cards, not the cards that come in packets of English cigarettes, but cards made elaborately out of the cigarette packets themselves. The cards had different values according to brands, with English Gold Flake scoring highest and Australian Craven A scoring lowest. You flicked your card at a wall. The one who finished nearest the wall got a chance to toss all the cards in the air at once. The ones that fell face up were his.
>
> Bottle-tops worked roughly the same way, except that the one who got the closest to the wall stacked all the bottle tops on his upturned elbow then swiped downwards with his hand, getting to keep as many of the bottle tops as he could catch between hand and wrist. It is difficult to describe and even more difficult to do. I always lost. I wasn't bad at Cock-a-lorum, but falling over on the asphalt playground added painfully to my usual array of sores and scabs. The craze I hoped to be good at was dongers.
>
> A donger was an ordinary handkerchief folded into a triangle. You held each end of the hypotenuse and twirled until the handkerchief

had rolled itself tight. Then you held the two ends together in one hand while you rolled the fat centre part even tighter with the other. The result was then soaked in water to give it weight. The more reckless boys sometimes inserted a lead washer or a small rock. The completed dodger was, in effect, a black-jack. Every play-time, with me hovering cravenly on the outskirts, donger gangs would go into battle against each other. The brawls looked like the Battle of Thermopylae. Finally the teacher on playground duty would plunge into the melee and send everyone in possession of a donger up to the Deputy Headmaster to get six. With me still hovering elsewhere, solo desperadoes would then creep up on their victims behind the teacher's back. The idea was to clobber the target before the teacher turned around. He always turned around because the sound of the donger hitting someone's head was unmistakeable. It sounded like an apple hitting concrete."

Melanie Ryan recalled her favourite outdoor games:[11]

'Elastics', starting with the rhyme 'England, Ireland, Scotland, Wales, inside, outside, donkey's tails', which was then followed by a bunch of other set challenges jumping on and over the elastic. You started at ankle height and, if you were good, might finish at 'over headsies'.

'Sevens', which was played with a ball with challenges in sets of seven reps. When you completed all the first level challenges you made the next lot more challenging with claps, double claps, spinning around, under leg,

'Tag Games'. Surely one of the most enduring and mysterious childhood games is chasing. What appears simple can be complex, and a child's world allows the game to take place anywhere and with numerous rules or 'non-rules'. The point of the game is to chase and be caught. Sometimes, there is one designated chaser, and at other times, several. The role of 'it' can be chosen at the game's start or cumulatively, as those tagged join the game as 'it'. One standing rule common to most games of chase, tag, tick or tig, or whatever it is called, is that the chaser must allow an agreed time lapse before he or she can re-tag someone who has just been caught. Australian children will often be caught and immediately say 'no returns', meaning the chaser cannot immediately grab or tag them a second time. They must have time to escape before being chased and caught again. Children seem quite happy to change game rules, often mid-game, and sometimes these changes become what, to adults, a completely new chase game. It would be true to say that chasing games, and they are real games rather than simply chasing, are some of the most inventive children's games in folklore. In *The Lore of the Playground,* Steve Roud sums up chasing game rules. [12]

> The terminology involved in the basic chasing game is fascinating and confusing in equal measure. Children manage perfectly well when conversing among themselves, but when they talk about their games to grown-ups and outsiders, inherent confusion surfaces, and children have been known to get quite exasperated when adults cannot grasp what to them is very simple.

The wonderful thing about chase and tag games is that they can be played anywhere, anytime, from a few minutes to an hour. Chasing tag games can be organised anywhere from the schoolyard to a designated area within the school playground, the beach, swimming pools, trees or the backyard. Sometimes 'home', a safe place, is agreed upon. The tag itself changes and can be very inventive. 'Hospital Tag' rules that you cannot use the body area tagged, so, for example, if your arm was tagged, you have to hold it like a 'dead arm'. 'Aeroplane tag' rules that when tagged, the player must hold their arms out, like wings, and can only be released by another player diving under the arms, like a low-flying plane. 'Feet-off' rules that a player can avoid tagging by being suspended from the ground, hanging off a clothesline, climbing a tree branch, wrapping themselves around a pole, etc. 'Chain tag', a popular variant, has the tagged people form one 'it' chain by holding hands and running around to trap players in their 'net'. 'Cops and Robbers' has been played in Australian schools for decades. Instead of a 'home' or safe place, the game has a designated prison area where tagged players must bide their time until the game concludes. There is often an 'escape' rule.

SKIPPING. One of the most enduring play activities, especially for girls, is skipping. It can be done solo, duo or in groups. There are numerous rhymes associated with skipping. There are also numerous styles of skipping.

A popular family magazine in 1903 detailed the varieties of skipping in Australia.[13]

> 'Going to School' is a pretty form of skipping. Two girls lock arms, or each places an arm around the waist of the other and, with the disengaged hand, holds one end of the rope. They then turn it over themselves, varying their steps in unison as they fancy.
>
> In 'Going a-begging,' two girls turn, and two others jump in and skip side by side. Then, while still skipping, they change places with each other. One of them says as they pass, "A piece of bread and butter," and the other replies, "Try my next-door neighbour." This is kept up until one of them trips.
>
> In 'Winding the Clock,' the girl skipping turns completely round with each skip, calling out, "One, two, three," and so on up to twelve as she does so.
>
> 'Baking Bread' is played by a girl taking a stone in her hand, and as she skips, laying it down on the ground without a check in her skipping, and then picking it up again. She repeats the operation as often as she can without tripping.
>
> In 'Double Rope,' the skipper has a short rope herself. While the two girls turn the long one over her head, she skips and turns her own rope, a double movement that is quite difficult.
>
> In 'Chicago,' the two girls who turn have a rope in either hand and turn them alternately, the skipper having to jump in and out with marvellous rapidity to avoid being caught.'

'Oranges and Lemons' a game with a traditional rhyme. MV DH/JF

STRING. It seems odd to think that string has had such a long history with childhood amusement. Indigenous communities made their own string and used it in play, including tying up a round bundle of leaves, ferns, etc, to fashion a ball used with football and other games. Colonials also used stringy-bark and green-hide as a form of string, including, in the absence of nails, in constructing huts. There appears to have been a craze for string games in the nineteen-thirties; perhaps because factory-made string became more affordable. More likely, the Depression steered folks into more thrifty toys. In 1937, when an infectious disease forced many schools to close, newspapers offered suggestions on how to amuse the homebound.

This somewhat strange, hilarious 1930s description unintentionally evokes *50 Shades of Grey*.

Fun With String [14]

Are you one of the many children whose school has been closed as a safeguard against the spread of the Infantile Paralysis epidemic? Time must often weigh heavily for you if you are. But there is no reason why it should. Try these indoor games with some piece of string and a companion. They will afford you a lot of good fun.

Fun with string. What were they thinking! *The Argus,* Aug 1937

Tell your friend that you can tie him up with two pieces of string, each only a foot long, in such a way that he cannot get free even by using a knife or a pair of scissors. He may find it hard to believe, but if you tie him up in the following manner he will find it quite impossible to free himself.

Make him kneel down, and while he is in that position tie his right wrist to his right foot and his left wrist to his left foot. You may then place a pair of scissors in front of him and ask him if he would like to cut himself free. He cannot move either hands or feet; in fact, the only movement he can make if he tries to get hold of the scissors is to fall over, tied in that position, he will be helpless.

Another good string game is to tie two people together and ask them to release themselves without cutting the string or untying the knots. They must be tied, as you see in the picture.

The first boy, whom we shall call "A," has his wrists tied together with a long piece of string, having one end tied around one wrist and one around the other wrist. The second boy, "B." must have his wrists tied similarly. But before the second knot is fixed, pass the string behind "A's" string so that the two boys are linked together. People who do not know the trick will probably try to step out of the string and, in so doing, get themselves very tied up.

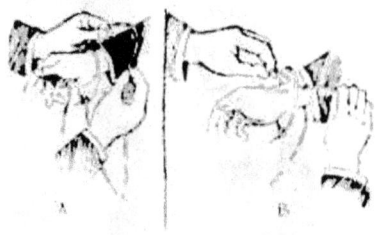

Fun with string. *The Argus* second image

To do it successfully you must take hold of "B's" string in the centre (as you see in the second picture). Take the loop you thus get behind either or "A's" wrists, pass through the piece that goes round his wrist, and slip it back over his hand. Then, If "A" draws his wrists away he will find that he is free. if you watch the way in which the string slips out at the wrist you will be able to reverse the process and link the two boys together again.

A West Australian newspaper followed the trend.[15]

A string-winding race. This is an amusing race which must be played in pairs. The players stand opposite each other, holding a connecting string to each end of which is attached a piece of stick. At the signal for the start, the couples begin rapidly to wind the string on the sticks, which each holds until the partners meet. Then, taking hands, they run to a spot selected as the winning point, and the first couple to reach it and who can show that their sticks are fully wound up win the game.

Not to be outdone, a Brisbane newspaper followed suit and offered tips:[16]

Fun With String. It is surprising what amusement can be had merely from a piece of string. Here is a trick which you will enjoy doing. It originated from the Aborigines and represents a boy climbing a tree.

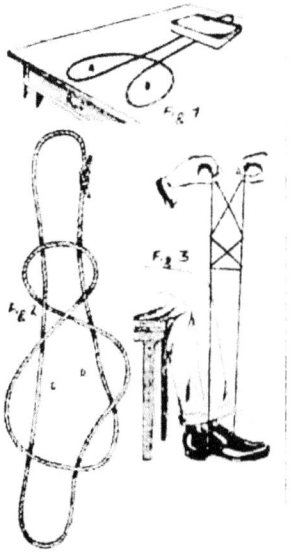

Fun With String Fig 1, 2 & 3. *Brisbane Courier Mail,* 1932

Lay a loop made from a piece of string about 7ft. long flat on the table, with a book on one end of the loop, and then, doubling back the other end, make a second, as at Fig. 1. Now twist both loops, A and B, so that they form the pattern shown at Fig. 2. Lift the parts C and D between the finger and thumb of the left and right hands, respectively. Then, slip the loop from under the book and put it under the foot; the string figure then shown in Fig. 3. The crossed strings and loop represent the boy, and the two parallel strings represent the tree. Pulling with both hands causes the boy to stop still, but by working the strings over the thumbs with the aid of your fingers, you can make the "boy" climb the "tree" in a very uncanny fashion.'

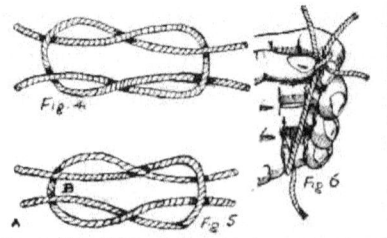

Fun With String Fig 4, 5 & 6. *Brisbane Courier Mail* Nov 1932

With this next trick you can have a good deal of fun with your friends, and mystify them quite a lot. But the success of the trick depends on the way in which it is explained before the trick is performed, and also upon your dexterity when doing it, so practise it first, so that you get it to perfection, and then try your luck. Tie an ordinary knot (shown at Fig. 4), in a piece of fairly stout, smooth string. Draw it tight, and then ask someone to unfasten it. Naturally, the unfastening takes some time. You chaff your friend about being such a long time over the job and offer to show him that you can untie it in a moment and with only one hand. Then you tie what appears to be the same sort of knot, but really is a different tie-one arranged as at Fig. 5. Then, taking hold of the string at the part A, twist it around the little finger, and hold the knot in the palm, concealing it by the second and third fingers. By pulling part B outwards with the finger and thumb, as shown in Fig. 6, the knot immediately comes undone.

Readers - if you have accidentally tied yourself in knots - you are forgiven. WF

Looking for Easter Eggs. Children of the YWCA free Kindergarten, Richmond. *The Argus*, 1935

"A HUNTING WE WILL GO, a hunting we will go, hi ho the merry-o, a hunting we will go". Children love a hunt, be it for Easter eggs or, as once was popular, peanuts. Hunts can be inside or outdoors, and there's no limit to the number of players;, the more, the merrier as kids scramble to discover the treasure. Of course, having lots of treasure helps create a fairer playing field. Some hunts involve clues, a map, or a series of riddles leading to the ultimate prize. The real fun is being in the chase, the hunt, and not necessarily the treasure.

Children hunt for treasure on St Kilda beach. 1929

Children's Treasure Hunt At St. Kilda. [17]The hunt for buried treasure, which appeals to every child, took hundreds of little folk yesterday to the St. Kilda beach, where the Mayor of St. Kilda (Councillor J. Levi) had buried a "treasure trove" as an attraction to the seaside suburb in connection with this week's charity carnival. The children entered thoroughly into the spirit of adventure and moved tons of sand in their search for the casket.

PARLOUR GAMES. Both adults and children of the Victorian era loved to play what they called 'parlour games'[18]. Many older games were written down and published for the first time, and many of these books found their way to Australia.

'Blind Man's Banquet'. Blindfold games are always popular at a party, and one of the funniest and most entertaining is the 'Blind Man's Banquet'. Two of the juniors are blindfolded, and seated on the carpet about a yard from each other, and near each is placed a plate or two or three small pieces of bread and butter.

The players are not supposed to speak and to use only one hand, and at a given signal to feed each other. The task is a good deal more difficult than it appears, and the attempts to find each other's mouth cause great merriment. Time for the completion of the meal is taken and compared with that of another couple, the shortest period gaining the prize.

Games for Summer Days. There are days when the only place to play — except when it rains— is out in the glorious sunshine. The games I shall suggest will, therefore, be out-of-door games for summer days.

To play 'Midnight', mark off a corner of the garden, which is the fox's den. Mark off another larger corner which is the sheep fold. Choose one player to be the fox. The rest are the sheep. Both fox and sheep venture from their corners, their den and their fold. While they are out in the open, a sheep every now and then asks: 'What time is it?' The fox may answer any hour he chooses, such as: 'Nine o'clock,' 'Two o'clock,' or 'Twelve o'clock midnight.' Nothing happens when any of the hours except twelve o'clock midnight is answered, but when the fox says, 'Twelve o'clock midnight,' all the sheep run for the sheepfold, and the fox tries to catch one or more before they get there. As soon as the fox catches a sheep that sheep changes places with the fox and becomes a fox itself, and the game goes on as before.

'Hop and Choose'. The two tallest players choose sides. The ones chosen by each of these captains then stand in rows six feet apart with their backs facing. At least 15 feet in front of each row, the captains place in another row, as many small objects as there are players in a row. These objects may be any things that may be picked up quickly and that do not have sharp or pointed edges.

After this preparation, the captains say, 'Ready,' and the players in each row hop on one foot to the row in front of them, snatch one of the objects and hop back, without once having had their weight on two feet. As soon as a player is back in the first line, he may choose any one of his opponents who has not yet succeeded in returning to the original line. These chosen are out. The objects picked up are then replaced by the captains and the business of hopping, snatching, returning and choosing an opponent goes on until all on one side are out. If a player puts his weight on both feet during the voyage from the starting line and back again, he too is out.

'Hunt and Huddle'. This game is played best out in open country, preferably in wooded grounds. Two sides of an equal number of players are chosen by captains or drawing lots. One side is then the hunters; the other is the huddlers. Huddlers are furnished with slips of paper coloured red, green, blue and yellow. Red means north; green, south; blue, west; yellow, east. The hunters remain at the goal at the start, while the huddlers set out, leaving a trail by means of the coloured paper. They must travel in straight lines, changing to another direction of the compass whenever they wish, but in each case leaving a slip of paper to show the new direction. When the huddlers hide, they huddle in one group. When the hunters go out to seek them, they travel with hands joined. The search begins within a certain time after the huddlers have gone forth. Whenever then, the hunters find the huddlers, they join hands and encircle them. If the hunters pass by the huddlers, the latter may rise up and run back to the goal. The hunters will also return to the goal, no longer having to keep their hands joined. As a player gets back, he touches the goal and yells, 'Goal.' if the huddlers get back before the hunters, they may be huddlers again; if not, the hunters become huddlers and' the huddlers become hunters. Also, if the hunters succeed in forming a circle around the huddlers, the two change places, and the game goes on.

MOST CHILDREN PLAYED versions of 'Cowboys and Indians' up until the 1960s when, as if by magic, it was realised the Indians never won, were typically portrayed as 'bloodthirsty savages' (except the tales of Pocahontas), and the Cowboys were innocent ranchers. Versions of the game are undoubtedly still played; though hopefully, we have a better understanding and appreciation of indigenous peoples.

COWBOYS AND INJUNS. [19]

'Indians. Players are divided into two groups, one of which is larger than the other. The large group is the Indians, and the other one is the Family. The Family chooses a Father whose duty is to watch over them and keep them from all harm. The two groups then take up places at opposite ends of the garden or playground. As soon as the members of the Family have settled down to sleep, the Indians creep up silently. When they have approached near, the Father who is on guard discovers them and cries, 'The Indians are coming! The Indians are coming!' At this, the children of the Family awake, jump up, and race the Indians back to their camp. All the Indians who are tagged before they get back are prisoners of the Family, and are out of the game. The game continues until all of the Indians are caught.'

Elizabeth Hawkes recalled disliking the game because, as the younger sister, she would inevitably be tied up by her brothers and who would then leave![20]

~

MEMORIES OF A QUEENSLAND CHILDHOOD *in the Nineteenth Century*, written in 1911.[21]

> Some of the happiest memories of my Childhood are connected with the games I used to play. "Blind Man's Buff" was my great favourite, but "Oranges and Lemons" ran it very close, and I regret to say, "In and Out the Window" says a Woman writer in an interesting article in "The Queen." The repetition of these rhymes will show how Queensland daughters have followed the traditions in games of their British mothers. Even now there are a good many of us who are quite ready to join in the games at Christmas-time, or any other time when the children beg for a grown up to help them. We know all the games so well, we played them almost as soon we could run, that it seldom occurs to us to inquire their origin. This very fact shows their antiquity. If these games were made by our mothers, or even our grandmothers, we should be able to repeat their history as easily as we enumerate the wars of Queen Victoria's reign (Many of these much-loved games had a certain preliminary known in England as "counting out," in Scotland as "chapping out." We stood in a ring, and one in the centre, with finger pointing, went through some doggerel, which satisfactorily and with absolute fairness decided which should be "he" or "it" or "blind man" or some other important and responsible person. One rhyme most of us knew was as follows :
>
> > One-ery, two-ery, dekery, Ann.
> >
> > Fillery, fallacy, Nicholas John,
> >
> > Quever, quaver, English knaver,

Stuckellem, atauckelus, Jericho, buck.

Another was so haunting that now I can say it without the slightest effort at remembrance:

(editor's note. Here is another game with the stereotypical racist reference of the dreadful word 'nigger'. It has to be noted this was written in 1911, only a decade after the introduction of the White Australia Policy. It was, of course, unacceptable then, although in common circulation, and impossibly unacceptable now. WF).

Ena, dena, dina, do,

Catch a nigger by his toe;

If he hollers let him go,

Ena, dena, dina, do.

One, two, three-out goes he.

It may at first seem us if these rhymes are just a mixed jingle of words, as children might easily compose, but the fact that we now use expressions like "hocus pocus," originally "hoc est corpus"[22] and "Punch and Judy," once meaning "Pontius Pilate," suggests there may be something deeper below this apparent nonsense. Very probably these rhymes are a relic of the time when such counting out was used for selecting a victim for sacrifice - this, of course, in heathen days. A strange likeness exists between these rhymes in many different countries. A great number of the so-called English rhymes are used among the children of other European, and often Asiatic nations. Children of every nation play games, many very similar, and all children in every part of the world perform the initial act of "counting out."

A magic charm-or a religious charm was certainly only a mixture of strange words and sounds; the more strange they were the more they impressed the bearers. The charm which Faust says when invoking the devil is a good example of this, and we know that savage nations use doggerel for their incantations.

Other counting rhymes:

One, two, buckle my shoe; Three, four, knock at the door,

and the strangely sweet ;

One, I love; Two, I love; Three, I love, I say;

Four, I love with all my heart; Five - I cast away

sung to the falling daisy petals, are much younger than the "counting out" rhymes. They are probably the work of the last two centuries.

The games - and there are many - in which the lover pursues his lass or the lass seeks shyly her lover have come to us from that barbaric time when most marriages were the result of capture. The final verse of "I sent a letter to my love":

Now you're married you must obey;

You must be true to all you say.

You must be kind, you must be good,

And help your husband chop the wood

substantiates this idea by its many commands of obedience and service laid on the wife, and the total liberty from obligations which the husband is to enjoy. "In and Out the Window," in which the girl is followed through all kinds of obstacles - nothing worse to-day than soft linked arms and plump childish forms quite reproduces the efforts of the seeking husband and the reluctant wife. This reluctance is by no means so marked in "Poor Mary sits a-weeping." At the question being asked, "Pray, tell me what she's weeping for?" the answer is given promptly, "She's -weeping for a sweetheart.".

"Lady Queen Anne," whose complexion is described as "fair as a lily, as white as a swan." and "The Quaker's Wedding" are also games of courtship.

There are not many funeral games left, but "Jenny Jones" is quite the most lugubrious.

Games which prove our ancestors were men of war are often the greatest favourites among children. "Nuts in May" (usually known as "Nuts and May"),

"Oranges and Lemons," "Twos and Threes," "Tom Tiddler's Ground," are all grand games of prowess and strength, and sometimes subtlety, - as in the last one mentioned. "Twos and Threes" is often known as "French and English," an immortal reminder of the fact that the neighbours across the Channel were not always on such good terms as they are now.

"London Bridge," with its somewhat gruesome reiteration :

London Bridge is broken down,

Dance over my Lady Lea :

London Bridge is broken down,

With a gay ladee

hints at the ancient custom of sprinkling a bridge with the blood of children or women. "Oranges and Lemons" is patently a London rhyme for all the oldest churches of the City are introduced into it. "Nuts in May" was originally "Knots in May," immortalising the custom of picking bunches of the white hawthorn on May Day and wearing them during the festivities.

"Oats and Beans and Barley." a little known game, which comes from Dorset-shire, is a harvest game, so is "Barley Bridge," a version of "How many Miles to Babylon?"

"Cat's Cradle," a game for which I had a passion, stands apart as a game for two, though other players are sometimes allowed to take a hand. This game, very little different, is played by the people of Torres Strait.

SIMON SAYS. A simple game based on anticipation of reflexes. One player is elected as Simon, and the players stand in a line or circle. The game follows the leader, and whenever Simon commands, the others must follow - unless he commands without saying, "Simon says'. For example, the leader calls, "Simon Says, hands on heads." He executes the command by placing his hands on his head. But if he says "Forward -march." (without prefixing it with Simon says") everyone who moved forward is out.

'**Light as a feather race**'. Each player carries four small feathers in his hand and has to run without them blowing away.

'**Sugar-lump race**'. Players try to balance a sugar cube on their noses as they walk or run.

'Pass the potato'. Using a spoon held in the mouth to take and balance the potato.

ALAN WALKER DESCRIBED PLAYING the game of Flickers: [23].

> This was a game we used to play, probably in the late forties. I certainly was not playing it until 1951, when I started high school. The game was played with empty cigarette packets folded flat. The tray inside the packet was used to lock the folded packet flat. The folded packets were flicked towards a wall, and the one closest to the wall won. The winner took the losers' packets. We played this game on the front verandahs.

Arthur Elliott, Brisbane, recalled his games in the 40s and early 50s.[24]

> Fly – a game involving any number of (usually) boys. Two sticks or twigs about a foot long were placed parallel to each other, some small distance apart. The "Fly" or boss of the game (this changed for each game, often depending on who won the previous game) nominated the number of steps that all players had to make within the space between the sticks (if you touched a stick, or took the wrong number of steps, you were out.) He went last and would take a large final step beyond the second twig. Where he landed became the position where the second stick was now placed. And so on, the gap became wider with each round, although the number of steps stayed the same. Players gradually were eliminated, sometimes including the Fly himself. Whoever was the last person remaining became the Fly for the next game. There was a Mosquito, too – I think he was the first person in the line of players.
>
> Red Rover is a well-known playground game in which you run from the safe area at one end through increasing numbers of players in the middle trying to catch you to the safe area at the other end. If you were caught, you stayed in the middle. A variation was Blue

Rover, in which you weren't allowed the three-step dispensation over the line that Red Rover gave you.

Defenders is a tennis ball game played between two teams. It starts with a bounce, and the team that gets the ball has to keep it away from the other team. There are no goals. It was eventually banned from my school, as too many shirts and other items were being ripped while playing it. It was very popular.

Brandy is another well-known game played with a tennis ball. One person has the ball and tries to hit anyone else playing by throwing it at him. If successful, that person becomes "it." A variation is Wall Brandy, where players line up against a wall, and the person with the ball throws it at them. It is quite hard to dodge the ball, as the target is quite a confined area. It could be rather painful.

Bedlam – very popular. Two teams were chosen. One team had a designated base (say, an area around a tree, marked by a scratched-in line), and it was their job to hunt members of the other team, capture them, and "imprison" them in the base. The prisoners could only escape if an un-captured member of their side managed to run through the enemy's base. When all of one side was captured, the teams changed over."

Australian children playing Crack-the-whip

Crack the Whip is a simple outdoor children's game involving physical coordination and is usually played in small groups on grass or ice. One player, chosen as the "head" of the whip, runs (or skates) around in random directions, with subsequent players holding on to the hand of the previous player. The entire "tail" of the whip moves in those directions but with much more force toward the end of the tail. The longer the tail, the more the forces act on the last player and the tighter they have to hold on. As the game progresses and more players fall off, some of those who were previously located near the end of the tail and have fallen off can "move up" and be in a more secure position by grabbing onto the tail as it is moving, provided they can get back on before some of the others do. There is no objective to this game other than enjoying the experience.

Snap the Whip, Winslow Homer *(1872)*

Playing on the Monkey Bars – round and round the monkey bars and doing "deathdrops". Using steel frame equipment.

Round and Round the monkey bars . – Hook one leg over the bar. Both arms under the bar and over your leg. Then spin around the bar.

Deathdrops: Hang from the high bar by the back of your knees. Either swing and drop to the ground onto your feet without using your hands, or no swing and drop onto your feet.

An early cartoon of children playing tag, 1860s

TAG IS a playground game in which two or more players chase other players in an attempt to "tag" or touch them, usually with their hands. Many variations exist; most forms have no teams, scores, or equipment. Usually, when a person is tagged, the tagger says, "Tag, you're it."

These are the most popular versions of tag, although it's difficult to specify popularity when game rules and names change so often. The seemingly simple game of tag, an exercise in children healthily running around a play area, has also attracted criticism for being 'too rough' and even 'dangerous'. There have also been schools where the game is banned because elimination games can create 'self-esteem issues' in nominating one child as the victim. In some schools, only supervised tagging is allowed, sometimes with a type of tagging called 'butterfly tagging' - a light tap on the upper body.

British Bulldogs (also known as Red Rover, etc.) is a tag game that has been popular in Australia for over a century. One or two players start as the 'bulldogs', who stand guard in the middle of the play area, while the players stand at one end of the yard. The aim is to rush from one end to the other without being caught by the bulldogs. When a player is caught, they become bulldogs. The winner is the last survivor. Some schools have banned this form of tag as being too dangerous.

Chain tag is a variant of Build Ups in which each person caught joins hands with 'it', and the chain must remain unbroken until everyone is caught. The more people caught, the longer the chain, and the more difficult it becomes to remain free.

In Freezers or Zombie Tag, the captured players freeze when they are tagged, extending their arms like zombies until they are unfrozen.

Cops and Robbers (also known by several names) has a designated jail area, sometimes drawn with a chalk border or, as often as not, an accepted area. The players are divided into cops and robbers, and the cops chase the robbers, tagging them and taking them to jail. Some versions allow the robbers to stage a jailbreak by tagging one of the prisoners without getting tagged. The game ends if all the robbers are in jail.

What's the Time, Mr Wolf? (or Dingo) One player is chosen to be Mr Wolf and stands facing away from the other players at the opposite end of the playground. All players except Mr Wolf chant in unison, "What's the time, Mr Wolf?" and Mr Wolf will answer in one of two ways: Mr Wolf may call a time - usually an hour ending in "o'clock". The other players take that many steps towards Mr Wolf. They then ask the question again. Alternatively, Mr Wolf may call "Dinner time!" and turn and chase the other players back to their starting point. If Mr Wolf tags a player, that player becomes Mr Wolf for the next round.

Builder - where the game starts with one tagger and builds as new children are tagged and added until everyone has been tagged is the most popular. It is simple with one main rule: avoid getting tagged, requires precisely what is needed after being seated most of the morning - an opportunity to run around as exercise.

The march of technology has also been tracked in the playing of tag and hide and seek. Computer tags allow players to use GPS tracking devices on their mobile phones to locate players. The commercial game of Pokemon, where mobile devices are used to track and collect 'pocket monsters', is another example of technology meets playground games.

. . .

Spinning Tops, Hula Hoops and Yo-Yos

Recalling his days at Bendigo High School in 1957, Peter Ellis remembered a schoolyard craze.[25]

> That year, small wooden spinning tops became popular. They were solid wood, cone-shaped and burgundy or maroon red or green with a small metal tip at the base. You drove a small nail into the top, looped the string over it, and then wound it around the top to make it spin as you flicked it down on the ground. As it hit the ground, you gave the string a back tug and, on releasing this, straightened the top. Some of the boys were very accurate with their tops and could land them on the marbles splitting them in half. That put an end to any marble games from then on. Yo-yos became popular at that time with all the tricks such as circling overhead and 'Walking the Dog'. Hipping the hula hoop for girls had also become a favourite pastime… causing a loss of interest in Skippy and Hopscotch.

Which hand? A.F.U.

Hand Games

'Chopsticks' is a seemingly simple hand game with many rules. As the name implies, its origin probably dates back to Ancient China. It is a hand game for two players in which players extend several fingers from each hand and transfer these scores by taking turns to tap one hand against another. 'Chopsticks' is an example of a combinatorial game and is solved in the sense that with perfect play an optimal strategy from any point is known.[26] It's complicated!

> Each player uses both hands to play the game; the number of fingers extended on a hand shows the number of points the hand has.
>
> Both players start with each hand having one point — one finger extended on each hand.
>
> The game's goal is for a player to force their opponent to extend all their fingers and thumbs on both hands or to force the player to extend all their fingers and thumb and one hand if their other hand is already out.
>
> A hand with all fingers and its thumb extended is called a dead hand and is taken out of play.
>
> Players take turns to tap their live hand(s) against another live hand (either their other hand, or one of their opponent's). You can tap any live hand per turn, but only one.
>
> The number of points on the tapping hand is added to the number on the tapped hand, and the player with the tapped hand extends their digits to show the new score. The tapping hand remains unchanged.
>
> A player may tap their two hands together to transfer points from one hand to the other. This is called a split. For example, if a player has 4 on one hand and 2 on the other, they could split to have 3 on each hand. Additionally, if a player has one hand out (0 fingers) and two fingers on the other hand, they could split to have one finger on each hand. You are not allowed to "swap hands" or switch the number of fingers between hands without splitting (going from 4 on one hand and 2 on the other to 2 on one hand and 4 on the other).

'**Rock, Paper, Scissors**'. One of the most enduring hand games is 'Rock, Paper, Scissors', which involves two players making shapes with their hands. Usually, the words rock, paper, and scissors are recited, and immediately at the end, the player must form a shape. The key to the game is that rock blunts scissors, scissors cut paper, and paper wraps the rock. The closed fist represents a rock, a flat hand, paper, and a two-finger V for victory sign, scissors. The game is often used to decide who will go first in other games, similar to tossing coins for a head or tail.

Another popular hand game, particularly for boys, is 'Bleeding Knuckles' or, more simply, 'Knuckles'. It employs speed, strength, and tolerance. It is a bully's game as the two players holding the clenched fists of one hand meet their opponents and, on a count, with no flinching, attempt to bring their knuckle down on their opponent, hence the game's name.

A more civil game is 'Pat-a-Cake'… well known for its traditional rhyme used as a simple clapping game with alternative claps exchanged between partners.

> Pat-a-cake, Pat-a-cake,
> Baker's man,
> Bake me a cake,
> As fast as you can.

'Thumb Fighting' is a hand game where the player's thumbs simulate fighting. It sounds easy but can be complicated. It is sometimes called Pea-Knuckle. '(following Wiki: The players face each other, hold out their left or right hand in a "thumbs up", and link hands such that each player's fingers curl around the other player's fingers. Gameplay has several tactics such as "playing possum", aiming for the knuckle rather than the nail for a pin, going for a quick strike, and waiting for one's opponent to tire. Variations include making the thumbs "bow", "kiss", or both before war and going to war with both hands at once, or sneak attacks, which involve using your pointer finger to take over the opponent. Players may also engage in a 'Rabbit Hole' manoeuvre to escape imminent defeat. Players may not use any of the fingers except the thumb to pin down their opponent's thumb. This is when you duck your thumb down into your palm.

The game is typically initiated by both players uttering the rhyme "One, two, three, four, I declare a thumb war," passing their thumbs over each other in time with this rhyme.

Another relatively simple hand game is 'Odds and Evens'. Each player chooses whether they are odds or evens, and after agreeing on whether the result will be an odd or even, on the call of one or two shouts, players extend one or two fingers until the winner emerges. The winner is usually the best of three games.

Clapping rhymes change with the times and often reflect either pop songs or commercials. This one seems to bring in McDonalds, Coco-Pops and some lines from a pop song. It was collected from girls in a primary school in Flemington, Victoria, in 1985.[27] It is not unusual for American and British clapping rhymes to enter Australian circulation.

> RONALD MCDONALD, (CLAP, CLAP) BISCUIT.
>
> Ronald McDonald (clap, clap) biscuit.
>
> Ah, shoo shoo, walla walla, biscuit.
>
> I've got a boyfriend, biscuit. He's as cute as a biscuit.
>
> Ice-cream soda with a cherry on top,
>
> Ice-cream soda with a cherry on top.

Sweet sweet baby, I don't want to let you go,
Downtown baby, down by the roller coaster.
Shimee shimmer coco-pops,
Shimmee shimmer pow.
Shimmiee shimmy coco-pops,
Shimmee shimmer pow!

THIS HAND and body clap is based on the words of a 1975 pop song: 'That's the Way I Like It' by KC & The Sunshine Band.[28]

1, 2, 3, HIT IT!
That's the way, uh-huh uh-huh I like it,
uh-huh uh-huh,
That's the way, uh-huh uh-huh I like it,
uh-huh uh-huh,
Truth, love, peace, full stop!

Two girls on the high swing. 1923

PLAYGROUND BALL GAMES have an extremely long history, ranging from easy to complicated, strenuous to simple. The main categories are bat and ball games, such as cricket, rounders, stickball and baseball; racquet and ball games, such as tennis, squash and badminton; hand and ball-striking games, such as handball and rebound handball; goal sports, usually team sports such as any football and hockey; non-racquet net sports, such as volleyball and basketball; and target sports, such as bowling and croquet. Children are particularly good at adapting ball games and inventing new ones.

'Hopscotch' is an ancient game that possibly dates back to Ancient Roman times. It is still popular throughout the world, including Australia. The game is played mainly by girls. The popular Australian version of the game uses the standard layout of triangles and rectangles drawn on the ground with chalk or even traced out on dirt. Some schools and play centres have permanently painted Hopscotch courts. The local version has the game in three stages and can be played solo or with a group. The first stage involves the player hopping the circuit; the second requires the player to jump, landing on both feet; the third, called 'sizzles' or 'scissors', requires a jump landing on crossed legs. The end of the court is 'safe' or 'home'. If a player lands on a line, they are demoted and have to start again from that level.

Skipping is a playground activity usually associated with girls, but not exclusively, and to be a good skipper requires stamina and skill. There are many skipping games and, no doubt, more still to be created. Rope jumping requires the swung rope to pass under the skipper's feet and over the head. Skipping can be solo or with others. The five popular categories in Australian skipping are single freestyle, single speed, pairs, three skippers ('Double Dutch'), and three-person freestyle ('Double Dutch freestyle').

For the sake of historical documentation, this collection includes some very old Australian game rhymes. Some use words that we now feel offensive, like 'Chinaman' and 'Black Gin'. Racial stereotyping was the usual fare for earlier playground rhymes and stories. Such use was then innocent, and if we are to learn from history, their inclusion here will serve as both documentation and a warning. One of the aims was to show that although a large portion of our children's folklore was transplanted, mainly from England, Scotland and Ireland, we had the creativity to adopt and adapt, localise and make the rhymes Australian in word use and intent.

Counting Out Rhymes

The following rhyme was printed in *The Bulletin Magazine*, Sydney, 9 April 1898. Its contributor, John Peat, added, 'another local girls' game-rhyme - a Woolloomooloo classic'

BAKE A PUDDING.

Bake a pie,

Take 'em up to Bondi;

Bondi wasn't in,

Take 'em unto black gin;

Black gin took 'em in -

Out goes she.

Nonsense rhymes are always popular with children who, often to the amazement of adults, have little trouble getting the jumbled words out of their mouths.[29]

Ibble abble black bubble

Ibble abble out.

Eeny meeny miney mo,

Katawheela whila wo,

Each peach, pear, plum,

Out goes old Tom Thumb,

O-U-T spells out

And out you must go.

Inky pinky ponky

Daddy bought a donkey,

Donkey died, Daddy cried,

Inky pinky ponky.

Melbourne City Council, one, two, three,

Melbourne City Council, you're not 'he'.

'ONE POTATO' is a counting-out rhyme with a hand game of the same name.

Players hold their fists out, and the counter counts them off; the last one touched (on 'more') drops his or her fist; the owner of the last fist left in is 'it' or 'he'

> One potato, two potato, three potato, four,
> Five potato, six potato, seven potato more.

Skipping[30]

> All in together, girls,
> This fine weather, girls,
> When you hear your birthday
> Please run in...
> January, February, March etc...

Girls progressively join the skip, entering when their birthday arrives.[31]

> Andy, Andy, sugar and candy,
> French almond rock,
> All the boys in (Loftus) school
> Wear dirty socks.

> All in together
> this fine weather.
> i saw a nanny goat
> peeping up my petticoat,
> Crash, bang, fire.

After the child has skipped this rhyme, she crouches and repeats the rhyme while the rope is turned over her. When she gets to 'fire', the rope is brought down, and she must jump over it. The pattern is repeated until she is out."

The introduction and popularity of early television can be found in several traditional playground rhymes. Today's children's television is a slick machine compared to the 1960s and seventies. Sunday newspaper comics were also an influence, and the following are two well-known cartoon characters, Blondie and Dagwood Bumstead, from the 1960s.[32]

> Blondie and Dagwood went to town,
> Blondie bought a dressing-gown,
> Dagwood bought a newspaper,
> And this is what it said:
> Close your eyes and count to ten,
> If you don't, you'll take my end.
> 1, 2, 3, …10
>
> Teddy Bear Biscuits are the best,
> North, south, east and west

On 'south,' the skipper crosses her feet; on 'west,' she traps the rope by straddling it.

> There was an old lady who lived in a shoe,
> She had so many children she didn't know what to do.
> How many children did she have?
> 1, 2, 3, 4, …
>
> Apple tart, strawberry tart,
> Tell me the name of your sweetheart.
> A, B, C, D.
> (David, David) come to tea,
> (David, David,) marry me.
> What shall we get married in?
> Silk, satin, rags, bags.

> What shall we go to the church in?
>
> Coach, cart, carriage, wheelbarrow.

Divination rhyme. The skipper's future is told by the letter or word on which the player fouls the rope.[33]

Another skipping rhyme group is based on questions rather than answers.

> My father is a butcher,
>
> My mother chops the meat,
>
> And I'm a little frankfurt
>
> That runs around the street.
>
> How far do I run?
>
> 1, 2, 3, 4, ...

> There was an old lady who lived in a shoe,
>
> She had so many children she didn't know what to do.
>
> How many children did Mother Hubbard have?
>
> 1, 2, 3, 4, ...

Edel Wignell recalled a nonsense rhyme from her childhood in the 1940s.[34] This appears to be a child's version of what was commonly known as a 'stump speech'. These nonsense speeches typically invoked political grandstanding speeches.[35]

> Ladies and gentlemen, reptiles and crocodiles,
>
> I come before you to tell you a story I know nothing about.
>
> Last night, at six o'clock this morning, an empty house full of furniture caught fire. The people being out rushed downstairs and fell into a bucket of cold water, and were badly scalded. They now lie in the Hobart Sydney Hospital in the best of health but are expected to die at any moment.

Hand Clapping

>Mary Mack, dressed in black,
>Silver buttons down her back.
>She likes coffee, I like tea,
>She likes sitting on a Chinaman's knee.

clapped in a 4/4 time between two players [36]

>My mother said I never should
>Play with the gypsies in the wood.
>If I did, she would say,
>"Naughty girl to disobey."
>The wood was dark, the grass was green,
>By came Sally with a tambourine,
>I went to sea, no ship to get across,
>I paid ten shillings for a blind white horse.

The following uses a line from a popular 1960s song, *'I Told The Witchdoctor'* [37]

>I went to a Chinese restaurant
>To buy me a loaf of bread, pom, pom,
>He wrapped it up in a five-pound note
>and this is what he said:
>Oo ee oo ah ah,
>Ting tang walla walla bing bang.

Ball-Bouncing [38]

>Big Ben,
>Strike ten,
>Touch knee,
>Touch toe, Clap hands, Through you go.
>Oliver Twist, can you do this?

If so, do so.

Number One, touch your tongue.

Number two, touch your shoe.

Number three touch your knee.

Number four, touch the floor.

Number five, jump up high.

Number seven, fly to Heaven.

Number eight, shut the gate.

Number nine, drink some wine.

Number ten, start again.

>Old Mother Mop
>
>She had a big shop
>
>and all she could say
>
>Is candy pop pop
>
>Candy pop pop
>
>A penny a sop
>
>Catch the ball
>
>And don't let it drop.

Dorothy Howard 1957 noted, "The game was played with three balls; two were thrown against a wall alternately with one hand; the third was thrown into the air with the other hand on 'op'.[39]

>P.K. chewing gum/
>
>Penny a packet//
>
>First you chew it/
>
>Then you crack it//
>
>Then you stick it/
>
>To your jacket//
>
>P.K. chewing gum/
>
>Penny a packet//

This game is played in pairs. on//, the left-hand throws the first ball underhand against the wall; on //, the right-hand throws the other ball overhand against the wall.

THE SCHOOL PLAYGROUND has undergone considerable physical change over the past decades. In many schools, the need to construct more buildings has seen the continual loss of green space; drought has also taken its toll on lawns, and bitumen is far easier to maintain! Sheds now replace shady trees, and recreational space diminishes as overall school numbers grow. There are also imposed rules and a lot of banned activities. Here's a general list of playground rules reported in a 2007-2010 play Childhood, Tradition & Change study.[40] No doubt, more than a decade later, this list is longer and scarier.

> Rules Impacting on Play • No hat, no play [in summer] • No running on concrete or paved surfaces • No running on the play equipment • No climbing trees • No playing with sticks or rocks • No playing in the gardens • No scratching or digging in the soil surface • No picking leaves or flowers • Each Year level to play in their designated playing area • No playing in out-of-bounds areas • No bringing toys from home • Pokemon cards are banned

DIVERSITY in the Playground[41]

Australia now claims more ethnic diversity than any other country on earth; more than the United States, Canada and the United Kingdom. We salute our Indigenous history and more than two hundred years of welcoming people who were quaintly referred to in the mid-twentieth century as 'New Australians'. Many came as early settlers, many came to seek their fortune on the goldfields, later emigrants came over in giant clipper ships for a new life in a new land, and many came as participants of our government's post-WW1 and WW2 'populate or perish' campaigns offering assisted-passage.

There have also been refugees. Dispossessed people seeking asylum. All emigrants, whatever their reasoning, bring baggage. Sometimes, as for refugees, this baggage is little more than memories and family customs. Children, often reluctant travellers, are usually the easiest members of the family to become settled. They fit into our society easily as just another child eager to learn and play. Games played in their original land, some variants of known local games, and some completely new ones are quickly introduced and assimilated. Childhood is a great welcoming leveller for migrants and an important part of today's and tomorrow's story. In 1986, Heather Russell, assisted by Gwenda Davey and June Factor, undertook fieldwork research at the Hightown Primary School, Melbourne, as a snapshot of play at that moment in time.

At the time of the study, Hightown Primary School had 342 pupils, with 82% of the children coming from non-English-speaking backgrounds. Most of them came from low-income or assisted housing. Many came from refugee families. The school itself, including play areas, was in porr condition.

The document is a fascinating study of multicultural diversity in the playground. Its overall finding showed that children have a remarkably strong urge to play and a resourcefulness to make it happen. This finding was particularly important considering the multicultural nature of the school and the fact it was a primary school with mainly recently arrived migrant children. Normally, a primary school would have many verbal traditions, including rhymes associated with skipping and clapping games; however, because of the non-English speaking background of the school mix, the Hightown study showed extremely limited verbal use in games.

The study identified three main play areas at the school: the concreted area connected to the classroom building, the three designated adventure playgrounds with equipment appropriate to different age groups, and the sport's oval. The concreted area was used for the standard play games, including hopscotch, elastics, cricket, kickball, statues, marbles, hide and seek, ball wall games and the now inevitable rap-dancing. The play sessions in the three portioned adventure playgrounds were generally unstructured, with children taking advantage of the equipment such as slides, climbing logs, etc. Play is described as 'having few special rules and rituals, and involves more informal social and physical interaction. Climbing and balancing are the main skills for playing on adventure playgrounds. This type of play is less energetic and requires fewer motor skills than games like elastics, high jump and down ball." The study also found age difference was accepted in this style of play, "it is not uncommon to find a Grade 4 boy playing on the slide with four or five prep children."

Adventure playground 3 proved the most popular, with up to thirty-five children often playing on the equipment at once. "Children of both sexes and from all ethnic backgrounds. The equipment consists of a slide, a chain walk, a ladder with a platform at the top, a tyre walk, and a platform connected to the ground via a pole and a ladder and all these pieces of equipment are connected."

Elastics is probably the most popular playground game for girls in Australian schools. At Hightown Primary, it was "common to see six or seven games of elastics going at one time, each involving four or five players."

This study on multiculturalism showed that girls who engage in game-playing prefer to play in groups where girls share some cultural similarities rather than in multicultural groups. It also showed that Indo-Asian girls were the keenest players. "They participate in various games and seem to possess greater skill and physical dexterity than their classmates. These Indo-Asian girls treat their games seriously and will practise and play more than other children in the playground. Many games they play represent a carry-over of play traditions from their country of origin (most were born in Vietnam). These girls value their play culture highly and are prepared to teach their games to others."

The boys at Hightown Primary played typical boy's games, including marbles, football, chaser, poison ball, off-ground piggy, statues, four squares and skippy. The report noted, "It should be noted that although, during the two-month observation period, boys were observed playing as many different games as girls, boys generally play these games less frequently than girls." They also played in multicultural groups rather than mono-cultural groups.

Evidence of cross-cultural influences in both boys' and girls' games was noted. In Marbles, the ever-important flick action has seen the introduction and growing popularity of the so-called Chinese flick. Vietnamese and Chinese girls have also introduced a rule into elastics that involves twisting the elastic around one leg and jumping out.

7

WONDER AND EXCITEMENT

Section of lantern slide showing kite flying

Childhood wonder comes in many forms. Our perception of what is mysteriously wondrous changes over time because of uncontrollable influences, especially in technology connected to popular culture. Children were once fascinated by spinning a top or turning the end of a kaleidoscope, producing endless patterns. Magic lantern slide shows, a simple projection device produced gasps of awe, and good old Punch and Judy encouraged boos, hisses and uncontrollable laughter as the audience imagined themselves up there on the puppeteer's tiny stage. Listening to the wireless, imagining the pictures in your head, was a wonder; then television and internet-connected devices arrived to spoil the fun. Fifty years seems like a short jump in history, yet five years is a mammoth leap for young children.

Many innocent pastimes have slipped away, replaced by glitzy screens on hand-held devices like smartphones or tablets or expensive units like the Xbox. Children who were content to hear a bedtime story or song now demand moving images and sound. Everything else seems passé.

Yet, children still manage to find wonder in simple things. Peek a Boo, even if just the hiding and revealing of a line of sight with a hand, can make an infant giggle with delight. It is easy to be cynical. However, all parents and educators know that despite all the changes in the world, a young child has an explorer's mind, a yearning to explore, and, above all, the determination to find wonder where adults never look.

Kaleidoscopes, Thaumatropes. Zoetropes & Strobotropes

The early kaleidoscope, popularised in the 1800s, was a tube that turned utilitarian mirrors, allowing viewers to explore concepts of light, colour and optics. Near the end of that century, the kaleidoscopes used a rotating wheel and tiny ampoules that separated the liquids to produce even more possibilities. They were referred to as 'philosophical toys' that served a double duty of entertainment and sharing scientific advancement. Seeing wonder and sharing wonder is part of childhood discovery and leads to a questioning mind, a curiosity, which aids education from a very young age. Other 19th-century 'philosophical toys' included the Stereoscope (a device with two images that, when viewed together, gave a perception of depth). Thaumatrope (images on the reverse side of a disc that were spun on a string until they appeared to be a single image), Zoetrope (a cylinder with drawings on the inside that were viewed through slits on the opposite side as the cylinder rotated), and the Stroboscopic Disc (a device that provided a series of images in rapid succession, allowing the impression of movement).

1818 print of a man using a Kaleidoscope 'Human Nonsense'

Thaumotrope *Muséums Victoria Collection*

Zoetrope

Stroboscopic Wheel - when rotated the boys leap-frog

Fortune-telling Fish

How many Australian children have had their fortune told by a fish? - a magic fortune-telling fish. The fish, made of cellophane, sits flat on the hand and, with a little body heat, twists and curls, and each position tells your fortune. Moving head = jealousy, moving tail = indifference, moving head and tail = in love, curling sides = fickle, turns over = false, curls up entirely = passionate, and, if it is motionless = you're dead!

The Fortune-Telling Magic Fish

Shadow Puppets [1]

How wonderful to experience a puppet show performed entirely with hand movements. The wrist becomes the head of an animal like a dog, cat, lion, camel, bird or horse, and then it moves, wriggling ears, twitching the nose, opening the jaw and so on. Shadow puppets were used in some primitive communities as part of their great storytelling tradition, often combined with epic songs.

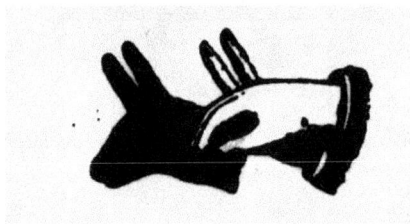

> A simple form of amusement is making shadow animals on the wall with one's hands. For example, we give a small illustration representing a rabbit or something similar. A large sheet of white paper should be pinned to the wall, and a candle should be arranged on a small table close at hand to throw a well-defined shadow on the paper.

Punch & Judy

The puppetry of Punch and Judy (sometimes Punch and Toby) has a fine pedigree. With Mr Punch's hooked nose, humped back and menacing club, he surely terrified many youngsters over his centuries of misbehaviour. Australian Punch & Judy 'punch-man', the late Dr. Bruce Rosen, described the history as:[2]

> By the middle years of the nineteenth century, the Punch and Judy show had entered its golden age. Punch-men performed wherever they thought they might draw a paying audience, including country fairs and seaside resorts, London, and other population centres in England.
>
> Punch himself is based on the Commedia Dell'arte character,

Pulcinella or Punchinello, to whom has been added many of the characteristics of the medieval English fool or jester. In the play, which is often coarse and satirical, Punch first kills his infant child when the baby will not stop crying. He then beats his wife to death. The story rambles on with Punch meeting, arguing with and finally beating--often to death--a series of characters. He outwits the hangman, who hangs himself, and finally vanquishes the devil through either trickery or combat.

Although the plots vary from one version to the next, the nineteenth-century play usually included, in addition to Punch and Judy, Judy's ghost, the baby, Toby the Dog, the Beadle, the black servant, the Hangman and the Devil. Except for Toby, these were puppets, but by the nineteenth century, it had become a common, if not universal practice, to have a real dog playing the role of Toby. Indeed, some Punch-men even taught their dog to sit and hold a pipe in its mouth.

Magic lantern glass slide of Mr. Punch

George Cruikshank's drawing of a Punch & Judy Show. *V&A*

Punch's voice, high pitched and squeaky, is produced through the use of a swizzle or squeaker. Victorian writer Henry Mayhew, interviewed one Punch-man who referred to it as a "call" and said:[3]

> They ain't whistles, but calls, or unknown tongues, as we sometimes names 'em, because with them in the mouth we can pronounce each word as plain as any parson. We have two or three kinds: one for out-of-doors, one for indoors, one for speaking and for singing, and another for selling.

Of course, the violent theme of the typical Punch and Judy show is now frowned upon, or, worse still, has been replaced by the dull, expurgated story. Perhaps it is a case of T.M.I. (too much information), and despite children squealing with delight at the beating of Judy, the reality of domestic violence is now well-known and possibly too confronting for tender eyes and ears. There are still a handful of 'Punch' shows in Australia.

Magic Lantern Shows

Magic Lantern shows were very popular in Australia, and our major heritage institutions hold extensive collections of glass slides and projectors. For example, the Australian Museum in Sydney has over 30,000 slides on natural history and anthropological nature. The National Film and Sound Archive has thousands, many still uncatalogued. The origins of the magic lantern can be traced back to the mid-1600s, almost two hundred years before the first photographs were made. In Australia, the slide shows were staged as part of public lectures, missionary work, and entertainment. The founder of the 'Flying Doctor' the Reverend John Flynn, had a large collection depicting bible stories and natural wonders. The Salvation Army also used shows in their evangelical work. Magic lantern shows entertained Australia for over 100 years, from around the 1840s onwards. Images were illuminated, first by candle, then by oil lamps and later electricity, onto screens or bedsheets in shearing sheds, goldfield's singing rooms, churches, Schools of Arts and other halls, private homes and even outdoor spaces. It even went to war and entertained the troops during the Boer and First World Wars. The magic lantern disappeared after the arrival of motion pictures.

The Magic Lantern show programs ranged from education to the bizarre. Hand-coloured views would dissolve, transforming before the viewer's eyes, ghosts would appear and fade away, and one early report tells of a slide of live bread weevils moving around—a very strange sight for young viewers. Joe Watson, a travelling magic lantern showman, told of a series depicting the Kelly Gang, and incorporated a 16-verse ballad [4]of Kelly's exploits to be sung as part of the entertainment.

A Magic Lantern show.

In the hurly-burly: limelight effects in Melbourne (*Melbourne War Cry*, 28 July 1894)

The wonderment of the slide

Magic, Hypnotism & the Spirit World

The latter half of the nineteenth and early twentieth centuries saw a wave of spiritualism sweep the Western world. Well-known figures like Conan Doyle, of Sherlock Holmes fame, fanned the interest, and performance artists, including the 'Great Houdini', questioned whether the 'dead can return'. What such nonsense sparked in the imagination of youngsters is unimaginable.

What youngster could resist such an offer?

In the 1870s, one of the world's most famous acts toured Australia; the Davenport Brothers, two young Americans, amazed audiences with eerie stories and sights, including a huge cabinet containing various musical instruments - which, when under their spell, would play by themselves. Sadly, the younger Davenport brother died in Sydney mid-tour and was buried at Rookwood Cemetery. When touring Australia, The Great Houdini visited his grave.

The Davenport Brothers in their magic cabinet

Eliza Chomley recalled children holding mock seances.[5]

The boys and ourselves often spent pleasant evenings at the Tripp's with various interesting games - sometimes a seance that had a dreadful fascination for me. We would all sit in the dimly lighted enclosed end of the verandah and take it in turns to tell the most horrible and blood-curdling ghost stories (murders sometimes admitted).

Kids seem to enjoy being scared witless, which is strange considering our human fear of the unknown. Perhaps the popularity of scary story books and ghost films is a carryover from times when storytellers and audiences revelled in tales about headless riders, ghostly encounters, cemetery stories, and even blood-sucking vampires.

Audrey Blake recalls listening to stories in the 1920s in working-class Melbourne.[6]

> Most of the time we didn't have toys but we did have two packs of cards and we delighted in euchre, spoons, sevens and rummy. After cards we would sometimes turn out the light and play 'findings'. When one child found another there would be a wrestling match in the dark with all joining the fray. Or we played ghosts, with Reg as storyteller, wonderfully disguised in sheets and face powder, a dark room artfully lit by candle; he scared us beautifully.

Look into my eyes, Look into my eyes.

Interest in the supernatural resulted in the publishing and advertising of booklets on spiritualism and magic. Many young people mailed away for booklets on how to learn Hypnotism and *How To Be An Escapologist*[7] and consequentially thought of themselves as possessing supernatural powers.

. . .

ONE OF AUSTRALIA'S favourite comics was undoubtedly the crime-busting *Mandrake The Magician* written and drawn by Lee Falk. Mandrake was evoked in many backyard games.

TABLEAUS

Empire Day tableau North Ryde 1934. *School House Museum.*

Government and schools promoted the fashion for tableaus, where students were involved in portraying welcoming commemorative messages or historical scenes. The word tableau comes from the French and means 'picture', a stationary picture: some involved thousands, others only a small group. The most notable tableaus were commemorative, such as a celebration of Empire Day, a royal visit or a coronation. To participate in a tableau would have been exciting for many children, especially if it was a large event with several participating schools. The tableaus were also in costume and usually involved pomp and circumstance with music and patriotic speeches. Children also arranged backyard tableaus.

Britannia and Daughters. Empire Day North Bondi School, 1933

In 1908 the arrival of The Great White Fleet, a show of power in the Pacific by the US Navy, was commemorated with a Hail Columbia tableau where 8000 children formed the American and Australian flags intertwined. The opening of the Sydney Harbour Bridge in 1932 had 4000 boys and girls form a replica of the great bridge at the Sydney Cricket Ground.

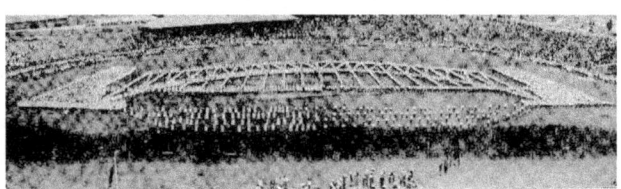

The Sydney Harbour Bridge Tableau. *Labor Daily (Sydney)* April 1932

THE LIVING ROSARY. In 1937, schoolchildren in Ballarat formed a large tableau to celebrate the coronation of King George VI. According to Marita Blood, the local Catholic college students formed a giant set of rosary beads a few years later. Marita wanted to be a 'bead' in the performance. Tableaus were not restricted to cities, and many country towns boasted their own tableau performances.

Australia also has a tradition of what was loosely described as 'historical pageants'. These costumed displays were similar to the tableau and usually commemorated an event in history, such as the first landing of Captain Cook, coronations, community centenaries, etc. Adults and children would dress in period costumes, often with props, and reenact the event. Tableaus were once a feature of Australia Day celebrations.

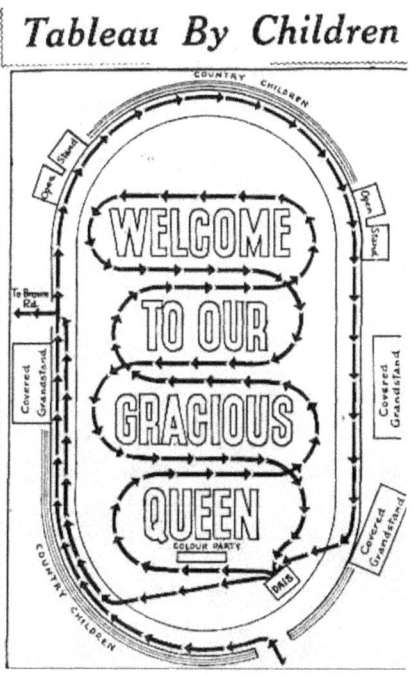

Newcastle's children spelt out 'Welcome to our Glorious Queen' for the royal visit 1954.

One of the largest tableaus was staged in the northern New South Wales city of Newcastle in 1954.[8]

> Seventeen thousand children will form a tableau of the words "Welcome to Our Gracious Queen' at the Showground tomorrow while the Queen and the Duke of Edinburgh are at the ground.
> The diagram shows the route of the Royal vehicles inside the ground. The Royal car will enter the arena at the dais end and make a complete circuit of the oval before pulling up at the dais. Later, the

Royal visitors will make a complete tour of the children forming the tableau and return to the dais again through the assembled ranks.

When the Royal car leaves, it will make a partial circuit of the oval and then take a route lined with 4000 Boy Scouts and Girl Guides on the way to the Brown-road exit. Most of the Newcastle and Lake Macquarie Shire pupils will be inside the arena, either forming part of the tableau or flanking it. Country children will have ringside and grandstand seats. In front of the tableau will be a group of school captains carrying their school banners. The children should have every opportunity to see the Queen and the Duke.

Massed Displays

Human flag for The Great White Fleet's visit, 1908, Sydney Cricket Ground. *State Records NSW*

Federation in 1901 and the visit of the American Great White Fleet in August 1908 were occasions of public celebration, and schools were harnessed for mass displays. Many participated in spelling out names, nations, and even flags by choreographed children.

Over 1500 Broken Hill primary and high school students formed the outline of Australia (without Tasmania) for the Broken Hill sesquicentenary, 1951. *State Records, NSW.*

Bonfires & Crackers

> Remember, remember, the fifth of November,
> Gunpowder, treason and plot!
> If you can't give us one, we'll take two;
> The better for us and the worse for you!

Undoubtedly, one of the most exciting annual events in the children's calendar of yesterday's Australia was Bonfire Night, alternatively known as Cracker Night, because fireworks were generically called crackers. For many, it came a close third to Christmas and birthdays in the anticipation stakes.

Tending the bonfire. Weekly Times (Victoria) 1912

Bonfire Night[9]

'Tis lots of fun, the children think,
To build a bonfire bright;
To see it blaze up toward the sky
Through the darkness of the night.
They pile on brush and old dry grass
Till the flames leap higher,
Then all the neighbours gather 'round
To watch the big bonfire.
It crackles, leaps and splutters, too,
Just feel its awful heat!
If you but stand an inch too close
'Twill scorch your face and feet!
No child will go into the house
To seek his comfy bed
Till every coal, yes, every spark,
Of the big bonfire's dead.

Guy Fawkes Night [10] marked the events of 5 November 1605, when Guy Fawkes, a member of the Gunpowder Plot, was arrested while guarding explosives a group of Catholics plotters had placed beneath the House of Lords. Celebrating King James's surviving the attempt on his life, people lit bonfires around London, and months later, the introduction of the Observance of the 5th November Act enforced an annual public day of thanksgiving for the plot's failure. It was celebrated in colonial Australia with references as early as 1824 when the *Sydney Gazette* reported:

"...the Royal Standard adorned the heights of the Dawes Point Battery the whole of the day." Four year's later the *Sydney Monitor* May 1828 reported: 'Guy Fawkes Day was celebrated in this city by the usual perambulation of countless urchins on Saturday last, tricked out in motley clothes, and chaunting a version of their doggerel chorus.

Guy, Guy, Guy - Stick him up high,
Put him on a lamp-post - And there let him die

A report in 1939 suggested the commemoration was headed for oblivion. TIt was very wrong! It would still be another thirty years before the last double-bunger exploded.[11]

> Fifth of November. — Yesterday being the anniversary of that memorable day, commonly called 'Guy Fawkes' Day', several parties of children were employed in the morning, exhibiting effigies of the old gunpowder plot gentleman, in order to raise a few pence. The commemoration of this day is fast falling into oblivion.

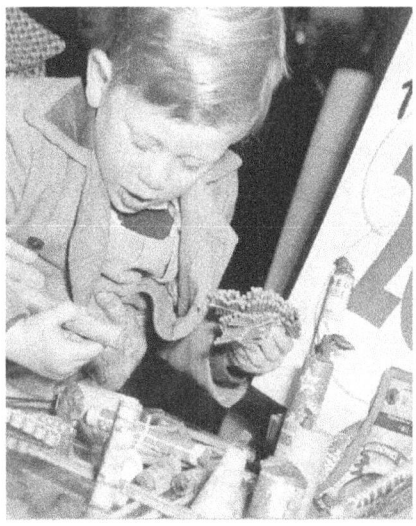

The fireworks stash. *Courtesy Paul Becher Collection, Newcastle.*

Reports of Australian Guy Fawkes sightings, bonfires, and fireworks continued during the nineteen-fifties and early sixties, and so did the safety debate. [12]

> Guy Fawkes Day—This being the 6th of November of gunpowder plot celebrity, we caution our juvenile friends against the danger or discharging fire-works in the public streets, as where there are so

many wooden tenements, the most serious consequences might result from wanton or careless sporting with fire. There can be no objection to a little harmless mirth in suitable situations on Guy Fawkes Day. As some real 'orthodox' fireworks may be obtained in the town, we suppose there will be no resisting the effigy-burning custom of Old England, although in many places, it has become nearly obsolete. The Police will be on the alert to prevent accidents and to apprehend parties who infringe the provisions of the Police Act.

On the death of Queen Victoria in 1901, it was decreed that the unofficial Guy Fawkes Day be replaced with Empire Day as a tribute to the monarch, an event to be celebrated on her birth date of 24 May. It was designed to be a day of pomp and ceremony with flags flown on public buildings, military gun salutes, parades, receptions and gatherings. In 1905, schoolchildren were granted a half-day holiday in Australia, and Empire Night became Bonfire Night. By 1958, Empire Day had run its course and became Commonwealth Day. Like the bonfire, it was to fizz out eventually.

Flicking Firework Matches. *The Australasian* 5 Feb. 1921

'Guy Fawkes Game'. [13] This is a good indoor game and may be played by two or more players. A box is placed on the table, and inside the box is set a jam jar. The box is the bonfire, and the jar is the guy. Several matches must be collected, and painted different colours, So as to allow each player a set of a dozen matches. One player has red, one green, and so on. The matches represent fireworks. The players sit round the table, the box having been placed in the centre.

Each player, in turn, flips a match towards the box, trying to get it in the box or, better still, into the jar. Each match that goes into the box counts one mark, and each match in the jar counts two. No player may be closer than two feet from the box.

The best method of flipping the match is for the player to hold it upright between the table and the first finger of the left hand. With the first finger and thumb of the right hand, he gives it a smart flip, releasing the pressure of the left hand finger. In this way, a match will travel a considerable distance.

Collecting for the Guy Fawkes[14]

Huge double-bungers, rockets tall
And every kind of noise,
Will soon the neighbourhood appall,
And gladden girls and boys.
They're building bonfires rough and neat.
The stacks they're piling high,
And here and there we hear the bleat:
"A penny for the guy."
Guy Fawkes Day comes once a Year
When youth must do its stuff,
While parents moan in natural fear:
"And once a year's enough"

SINGING and playing musical instruments around the fire was often part of Bonfire Night, especially in the early evening before darkness descended and excitement erupted.

Fireworks displays. These days, firework displays are highly regulated and typically public events like festival openings and closings. Pre-1970, building bonfires was a matter for the community and, in some cases, the individual. It wasn't unusual for entire streets to have their own bonfire built over weeks. Some were extraordinarily large, inflammable mountains made from anything that would burn. Children would work like ants pulling their billy-carts or wheelbarrows up and down the street, collecting old clothing, wood, and used car tyres. The latter was a problem because they emitted a thick black, acrid smoke - but they blazed, which was important. Some children carted large timbers for miles. The bonfires were guarded, sometimes day and night, as rival gangs were known to attempt to light the opposition's bonfire before the big night. You could never be too careful, and, in such a case, innocent children became quite paranoid, especially during Bonfire Night's lead-up day. The Guy Fawkes came in all shapes, sizes and dispositions, being ceremoniously hoisted to the bonfire tower on the day of the big burn.

Heap Big Chief Fire Cracker - Guy effigy Lambton Park. Newcastle Sun. 4 Nov 1954

The night usually started early evening, often with barbecues and singing, as kids compared their stash of fireworks with other kids. Some swapping was normal, and bags were held close to the body 'just in case'. Everything went crazy once the bonfire was lit. Up it went, and the bungers, rockets, candles and sparklers came out. Noise everywhere, sky exploding and smoke-smitten eyes. By 9 pm, it was all over. The fire doused, and the children were ushered home—such excitement. The following day, older children raced to the site at dawn - to collect 'fizzers', crackers that had not exploded or had been dropped.

Fireworks came in all shapes, sizes and colours and were purchased at department stores, sports stores and news agencies. Pre-packed bundles were available; however, most kids preferred to pick and choose their own. Children saved up play-money, did odd jobs, and collected refundable drink bottles. Buying your crackers was a matter of pride.

Favourites included Roman Candles, Black Devils, Mine of Serpents, Catherine Wheels, jumping jacks, golden rain, whiz wheels, flower pots, skyrockets, Vesuvius, silver fountains, bungers, double-bungers, thunders, Tom Thumbs, spitfires, sparklers, star shell repeaters and fizzles.

Pranks. One problem with the annual event was the nuisance pranks. Robert Inglis, writing in the *Newcastle Morning Herald* in 1954, asked a local fireworks salesman about young boys and pranks: [15]

> They're weak about the business. When we let 'em off, we let 'em off full-blooded. I was once arrested, following a caution for letting crackers off in the street. Of course, you know crackers can't be displayed in a shop window. The law forbids this since about 25 years ago, when a boy in Paddington started a big fire in a shop by holding a magnifying glass at the shop window onto the crackers inside. We used to tie crackers to cat's tails, throw 'em under horses' tails, in short, make a nuisance of ourselves.

'Fireworks Blast - Blaze in Shops - A Story Of Boy With Magnifying Glass. [16]

An explosion of crackers in a shop window in Elizabeth St., Paddington, today caused a fire that caused extensive damage and endangered the shopkeeper's life. Police say that the explosion occurred when a boy, aged 10, with a magnifying glass, directed the sun's rays through the plate glass onto the crackers. A second shop was also damaged by fire, and a woman was almost overcome by heat and smoke while rescuing her pets.

The worst pranks involved 'blowing up letter boxes', throwing jumping jacks at innocent people, and, worst of all, placing a brown paper bag containing dog faeces at someone's front door, setting it alight, madly knocking on the door, and running like hell. The unsuspecting resident usually opened the door, saw the flaming bag, and immediately stamped on it!

Fireworks are dangerous, especially in the wrong hands. Many came with warnings 'do not hold in hand after lighting'. Daredevils shot rockets in empty cordial bottles and, over time, newspaper reports of tragedies piled up. Eventually, in the nineteen-seventies, the sale of explosive fireworks like the double-bunger, were banned from retail. By the mid-eighties, most state governments had banned the sale of fireworks, and the bonfires started to flicker out.

KITE-MAKING & Flying

Kite-making and flying have a long history in Australia; most were homemade rather than today's store-bought kites.

Flying kites. Engraving by Michael Voltz 1828

There are numerous types of kites, the traditional and the box kite being the most popular. Australian newspapers regularly carried How To Make A Kite articles, usually aimed at boys. However, kite-flying is something for both girls and boys.

Flying a kite is not easy. You need to learn. Older boys taught younger children how to handle the kite when neighbourhoods were friendlier. It was usually a sort of internship - no one wanted to make a kite and then see it disappear into the sky forever. The most complicated skill is getting the kite airborne, followed by complex movements that send the kite swooping down to earth as close as possible before quickly turning and soaring up again. Children also delighted in kite fights - competing to see how close they could get to the opponent's kite without getting tangled. Kites were once a common sight, especially on our beaches; however, like the billy cart, they were deemed dangerous for fear of being entangled in overhead power lines.

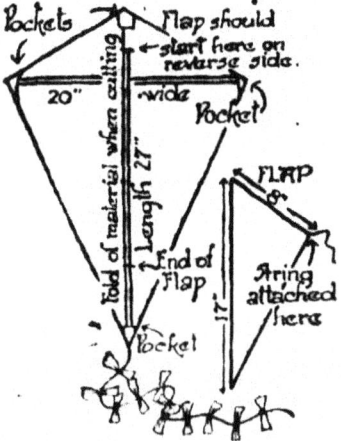

How to make a kite. *The Australasian 1929*

Here is a typical newspaper guide to making a kite.[17]

Make a Kite. This kite is especially strong as it is made from stout cotton material such as print or calico. Cut the material out to the shape shown in the diagram. If you make a fold down the middle of the staff, which should be 27in. long, and then cut through the double thickness, you will find it easier. The measurements on the diagram show how to shape the kite. The flap sketched separately should be sewn down the middle fold, starting about 3in. from the top. Next make a tiny hem all round, and then sew a tiny pocket at the top and bottom corners, and each side as well. These are for the sticks to fit into, and you can get two suitable thin pieces of wood for a penny or two at an ironmonger's or timber yard. The tail is made of string, with streamers of paper at intervals. The string to fly the kite is attached to the flap.

Holidays at last. Woolloomooloo Methodist Collection. Ted Hood 1938. *SLNSW*

Holiday Times

The Australian Christmas is topsy-turvy, and images of trees covered with snowflakes, rugged-up Father Christmas, snowmen, and reindeer-led sleighs do not sit comfortably with scorching heat and bright blue skies. It has a very different holiday feel from Northern Europe. Some northern traditions that have survived in Australia include decorating the Christmas tree, Christmas meals, traditional plum pudding, gift-giving, and carol singing. Some communities and churches also display nativity scenes, and others present nativity plays. Our Christmas is different, and the hot Christmas Day meal will likely be a relaxed barbecue or a beachside picnic followed by ball games, charades, or a scavenger hunt. One Christmas Day game destined to disappear is a Yuletide version of quoits where players flick Christmas cards into a bucket - hard to do that with online cards! Another game uses wrapping paper, and each player takes a sheet and has to turn around and rip their paper into the shape of a Christmas tree.

Easter is another holiday time with surviving traditions. Chocolate Easter egg gift-giving is widespread, including the annual promotion of Chocolate Bilbies rather than rabbits. Easter egg hunts in the garden are another children's favourite.

∽

Battling with Technology

Although this book is mainly about looking backward and celebrating the past, it also has an eye on the future. As we hurtle towards what increasingly looks like a one-world culture or possibly more defined Western and Asian one-world cultures, it is impossible to ignore the role of new technology in childhood entertainment. Of course, the revolution started years ago, and mention has already been made of extremely young children using smartphones and other devices for amusement. The software being developed for these carriers has become increasingly sophisticated and affordable. Where the market is in the multi-millions, the unit price comes tumbling down like Humpty Dumpty. Many will defend these new amusements because we live in a connected society where more than sixty per cent of the world's people are connected to the internet. There is also an argument that children need to be able to master technology at the very youngest age, for this is their future. Others will present the extraordinary educational value of the software. Producers like Tinybop, for example, have an excellent range of games that entertain and educate on science, geography, geology, machinery, mammals, plant life and space, to name just a handful. The Tinybop Machinery, for example, explores the playful side of physics by experimenting with levers, pulleys, inclined planes, wedges, wheels and axles, and screws. The player can test machines to destroy a building, make music, send satellites into orbit, and more. All for $4.99 and available in almost every language on the planet. Seductive? Educational? You bet. If there's a downside, it would have to be that children should be outdoors, running around and socialising. Is it a case of too much too soon? Many would say to let the child decide how best to be amused; others would firmly uphold that parents and teachers know better. Let the battle begin!

Today's children are growing up in the information age, where screens are an accepted part of everyday life. We are constantly tweeting, texting, Googling, and checking e-mail; consequentially, technology addiction is a real concern for today's children. Yet parents are often unable to unplug from their own digital devices, setting a double standard when attempting to reduce their child's screen time.

On average, most Australians spend more time in front of a screen than sleeping. That's around a third of a day, 9.4 hours, 143 days of every year glued to a screen. These are frightening statistics, yet most Australians believe they monitor their use appropriately. The dangers are obvious: technical addiction, reliance on computer information, play substitution, health implications and a general disconnect from family and society.

We already know the effects of sedentary behaviour, and hollow calls to action generally follow the increasing child obesity figures. Action in the information age is not easy. The Australian Government's Health Report of 2017 stressed reducing screen time, especially blue screen exposure in children. The official line was: [18]

> To reduce health risks, children aged 5-12 years, should minimise the time they spend being sedentary every day. To achieve this: Limit electronic media for entertainment (e.g., television, seated electronic games and computer use) to no more than two hours a day; lower levels are associated with reduced health risks. Break up long periods of sitting as often as possible.

To achieve this, adults need to set a better example and unplug themselves.

Now that schools actively use tablets in education, it is extremely difficult for parents to monitor their use. Homework is often done on the computer, and, for many students, the internet-connected classroom has been an immense advancement, especially for students in remote areas. While parents would like to think their children are using the devices for homework, chances are a large chunk of the time is spent playing online games or on social media sites. This begs the question - do parents know anything about the games their children are playing? Are they safe? Is there any educational value?

A 2018 *Digital Australia*[19] report found that 68% of Australians play video games, and 98% of homes with children under 18 have a device for playing video games. The preferred viewing varies with age and access; however, generally, most use tablets, consoles and smartphones as their primary device. Approximately 91% of all children play video or online games. Unsurprisingly, the video and online gaming business is growing exponentially. In 2024, the total Australian video gaming business was around 5.2 billion dollars (compared to the $1.69 billion book market). Further findings report that 39% of children aged 1-4 play video games, 91% of children 5 - 14 play video games, and then, with children 15-24, it falls to 84% as they pursue other activities.

Many children feel they compete with the screen to attract family attention. Parents continually in front of a screen send out a wrong message, with children thinking the screen is more engaging than them. There is also the danger that children will mimic parents in their use of screen time. There are, of course, many parents who willingly play these games with their children. They do so for several reasons, including considering it a way to spend time with their children, that it is fun for the whole family because their children ask them, and it enables parents to monitor when they play, what they play and how much they play.

A recent study in *Scientific American* [20] showed that greater use of technology among tweens and teens correlated with shorter attention spans, a preference for digital time over physical activity, and worse school performance. Toddlers and infants also have a harder time learning emotional and nonverbal cues because their parents constantly have what psychologists call the "still face phenomenon" from concentrating on mobile devices. It is not an attractive look!

The availability of online and video games is now quite staggering. They range from simple to extremely sophisticated and are available within targeted age groups, from babies to adults. They can be accessed on various devices, from computers to consoles to smartphones.

It is difficult to dismiss many video games because they are increasingly seen as beneficial to childhood development. Of course, there are many types of games, violent and non-violent; some are purely entertainment, and others are educational. The industry has even spawned a new definition - *edutainment*, for the increasing demand for educational and entertaining games. The major downside to gaming is addiction. Most games are extremely seductive and supported by very focused marketing. This, of course, is nothing new in the world of children's entertainment; however, nothing has ever been so competitive as the game market. It is growing larger than the music, book and film industries.

The negative side of gaming points to problems associated with addiction, exposure to violence, alienation from society, effects on health, and depression. The positive side points to improving spatial visualisation ability (i.e. mentally, rotating and manipulating two and three-dimensional objects), learning to set goals, physical manipulation dexterity, encouragement of curiosity, development in basic reading and numerical skills, relating to competition and general improvement in self-esteem. Some of these claims are debatable; most are not. Certainly, some children 'disappear' into virtual worlds. However, most children see themselves as a community member and being gamers allows them to build real friendships with other gamers at school.

Many would say the learning outcomes far outweigh the problems, and now that the problems are being addressed, especially monitoring screen time, the positives are becoming more obvious. Few would deny traditional employment is giving way to work associated with the cyber world. There is evidence, for example, that gaming spatial development aids in the training of microsurgeons.

Minecraft[21], launched in 2014, holds the top position in the world of gaming. It is primarily a game about human expression: a giant, Lego-style construction set in which every object can be broken down into elements and rebuilt in the shape of a house, an airship, a skyscraper, or whatever else a player can create.

Minecraft's universe is procedurally generated, meaning that an algorithm places each asset—every hill, mountain, cave, river, sheep, and so on—in a unique arrangement every time a new game is loaded so that no two players' worlds are exactly alike.

Player Unknown's *Battleground* (75 million) is another hugely popular game. In 2024, the Australian chart best-sellers offered Legend of Zelda, Hogwarts Legend, Star Wars Jedi Survivor, Call of Duty: Modern Warfare 2, Wizard Game, FIFA 23, NBA 2K 23, Grand Theft Auto, Red Desert Redemption, Mario Kart 8, Dead Space and Resident Evil 4. The inclusion of a basketball, soccer and grand theft auto alongside 'shoot 'em ups' and fantasy games points to an eclectic audience.

World of Warcraft[22] is also the world's most popular 'massively multiplayer online role-playing game (MMORPG) with, as of 2024, over 300 million accounts being created over its lifetime. Players say *Minecraft* is more like an experience than a game. It's more like a destination, a technical tool, a cultural scene, or all three put together: a place where players engineer complex machines, shoot videos of their escapades that they post on YouTube, make art and set up servers, online versions of the game where they can hang out with friends. It's a world of trial and error and constant discovery stuffed with Byzantine secrets, obscure text commands and hidden adventures. With over ten billion dollars in sales since its launch in 2004, it runs on a monthly subscription base of around $15. In the 1980s and '90s, earlier games have also notched up impressive sales, notable Pac-Man (43 million), *'Space Invaders'* (10 million). *Super Mario Bros*, a game about two plumbers working in the New York underground sewer system, has a staggering 600 million direct sales and above 200 million download sales. These older games still sell.

At the time of compiling this book, a game produced by Epic (USA) named *Fortnight Battle Royale*[23] was smashing the popularity stakes. It could possibly claim the title of the 'most played game in the world' and hold the number one spot in IOS revenue. In 2024, it sold 350 million copies, and its revenue from this one game (to date) was US$26 billion. These are extraordinary incomes in any language. The game covers exploration, tension, and building, and you can play with or without friends and achieve mastery by progressing your skills. Their details cite *Fortnite Battle Royale, a free 100-player PvP mode in Fortnite. One giant map. A battle bus. Fortnite building skills and destructible environments combined with intense PvP combat. The last one standing wins. Available on PC, PlayStation 4, Xbox One & Mac.* Like many online or console games, the kick is in players making in-game purchases. In the case of Fortune, you can use your V-Bucks, your in-game currency, to buy skins, emotes to make your character dance and prance, and other cosmetic items for the 'nude' characters.

In an interview with Justice Single[24], a ten-year-old experienced gamester, he explained:

> "Everyone is playing Battle Royale. I can play it on my Playstation and also on my smartphone because I hook into my account. The average game lasts about 15 minutes and I play every day for about an hour and three to four hours on weekends."

In *Battle Royale* the game starts with 100 players and only one can win. When asked if he thought the game was violent (the game carries a violence warning rating), he didn't think it was.

> "No, it isn't violent because it isn't real. It's cartoonish and not like some other games where the characters are more realistic."

Although you can play solo, duo or in squads, he prefers to play solo and up his personal best by reaching new levels within the game.
"Everyone at school plays it, but I try not to talk about it too much because everyone thinks they are the best".
He sometimes plays with a small group of close friends but is shy about skiting.

> "Anyway," he says, "Anyone can see another player's level by looking at their Stat Tracker."

Justice had been playing for six months and was level 54. His character in the game is a girl warrior who, he said, "Looked cool." He also added that lots of girls play Battle Royale. When asked how he knew this, he said he checks YouTube for videos about the game. He had already placed three YouTube videos. There is also a live streaming service called Twitch, where you can watch people play. Epic also runs a forum where players can explore deeper aspects of the game and hook up with like-minded players.

"For me, this is the game of the moment. Another will probably come along, but this one feels good to play. I have to think, move quickly with my fingers, listen for sounds through my headphones and have my eyes everywhere."

Game companies often offer parental control that allows various limits on playing time. Setting a daily or weekly limit or specifying an allowed playing schedule is possible. To control these settings, logging in with credentials different from those used to enter the game is necessary. It is also possible to receive statistics on the time spent playing. As well as controlling children, adults sometimes use parental controls on themselves. Companies support this kind of protection as otherwise the potential players or their supervisors may choose to uninstall or block the game permanently.

As the last word to what will be a long and challenging story, games played on computer devices and smartphones are here to stay. They have already been elevated from gaming to 'edutainment', and popularity and physical and mental achievement are already being studied as contributors to education and society. The game is on!

8

GIRLS WILL BE GIRLS

Little Miss Anzac - the true story of an Australian doll. By Mrs W. A. Holman. *1917.*

Over the past twenty or so years, a lot has been written about demystifying sexuality in children. We certainly understand more about sexual identity than ever before, and we also appreciate that difference is natural. Girls will be girls, and, in some cases, boys will also be girls. The same can be said for some girls being more comfortable identifying as boys. There is no doubt that in previous times, roles were cast for young people, often with damaging results. However, most girls want to play girly things, just as most boys want boyish pursuits.

What are girly things? It would be easy to say dolls, but we know from history that boys also like cuddly things, especially bears, monkeys and other soft animals. This is fine, except most young girls dream of a land of tea parties for dollies, dressing their little friends in various costumes and, in many cases, projecting personalities onto their doll family. Most of us have witnessed young children, either in a group or, more often than not, conducting an 'afternoon tea' with a cast of dolls and chatting away merrily in an imaginary world full of joy.

Friends for afternoon tea 1907. *Museums Victoria*

ACCORDING TO THE OLD RHYME, 'Little girls are made of sugar and spice and all things nice - that's what little girls are made of.' Meanwhile, boys are made of 'snips and snails, and puppy dog tails - that's what little boys are made of.' A contemporary clapping rhyme is more to the point: *Girls go to college to get more knowledge, and Boys go to Jupiter to get stupider*[1].

Dolls

Dolls come in all shapes and sizes. Today, they are mainly purchased because of mass marketing campaigns, usually generated as a spin-off from popular film or television programming. Like all fashion, dolls come and go, with Cabbage Patch dolls being the obvious example. Some, like Barbie, are more enduring. The recent success of Barbie - the film (box-office receipts of over US $1.3 billion worldwide) - prompted Mattel to announce a 14% increase in Barbie sales and an estimate that 90% of girls have a Barbie doll.

Originally, dolls were handmade, including knitted dolls with button eyes. Dolls serve three purposes: entertainment, teaching how to care for young children, and understanding family relationships.

Girls with their prams on Kepos Street, Redfern. 1950s.

Dolls were brought to Australia with the first settlers. They were primarily crude wood-carved 'babies' dressed for the occasion. They were certainly not as ornate or refined as the European dolls, especially the French and German dolls of the nineteenth century. Once the settlers had 'settled in', dolls were made of whatever was handy, giving them a naive, almost primitive look. Of course, looks didn't matter much and, as the old saying goes, 'beauty is in the eye of the beholder'. This must have applied to our early dolls, which were quite ugly, heavy, almost grotesquely painted with strange murky eyes and wearing rough-made cotton outfits, more likely than not, held together with a large safety pin.

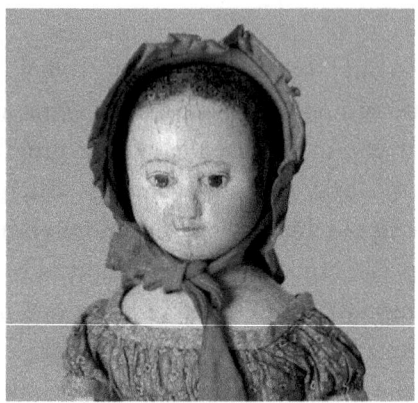

19th century doll with bonnet.

The following doll belonged to John Batman's daughter, Elizabeth. Its body is made of porcelain and leather, and the clothing is made of finely stitched fabric. It is dated circa 1820-1830 and is typical of the period.

Dolly. *State Library of Victoria.*

Portrait studio photography of children often portrays young girls with their favourite dolls. The following, of Hulda Lundager, was taken in Rockhampton, Queensland, in 1889. It is typical of the fashion of studio portraits.

Hudla Lundage's doll. *John Oxley Library Collection*

There is no accounting for what characteristics make a certain doll 'favourite'. She need not be the prettiest, most pliable or even best-dressed. However, children are drawn to love some dolls over others. Dolls, just like people! Elsie Joseph (aged 10), Flinders Terrace, Port Augusta, summed it up in a sweet poem sent to a South Australian newspaper in 1930.[2]

THE DOLL'S TEA PARTY

Miss Winifred Evelyn Constance McKee
Invited our dolls to an afternoon tea.
"Don't bring them all, for my table is small,
Just each little girl, bring her dearest and best," said she.
I felt in my heart it would not be polite
To take my poor Rosa, she's grown such a fright.
She's blind in one eye, and her wig's all awry,

For she sleeps in my bed with me all thro' the night.
I explained to dear Rosa just why she should stay,
And I dressed Bonny Belle in her finest array.
And then, do you know, when the time came to go,
I snatched up my Rosa and ran all the way.
And what do you think? of the six dolls that came,
There were two that were blind and four that were lame.
And each little mother explained to some other,
"She's old, but I love her the best, just the same."

Manufactured dolls commercially arrived in the twentieth century. The first doll registered in Australia was a composition-headed doll by Daniel Keily and recorded as being manufactured in 1916.

At the beginning of the 20th century, patterns for dolls were popular. American companies like Elms & Sellon produced pattern dolls imported into Australia. These simplistic dolls arrived around 1910 and included a sheet of cloth, 715 x 855, printed with the image of a doll in the form of a girl, with two smaller dolls for cutting, stuffing, and sewing to make a play doll, and instructions printed in English, German, French, and Spanish.

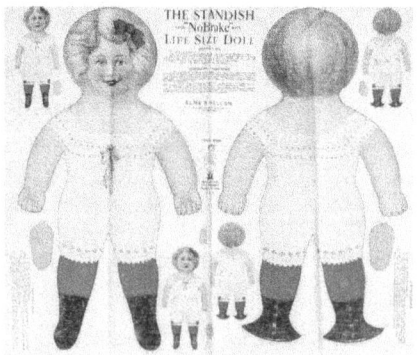

Early 20th century pattern play doll.

Doll's Houses

Dolls sometimes live in dollhouses, some elaborate and others as small as your hand. The imagination allows comfortable accommodation no matter the size.

When hosting a doll's party, you need cake. Dorothy Bock of Eaglehawk, Victoria, sent this recipe suggestion from 1939.[3]

> Thimble Cakes For The Doll's House
>
> Have you tried these tiny cakes for your doll's tea party? Next time your mother is making some pastry ask her for a tiny lump of dough. Roll out the piece quite flat and then cut a lot of little cakes out with a thimble. Then get your mother to bake them for you. When they are hard you can make tiny jam tarts by dabbing a touch of crimson paint in the centres, or they can be currant buns by dotting them over with black paint. They will look very grand in the doll's house.

Nineteenth-century newspapers encouraged children to be creative and build things. Many articles included instructions on how to build a doll's House and equally as many on how to build furniture for it. Some were quite elaborate affairs, like 'Pendle Hill'.

'Pendle Hill', *Museums Victoria*

Room 16 of 'Pendle Hill', *Museums Victoria*

'Pendle Hill' is a stunning 21-room, four-storey doll house depicting a grand, fully-furnished Georgian-style country house. Presented in the mid-19th century style, with some remodelling representing new fashions in interior design, the house contains grand family rooms and 'below stairs' areas, such as the kitchen, laundry and staff quarters. It is very Downton Abbey! 'Pendle Hill' was created by Felicity Clemons. She began working on it in the 1940s when her grandmother gave her daughter Antonia, then about three years old, a three-roomed doll house. Mrs Clemons was unhappy with its scale or authenticity, so a rebuilding project began for about 40 years and resulted in a four-storey grand house, now known as 'Pendle Hill' began.

Golliwogs and Teddy Bears

The fashion for dolls changes over time. Who can forget the curiously featured Golliwog? While such a doll would be totally inappropriate nowadays, it must be noted here because of its popularity right up until around the early 1960s.

Toy theatre Golliwog. *National Museum of Australia*

The popularity of Golliwogs most probably had a lot to do with the popularity of equally inappropriate minstrel shows where white people 'blacked up' and sang plantation songs. Minstrel troupes toured Australia from the early gold rush days, and many local troupes were established. Nobody thought of the racial discrimination and stereotyping caused by either. There was even a Golliwog biscuit marketed by the Guest Company until the nineteen-sixties.

W. P. Thornton, writing in 1953, described a very peculiar custom of making 'Picaninny dolls' for young girls.[4]

> The bush girl was delighted with a black Picaninny doll as a gift. Yet, it cost practically nothing, for it was fashioned out of one of mother's old black woollen stockings. Glass beads or small buttons were used for eyes, and coloured wools added to its attractions. For filling, mother used scraps of old clothes cut into small pieces. In these days, of course, mother wears nylons, and it's to be doubted whether you could make much of a Picaninny doll out of an old nylon stocking.

The Golliwog and Picaninny doll has been relegated to the past. Coloured baby dolls are now commercially available and, of course, respectfully reflect Australia's multicultural spectrum.

Koala plush toy

Cuddly Teddy Bears first crawled onto children's beds (and into their hearts) in the early 20th century. The stuffed toy was named after American President Theodore 'Teddy' Roosevelt in 1902. The first soft toy koala bears appeared in the 1920s and were made of koala, wallaby or kangaroo fur, with jointed arms, legs and head. Eyes were made of leather show buttons with a pure rubber nose.

Peg Dollies

Dolls can be, and have been, made out of everything from bottles to clothes pegs. Wooden clothes pegs have now disappeared from the supermarket shelves. It would be impossible to make a similar doll out of a plastic peg clip

A Hop, a Skip and a Jump

Clothes peg dolls from a time before the clothes dryer

How To Make Peg Dolls

Sydney Morning Herald 1952

HOW DO you make a clothesline wooden peg into a doll, and how do you dress her? [5]

How To Make Peg Dolls

'Madame Pompadour' and the 'Hula Girl' can be simply made from pegs to delight children.

Making peg dolls can provide endless entertainment for children, and adults can also exercise great ingenuity in making dolls for Christmas stockings. Cotton wool, wool, crepe paper, scraps of fabric, raffia, pipe cleaners, silver paper, and other oddments can all be used to transform a clothes peg into a doll.

Drill a hole through an old-fashioned peg just below the head and insert a pipe cleaner to make the arms. Glue a round disc to the bottom of the peg as a stand or make one of plasticine. If crepe paper is used to make frocks, eliminate the stand, as the paper's stiffness will hold the doll upright.

Here are suggestions for dressing the dolls

Hula Girl: Skirt: raffia plaited at the waist. Lei: gathered thin material. Ukulele: a shell and matchstick glued together. Hair: glue a little real hair onto the head.

'Madame Pompadour': Wig: cotton wool with pearls stitched on as earrings. Dress: three tiers of crepe paper glued to the peg for the skirt and silver paper to make the bodice and sleeves.

Peg people loved to dress up. *AFU*

Mountain Devils

Made from a bush nut and pipe-cleaner, these little devils were sold as souvenirs, especially in the Blue Mountains of New South Wales. No trip to the mountains was complete without a devil souvenir.

Little Devils. Here's an account from 1926 where Albert Mitchell commented on the Mountain Devil's popularity.[6]

> There are devils in the mountains, profitable, rakish little devils created by humans, especially for the downfall of humans. The men say they are cute little devils and secure them to adorn the office table; the ladies term them 'just lonely.' They collect one or two for their dressing table.
>
> In the Mountain resorts, the devils haunt you, taking you

unawares and filching hard-earned shillings from the pockets of your flannels.

Nobody seems to be able to resist the devils. They are the souvenir deluxe and have an Australian appeal that is all their own. Just a bush nut bead, cleft skull and ears a-cock, pipe-cleaner limbs, and a woolly body. There are tennis devils, golf devils, football devils, cricket devils, and just plain devils. They tell me the devils travel far, for nearly every overseas visitor to Australia takes one or two away. They may seem just woollen absurdities to you and me, but to their creators, I should imagine, they are golden devils.

A crafty little devil from Katoomba. *Australian Womens Weekly.*

The Mountain Devils were so popular that the tourist shop at Echo Point, Katoomba, had a life-sized version with which you could be photographed.

Life-sized Mountain Devil. *Blue Mountains Library.*

Mountain Devils 1960s, *Australian Woman's Weekly.*

Cork Dolls

The Corker Family[7]

Any child can make the "Corker" family. They can stand, move their heads and limbs, and even sit on the table's edge. Everybody laughs at them, and they are splendid fun. Corks, hairpins, pins, beads, and scraps of old fur are all the materials required to make them.

THE "CORKER" FAMILY.

The Corker Family - made from corks.

Take an ordinary bottle cork. Bore a hole with a steel knitting needle at the base from one side to the other. Straighten out a hairpin and pass it through, bending one end down to form the leg and bending down the other end quite short and close to the cork. The leg will then move on a little pivot. Bore another hole across and do the same at the opposite side of the other leg. Straighten a third hairpin and pass it through from side to side for the arms, which are bent into shape. A head for "Mr Corker" can be made from a whole cork sharpened at one end for the neck; "Mrs Corker's" head is just a flat round slice cut from the end of a cork and sharpened for the neck. The eyes, nose, and mouth can be indicated in coloured beads or coloured glass-headed steel pins, Push a steel pin through the top of the head, slip a tiny circle of fur (if desired) on the point, and fasten the head and fur collar to the cork body. Pin a scrap of fur round the body, and put circlets of fur on the wires before adding the hands and feet. The latter are long flat pieces of cork, pointed in front and rounded at the back. The feet must be as long in the back as in front or "Corker" will not stand. The legs are forced into the centre, a drop of seccotine is added, and the fur circle is pulled down. The hands are just scraps of cork with a V cut out, and the fur is pulled to the wrist. A piece of fur doubled and pinned on the head finishes "Charlie Corker," "Mrs Corker" only needs a second cork instead of wire legs, as it is covered with a fur skirt.

Corn Dollies

Koorda Corn Dolly. *The West Australian 2018.*

An individual can often start a local tradition that will spread across the country. Corn dollies, small dolls made out of corn husk or sheaves of wheat, are part of a long tradition dating back to Europe when villagers believed spirits lived in the fields. At one stage in England, corn dollies were made at the end of the season and placed in the fields to honour the gods. They were also given to young women by admirers interested in marriage. Likewise, young men wore tiny dolls, usually the simple entwined three-looped 'dolly' on their caps if they were looking for work.

Corn dollies have been made in the West Australian wheat-belt town of Koorda for over one hundred years and are now made all over Australia.

Twig Dolls

Bush furniture is now a collector's item—sideboard cupboards made out of assembled biscuit tins, rudely fashioned chairs, etc., were constructed out of whatever was available. This children's column from the Sunday edition of *The Queensland Times* tells how to make children's toy furniture out of twigs!⁸

Making of Twig Toys.

You all love making your own toys, don't you, dears? so I am going to tell you just how to make the jolly little pieces of furniture for your dollies that you see in the picture.

First of all you must gather a good big bundle of twigs. Be careful to choose very thin ones, and also to use them whilst they are still fresh, and therefore able to be bent easily. Besides your twigs you must have a paper of pins. The little dress makers' pins, which are about half an inch long, are the best to use. First let us start upon the little chair, as that is the easiest to make. Cut two lengths of twigs three inches long, and having, if possible a cluster of buds at the end. These twigs are for the back legs; now cut two more twigs with buds at the end, only this time, they must be one and a half inches long. Besides these, you will want nine pieces of twig, one and a half inches long, and two about two and a quarter inches long; these are for the rigs, the seats, and the cross pieces at the back. Make the back part first. The twigs must be fastened together with your tiny pins, and you must use a thimble upon your finger, as this makes it easier to drive the pins in. Now fix the four pieces for the seat and fasten the seat in place with pins. The seat must be made of thin cardboard, and should be painted brown. The front legs and the rungs are now added. Your little chair is thus finished and I am sure you will find it quite simple to copy the table and the armchair when you have seen how the little chair is done. You will find that, with a little practice, you very soon get into the way of making these pretty toys, and many other articles will suggest themselves to you. For instance, a little girl whom I know has a really fine collection of twig toys. There is a doll's table, a little wardrobe, a pretty couch, and the best little bed you can imagine. She also has a big log cabin, but in the making of this she had her father's help.

If you are not quite old enough to make the toys by yourselves, I am sure big brother or sister will love to help you.

Australian Dolls

Dolls in the late twentieth century, and definitely in the twenty-first century, reflect the power of mass marketing and especially popular culture. There were and are thousands of doll manufacturers worldwide, and, no doubt, relatively few are in Australia because of our population size. Australian manufacturers, past and present, include L. J. Lindsay, L. J. Sterne Doll Co., Jakas, Netta and the Australian Girl range. It is difficult to do retail battle with mass-marketed dolls like the Barbie. However, one company, Australian Girl, has successfully produced a culturally relevant range and shows that we have diversity in our Australian doll style.

The Australian Girl Doll collection, Victoria 2018.

Another unique Australian doll success story is the Shibajuka Girls range created by Madeleine Hunter for her family company, Hunter Products. The dolls, priced at around $40 retail, are inspired by Japanese Harajuku fashion. They are now sold in over 60 countries and greatly contribute to the $943 million Australian toy industry.

The 1970s saw a wave of new dolls hit the world market including Kewpie, Tiffany Taylor, Sonny & Cher, Talk-a-Little, Shopping Sheryl, Talking Twin Kip, Dancerina, Miss Piggy, Dress-me-dolls, Cabbage Patch Dolls, Charlie's Angels, and, of course, the continuing family of 'Barbie', who considering she was 'born' in 1959, was already getting on in years.

It is difficult to imagine a child growing up without a doll.

Range of L. J. Sterne (Melbourne). Museums Victoria

Bush Jewellery

Families often gathered bush seeds and berries to make pretty necklaces and bangles for their daughters. One of the most popular seeds for this purpose was the quandong (Fusanus acuniinatus).

These pretty, wrinkled, pitted seeds were painted in various colours and threaded on a strong string.

Necklaces were also made with the highly polished brown seeds of the black scrub plum (Sideroxylon australe), the pretty rough-surfaced seeds of the blueberry ash (Elaecarpus reticulalus), and the bright scarlet and black seeds of the giddy giddy (Abrus precatorius). These last seeds were also known as "crab's eyes."

Finger Knitting and Knitting Nancy

There was a time, a fair way back in time, when most girls were taught to knit and crochet. For many, their first experience with knitting was with what was known as finger knitting.

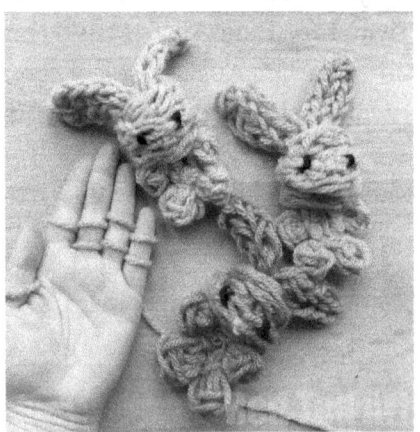

Finger knitting bunnies. Red Ted Art/All Created

Finger knitting is a form of knitting in which a knitted cord is created using only hands and fingers instead of knitting needles or other traditional tools.

A Sylko Knitting Nancy. *AFU Collection*

'SPOOL KNITTING'. Another popular child's knitting came with the availability of Sylco commercial cotton on a small wooden spool. These were ideal as a 'knitting Nancy', an improvised knitting machine. A few small nails on the top of the spool and away the fingers could fly. This technique was even better when thin strips of bright plastic became available. Boys and girls knitted long, brightly-coloured and mostly useless endless strands.

AS THE MOTHER OF INVENTION, necessity also allowed children to make a knitting machine using the centre cardboard of a toilet roll with four Paddlepop sticks adhered to the outer rim with heavy-duty masking tape. Ordinary wool was used to knit.

Knitted Animals

The era of young girls knitting has passed, and so too, after nearly one hundred years, has the publishing of patterns in newspapers and magazines. Some children, fascinated by the bobbing and weaving of wool and needles, still learn the art; however, cheap imported knits, often more affordable than buying patterns and wool and needles, have seen knitting almost disappear. It is now seen as quite old-fashioned. Once again, knitting toys were common during lean times. This letter to the children's editor of an Adelaide newspaper in 1943 is typical.[9]

Request For Knitted Toy Patterns

I have often thought of writing to the pages but never had the courage. I wonder if any readers have patterns for knitted dolls that they would lend me. As toys will be very scarce, I would like to make some. I would pay postage. Best wishes, 'Keen Knitter'.

Paper Toys

The plague broke out in Australian cities at the turn of the twentieth century. Bubonic plague, diphtheria, measles, and other infectious diseases became a problem, and many schools were closed. Children were detained at home, and children's wards in many hospitals were full. Newspaper columns offered suggestions on how to keep the children amused.

What better use for old newspapers than making them into pulp? In 1944, Patricia Harrison (14) earned a red certificate from *The Sun* (Sydney) for telling readers how:[10]

> Soak the newspaper in water for about four hours. Press it in your hands for about ten minutes and place it in a mixture of flour and water. Leave for a few hours, then shape it into animals. Leave for twenty-four hours, and then colour your models with paints.

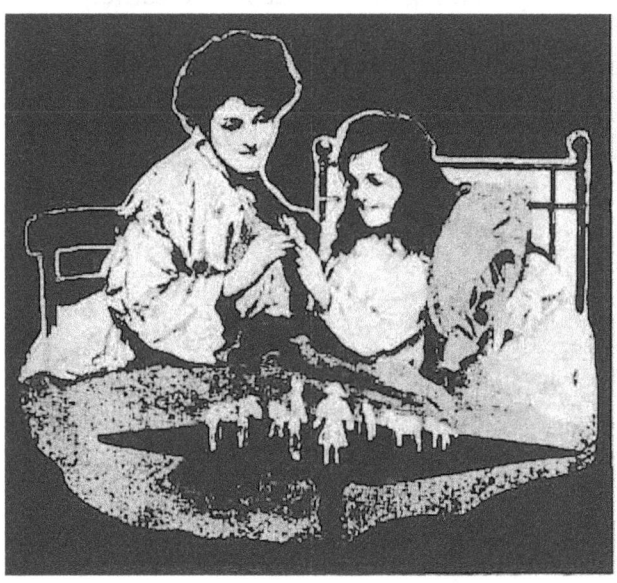

Making paper cut out figures. The Queenslander 1905

This report from a Queensland newspaper, complete with

disposal advice, suggested making paper toys as an activity for sick children. [11]

> The cutting out of paper figures is the most fascinating game for a sick child to watch, and skill in fashioning the little dolls' furniture, soldiers, sailors, or whatnot is soon acquired. These easily made toys are light for weak little fingers to hold, and can be burnt at once if the patient is suffering from an infectious disease. If a story is told as the paper hero or heroine is cut, so much the better. Convalescents between the ages of 8 and 14 love to do the cutting themselves when they are allowed to sit up. The pages of illustrated papers and pictorial advertisements are valuable materials.

Newspapers were used for many amusements—even made into fake clothing for costume parties. Women and young girls were particularly adept at using sewing machines creatively.

Paper Cut-Outs

One of the early favourites for working with paper was an early form of the Japanese art of origami paper folding. No doubt many older readers will remember making the head of a snapdragon - constructed correctly out of stiff paper, the snapdragon could be manipulated to snap snap snap.

. . .

JACKS. It was said that boys played 'marbles' and girls played 'jacks'.

Playing jacks in a Melbourne schoolyard 1955. Dr June Factor
Museums Victoria

Jacks, sometimes known in Australia as 'knucklebones', 'tali or 'firestones', is a game of ancient origin, usually played with five small objects or ten in the case of 'jacks'. Originally, the "knucklebones" (actually the astragalus, a bone in the ankle or hock) were those of a sheep, who were thrown up and caught in various manners. In earlier times, children would ask the local butcher for the bones, which were then painted in different colours. There is evidence that Aboriginal children played a similar game using wallaby or kangaroo joint knuckles. Modern 'knucklebones' consist of six points, or knobs, proceeding from a common base, and are usually made of metal or plastic. The winner is the first player to complete a prescribed series of throws, which, though similar, differ widely in detail. The simplest throw consists of either tossing up one stone, the jack, or bouncing a ball and picking up one or more stones or knucklebones from the table while it is in the air. This continues until all five stones or knucklebones have been picked up. Another throw consists of tossing up one stone first, then two, then three, and catching them on the back of the hand. Different throws have received distinctive names, such as "riding the elephant", "peas in the pod", "horses in the stable", and "frogs in the well".

In an article published in the Australian Children's Folklore

Newsletter in 1982, a child's description of a game of knucklebones from the 1930s explained:[12]

> Moves:
> Babies, Scatters, Babies non-move, Blind babies, Blind non moves, Tights ups and downs, Loose ups and downs, Skimming the milk, Pigsties in, Pigsties out, Low hurdles, High hurdles, Grandmother's teeth, Enemies (scats). Low candles, High candles, Clicks, Non clicks and Tidying.
>
> Rules:
> Cannot have 'touches' in 'non moves'.
> Cannot have 'tips' in 'enemies'.
> In 'low candles' you must not throw the knucklebone higher than your nose, and in 'high candles' you must not throw it lower than your nose.
> If in 'low hurdles', the knuckle bone lands on the back of your hand, it is out.
> A 'touch' is when you throw the knucklebone up and just 'touch' the other one on the ground without picking up, and then catch the one you threw up.

String Figure Games

String games, as described in chapter three, have had a long history in many cultures. Of the games people play, string figures seem to be one of the most widespread forms of amusement in the world: more cultures are familiar with string figures than any other game. The strings can be manipulated using solo or multiple people's fingers and involve the use of the mouth, wrist and even feet. Indigenous children learn them traditionally, as do all Australian children - primarily from parents or friends at home and school. Having a repertoire of these games is admired, and it seems that string games are as popular as ever.

Girl playing 'Bridge' or 'French lace'. 1954-55 *Museums Victoria.*
Dorothy Howard Tour

The most popular Australian string games include Cat's Cradle, Cup & Saucer, Queen's Crown', 'Parachute', 'See-Saw', 'Sydney Harbour Bridge', 'King's Crown', 'Soldier's Bed', 'Candles', 'Cat's Eye', 'Fish in a Dish', 'Hand Drum', ''Jail', Bow tie', 'Ironing Board', 'Telephone', Butterfly' and the curiously named 'Smelly Old Man's Trousers Hanging on the Line.'

Girl playing 'Parachute' 1954-55. *Museums Victoria/DHT/June Factor*

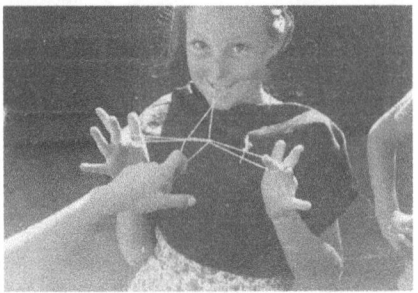

Girl playing 'See-Saw'. 1954-55. *DHT/JF. Museums Victoria*

Although playing string figures can be solo or with others, it is a relatively passive endeavour, often played sitting down. It can also have a social element, being played with a group watching. Australian children still play string games; however, as can be imagined, obtaining string these days can be a challenge.

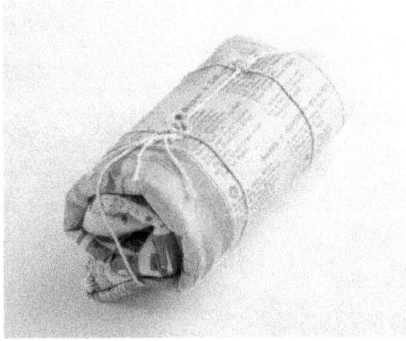

Necessity the mother of invention - a custom made football

Kicking the ball around

Kicking and throwing balls has always been seen as a boy's domain. This does not stand in our modern world, and even the most holy of ball games, cricket, took a surprisingly early feminist stand. The founding mother of women's cricket in Australia was the young Tasmanian Lily Poulett-Harris, who captained the Oyster Cove team in the league she created in 1894. Lily's obituary, from her death a few years later in 1897, states that her team was almost certainly the first to be formed in the colonies.

AUSTRALIAN GIRLS in the twenty-first century play tunnel ball, basketball, softball, baseball, virago, cricket, netball, hockey, volleyball, and several variations of football. The success and influence of The Matildas national football team have been a game-changer!

9

SECRET BOY'S BUSINESS

Woolloomooloo marble contest. *Courtesy Lynette Komidor*

There is little doubt that as boys grow older, they become more likely to follow a tribal mentality regarding dress, the 'slanguage' they use and the games they play. Older boys tend to play different games than girls. Rightly or wrongly, boys grow up conditioned to reinforce their masculinity, while girls, rightly or wrongly, reinforce their femininity. Segregated schools also reinforce the accepted characteristics of boys and girls and how they see their developing roles. That said, it is wrong to say a game is peculiar to one sex; as we know, rules are made to be broken, especially when it comes to play. Some progressive schools try to break down the expectations of stereotyping by actively encouraging role experimentation where girls participate in traditionally male activities like woodwork and football, and boys pursue traditional female activities like playing house or learning to cook.

Children like company; it makes them feel part of a community, it should teach them skills, and it should be a positive experience. Sadly, we know this is not always the case, and many children have been scolded for 'mixing with the wrong group', getting 'involved with the wrong crowd', and so on. Even the word 'gang', which used to have a friendly connotation, is now frowned upon as implying troublemakers. Possibly, we have become too protective of the child's well-being. Maybe programs should be developed to support youngsters forming gangs - for good outcomes. Maybe separating the sexes and encouraging gangs is only reinforcing the present-day problems of our communities, especially regarding equality. Can we trace the origin of boy gangs and relate it to how some men seek membership in all-male clubs?

It is fascinating how home and schoolyard play has changed over the decades. Although today's kids still run around like crazy, play ball games, and even invent new games, they have definitely succumbed to the digital era, especially the mobile phone. Many schools do not allow digital devices during school hours; however, as kids enter their late school years, the mobile phone in their pocket gets itchier.

Clearly there are games that fall firmly into the boy's or girls' camp. For example, boys are not inclined to play with elastics, which is strange because it takes physical dexterity and skill. Maybe it has to do with the fact that the first elastics were taken from women's bloomers and other garments. But remember, once upon a time, marbles was considered a boy's game... until the girls came along.

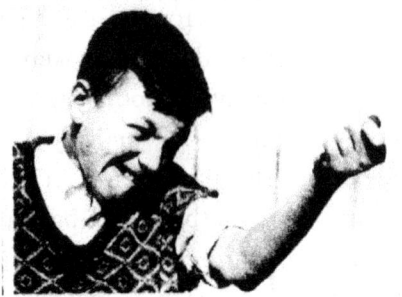

Determined marble shooter. *The Argus* 1939

Many schoolyard games were cyclical in the nineteenth and first half of the twentieth century. They would sweep the country for a month and magically disappear. In the nineteen-fifties and early sixties, for example, crazes included the Yo-Yo and Hula Hoop and the latest teen dances like the Madison, Hully Gully and Limbo. Whilst the dance crazes disappeared, never to return, the games did return, sometimes with new rules and even new names.

Boys playing marbles, 1954. *Museums Victoria/June Factor*

Marbles

Playing marbles has never disappeared; it was often called the 'king of games'. It was a male thing. Boys with balls. It was competitive beyond belief, and it wasn't unusual for boys to show off their marbles during the lunch break. It was important to have a complete set, including 'taws' or 'tollies' and your favourite shooters and lucky marbles.

Marbles, Newcastle, NSW. *Newcastle Sun 1953*

There are over forty different types of marbles, but the classic collection would have to include an aggie (being short for agate) glass and usually streaked ball; cat's-eye or devil's-eye (the pattern in the glass being similar to an eye); oxblood (looking like a streak of blood); a commie or common clay (they were way down on the collectable scale); clearie (or crystal) made from clear glass; alley (being short for alabaster); and, for the more aggressive player, the 'steely' made, not surprisingly, from steel (not a ball-bearing although they were also popular as 'weapons of mass destruction'). Kids scrutinised their mate's marbles for condition, size and eye appeal. Scratched and chipped marbles were mocked as inferior. Size wasn't everything; they had names. Smaller than standard were peewees or mini marbles, and the biggest was the billiard ball-sized grandfather, but it was difficult to flick skilfully. The slightly larger bonker, shooter, smasher and King Kong were far better. Some kids had big calico ball bags, but the average Aussie kid had about twelve marbles based on the three most important: the favourite, the tom-bowler, and the semi-bowler. The target marble was called the 'mibs' or 'kimmies'. Playing for marbles and swapping kept the marbles circulating like currency.

HOW TO HOLD YOUR MARBLE.

The rules of the game were strictly adhered to because most games attracted a ring of umpires ready to shout 'fault' or 'fudge'. The typical state of the play ran along the following lines: Firstly, the playing field must be defined; grass or earth was preferred, but failing that, gravel with a chalk circle. Players then knuckled down, crouched, ball in hand, ready to flick into the starting bunny hole, an imaginary goalpost area. You couldn't hit another player's marble (also known as a duck) until you had successfully entered the bunny hole goal. The back of the knuckles needed to be placed on the ground and stationary; otherwise, there would be a dissenting chorus of "disqualification". No part of the hand was permitted to be in front of the position where the marble had been resting on the ground. The thumb was usually used as the firing mechanism. If you happened to hit an opponent's marble before you entered the bunny hole (known as kissing another marble) – you had to start all over again. Confused yet?

The aim was to successfully hit your opponent's marble three times before you entered the bunny hole for the final time (known as the killer hit). If the game was for 'keepsie' you kept the loser's marble. You could withdraw without consequence if you agreed on 'quinsies' before the game. Like all sports, there were variations. If you called out 'elephant stomp' you were allowed to stomp your marble into the earth, level to the ground, making it difficult for the other player to hit yours. If agreed, and you were talented enough, you could also play bombs – where the player takes a couple of steps back and shoots mid-air. A ball-bearing flicked at a glass marble could easily shatter it let alone send it flying.

It was natural that many country boys should use quandong seeds as substitutes for marbles. The seeds were perfectly round and stood up to much knocking about. For several years, the makers of the modern game, Chinese Checkers, used quandong seeds as "men."

Peter Ellis recalled playing 'Quandong Kings' at Broken Hill, NSW, circa 1954.[1]

> This was a game fairly common among boys. It involved having a quandong stone and getting 'the old man' to drill a hole through it, so that a piece of string could be passed through and knotted on one side. The quandong stone could then be swung around. If boys so equipped met or had a suitably appreciative audience, one would challenge another. A penny would be tossed (heads or tails); the loser would place his quandong on the ground. The other boy would swing and bring his quandong down to hit and hopefully smash his opponent's quandong. The boys took turns until no one won or a player's quandong was smashed. The victor would then call his quandong 'quandong one'. If he won another contest it was then called 'quandong two'. If he lost a third contest to a novice, that person could then be 'quandong three' as he inherited the wins of his defeated opponent. The excitement and thrill of the game was exponential on the rare occasions of someone reaching 'quandong six' or more. So desirable was the esteem a successful player could muster that one boy got his old man to prepare a fake – an apricot stone! No one played with him. This game is similar to one in England where chestnuts are used and called 'Conkers'

Here is a description of how the game of marbles was played in Australia in the 1940s.[2]

Rules and Terms for Marbles. This week, I will try to clarify certain rules and terms used in marbles.

"Knuckle down, screw tight" is an expression often heard during a game. It applies when a player has lodged his taw very close to a marble or group of marbles, which it will be easy for him to hit the next shot, and his opponent cries, "Knuckle down, screw tight." The owner of the taw must then adopt a special method of firing for the next shot. He cannot raise his firing hand from the ground, rest it on the back of the other hand, or use any other method. The second joint of the first finger of his firing hand must be pressed to the ground ("knuckle down"), and not moved during the shot. "Knuckle up" is another term used to make a shot harder. It applies when a player is about to fire at another marble from a distance of two or three feet. His opponent may call "knuckle up" and the player must then raise his hand well above the ground and make the shot without any support. This is hard, as the hand is not so steady, nor the aim so good, in the position of "knuckle up." "Fat" is called when a taw sticks in the ring as it knocks out other marbles. When this happens, the marbles just knocked out must be replaced, and the player owning the taw must go last from where he aimed the shot. Players must not "fudge" when making a shot, that is, swing the hand holding the taw forward beyond the mark where the taw lay. If this happens, other players can demand that the shot be replayed.

Girls usually didn't play marbles in the schoolyard; however, as with all things, there were exceptions.
Australian writer Mary Eliza Fullerton, born in 1868, was a keen marbles player.[3]

Some of our games we found in action on the school playground. It seemed like a purloining to us; we were their inventors - or thought we were. l remember that in regard to some of these games we compromised as to our exclusive right to them only so far as to play them on the road to or from school. Top-spinning - our originals had been made from cotton reels; this was one of these, and marbles was another. For many a day I had my right thumbnail worn to tenderness from 'firing' my marbles from it. It was long before I could use my knuckle for that purpose, just as the boys and Claribel did. What rings we made on the dusty road! How many semi-truancies we played to finish a game against time! What searches in heather and fern for lost 'olleys' and 'glassies'! What squabbles over the ownership of 'taws'! What doughty battles, what streaked faces and dirt hands! and the worst of it - or the best - was that while other games had their season and came and went by tacit ordination with the phases of the calendar, marbles lasted the whole round of the year!"

Girls playing marbles. *Museums Victoria.*

Where did marbles originate? The English were recorded as playing World Marbles Championships in 1588 but were new to the game. Marbles have been found in the graves of ancient Egyptians. Yes, marbles have a very long history. However, the game is disappearing from Australian schoolyards, having fallen victim to competition, including virtual marbles, 'Candy Crush' and other games played on smartphones, and the fact that fewer schools have ground surfaces with grass and gravel. It's difficult to play the game on bitumen or cement.

. . .

Shanghais & Slingshots

A homemade toy that has all but disappeared, primarily because it could inflict injury, was the slingshot, or, as it was better known here, the shanghai. No source exists for why these projectile slings were uniquely called shanghais in Australia. They were also called catapults.

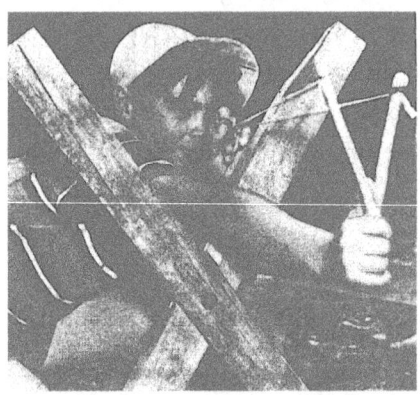

Boy with shanghai. *Melbourne Age, 1953*

The weapon and name 'shanghai' dates back to the larrikin gangs of 1870s Sydney and Melbourne. [4]

> The larrikin carries only one weapon, the catapult, known as the shanghai. Armed with this, he is able and always ready to avenge insults by providing work for the glazier, and he is not above knocking over a pigeon, hen, or duck should either bird come in his way.

Shanghai's are rarely seen today, and in most parts of the country are illegal - along with flick knives.

'Mumblety-peg'

Another dangerous yet widely popular boy's game was 'mumblety-peg' (or 'mumble-the-peg').

A game of mumble-the-peg. Painting

Before the 1960s, it was common for young boys to own a pen knife, which was extremely useful rather than being seen as a weapon. The game of mumbly-peg was right up there with marbles and jacks for popularity, especially in the 19th century. Bush workers like shearers and drovers also played this game.

THERE ARE different variations of mumblety-peg. One version involves two opponents standing opposite each other, feet shoulder-width apart. The first player throws his pocket knife at the ground so that it sticks into the ground as close as possible to his own foot. The second player takes his knife and does the same. The player who sticks his knife closest to his foot wins. A player could automatically win if he purposely stuck his knife *into* his foot! The second version explains the weird game's name: instead of getting the knife as close to your foot as possible, the aim is to get the knife to stick in the ground. This version is tricky because it involves progressively more difficult trick tosses. The first to successfully perform all the trick tosses wins and gets to drive the mumblety peg into the ground with the handle of his

One of the more complicated fancy throws in mumbly-peg

pocket knife. The loser has to pull the mumblety peg out of the ground with his teeth. You would not find this game being played in an Australian schoolyard today.

Knife Game and Pin Finger.

Another dangerous game for boys is the Knife Game or Pin Finger. Players place the palm of their hand down on a table with fingers apart and, using a pocket or pen knife, attempt to stab back and forth between their fingers, moving the object back and forth. The fastest player is the winner. It is a game of chance—a chance you could slice or stab your fingers!

Sword Fighting.

Most boys like to play sword games. Swords can be made with anything, such as fencing slats, plastic piping, short sticks, long sticks, and even pencils. And what better shield than the lid of a garbage bin?

On guard! Sword-fighting and survival of the quickest.

The *Star Wars* films renewed interest in sword fighting, and millions of brightly glowing, intergalactic Lightsabers were sold to swashbuckling would-be Jedi Warriors. Back in the days when pencils were used to write, pencil fights were a popular pastime. The aim was to snap your opponent's pencil. Wooden or plastic rulers served the same purpose.

Cockfighting & High Cockalorum

Joseph Verco grew up in 1860s South Australia and attended the Adelaide Educational Institute, colloquially known as 'Young's', after its founder, John Lorenzo Young.[5]

> "What games were played at Young's? Of course, the school ground was too small for games such as cricket or football. The only ones that were possible in Stephens Place were those that could be played in a very confined space. The following were some of these that the confined space would allow.
>
> Cockfighting A small boy mounted the back of a big boy; the bigger and bulkier, the better. Two such pairs, or more if there were two sides in the contests, attacked one another: the little rider grappling with his enemy rider and trying to drag him from his saddle, or the steeds in the persons of the carriers, the big boys bumping and jostling their opponents and striving to push them from the field of conflict.
>
> Another curious, rough and almost dangerous form of amusement was High Cockalorum. One boy stood with his back against the wall, a second bent forward with the head against this one's stomach and steadied himself by grasping the first boy's hips with his hands. A third pushed his head against the second one's tail and held on by his hips, and so did a fourth. The leader of the other side in the game from behind this line of bent bucks took a leap, as in playing leapfrog and putting his hands on the last one's back, jumped as far forward as possible and alighted (if one can use such a

word under these circumstances) on one of their heads, necks or backs. The three other boys followed his example till all were seated and had a good grip. Then, these all began to holler:

> High cockalorum jig, jig, jig, High cockalorum jig, jig, jig,
> High cockalorum jig, jig, jig, High cockalorum - jump off

It can easily be understood that if one of the unfortunates who was bending down happened to get one of these carcasses on his head another on his neck, and a third on his back, it was no easy task to bear the weight of them without giving way and sinking to the ground before these on top had completed their high cockalorum song. Should the feet of any of these who were riding touch the ground before their jig song was finished it was their privilege to repeat the process as before. In contrast, these pigmy Atlases were able for so long to sustain these worlds of flesh upon their shoulders, it was then their opportunity to bump down upon the necks or loins of the boys who had so used them. One would suppose this game to be very dangerous and that it might even result in a broken neck, but no catastrophe ever resulted.

Backyard Wars

In the Australian Children's Folklore Newsletter in 1991, James Lambert described a game of 'war'. This style of war game would be familiar to many Australian boys.[6]

> One of the most popular games the kids in our neighbourhood played was what we called 'Wars'. It was basically a role-play game like 'cowboys and Indians', or 'cops and robbers'. We chose two teams, usually of about five or more kids, depending on how many showed up to play. One team would stop around the front yard and wait a specified time - say one minute, or a count of 50. Meanwhile, the other team took up a defence position in the backyard, behind the hibiscus, the incinerator, in amongst the prunus, up the jacaranda or umbrella tree, under a plastic tarp, behind the wooden barricades we had put up for the game, etc.
>
> The team in the front yard would then proceed to attack, after

first yelling out something signalling their imminent advance; this warning was so that slowcoaches who had not yet found a place to hide could quickly scamper to some usually totally obvious and unsatisfactory place.

The attackers would then proceed up one side of the house, the other being out of bounds, and the battle began.

Basically, to kill another you had to:

(a) get a clear line of sight on them - trees, bushes etc were as solid brick walls even if you could see through them. (b) point your gun at them - guns were usually such things as hockey sticks, clapped-out tennis and squash racquets, plastic toy pistols, and homemade guns of various styles. We had one once that was fashioned out of a spear gun handle and a trigger and two pieces of black-painted wood, one forming the barrel, the other joined at right angles on the left side forming the magazine - it looked like a mock Sten gun; and finally, (c) make one of those raucous machine-gun sound effects that defy spelling (comic strips often transcribe as 'brat-a-tat-tat etc - which is nothing like what we used to say.)

When two players faced one another, the first to shoot (i.e. vocally) killed the other, even if the other made the gun noise. The philosophy behind this was that the one firing second was already dead so it didn't matter what he did. Who killed who in these situations often depended on where the guns were pointed exactly, and what the obstructions were in the way. If both shot at precisely the same time they both died. Usually, however, the decision depended merely on who was the most ardent and confident in his shooting.

This was a very effective use of paralinguistic communication. The loud machine-gun noise says, "I saw you first, before you saw me, and my gun was pointing at you split-seconds before yours was at me, and don't you even think of claiming that this was your kill!" The other noise, even though perhaps as loud, did not carry the ring of conviction and verity. It says, "Hey, I almost got you, so I'll pretend to be pretty cocky and shoot you and hope that you'll think that at least we killed each other." This communication usually decided whose kill it was without any further discussions such h as "I got you!" "Bull, you did."

After the game, according to James, the teams swapped positions, the attackers being the defenders and vice versa.

The team in which all the players were killed first was the loser, irrespective of how many were left on the other team. No score was kept.

D.I.Y. Making Models

'Home-made Cart and Matchbox Steamroller[7]

Home-made toys can be made from all sorts of odd things like matchboxes, nutshells, reels—not forgetting some nails and a little glue—so that they cost us hardly anything. Well, first of all make a little cart. For this take an empty cigar-box and remove the lid, being careful not to split the wood. This forms the body of the cart. The next things are the axle for the wheels to revolve on. For these we need two pieces of wood, each about 5 to 6 inches long and about half an inch square, which we nail on to the bottom of the box (from the inside) at points about two inches from the ends. You must make sure to get these measurements exact, for they are rather important.

The Queenslander April 1915

Next come the wheels, for which we want tin lids. Any sort will do as long as they are all of the same size, but cigarette tins with the lids off do beautifully. Punch a hole in the centre of each (you had better get a grown-up to help you with this, or you might hurt yourself) just large enough to take an inch nail without letting the head slip through, and then nail them to the ends of the two axles, taking care that the nails are driven in far enough to prevent the wheels from wobbling and yet not so far as to make them tight. Make the outsides of the lids face outwards, as they run better that way. Then screw a little hook into one end of the cart, and it is finished.

For the steam-roller we need three corks, two ordinary large bottle corks and one a trifle wider, a small matchbox (one of the inch and three-quarter ones), and a round peg like brewers use for barrels —perhaps your big brother could make you one by shaping the pointed end of a clothes peg. To begin with, glue one of the ordinary corks to the matchbox, and this will provide us with the engine's cab and boiler. To make the front roller cut about an inch and a quarter from the other cork, and fasten it to the boiler by a narrow strip of cardboard bent twice at right angles; you'll see in the picture just what is meant. Fix the short ends of the cardboard to the centre of the ends of the cork by means of pins, which serve as axles on which the rollers can turn. For the two back rollers cut the wider cork into two equal parts. A piece of broken knitting needle will make the axle for these, and after driving this through the match-box at the right height, push the corks on and keep them in their places with sealing-wax. Then push the peg into a hole on the top of the boiler-cork, and the steam roller is complete.'

Match Box Toys.

Making toys from matchboxes was also popular and inexpensive.

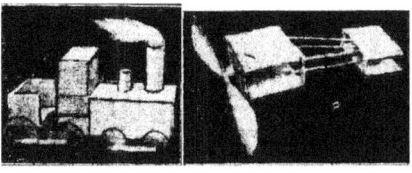

Matchbox toys. *AFU*

This description, from 1930 depression Australia, shows young readers how to construct a train and an aeroplane.[8] Could kids do this nowadays?

> Matchboxes can be used to make the most delightful toys, and a greater variety is possible if smaller matchboxes are used as well as ordinary-sized ones. Besides the matchboxes, a tube of seccaline or some such gum will be required to make matchbox toys, some small wooden button moulds like those used for covering with material for decorating frocks, and some stiff cardboard.
> A Model Engine.
> An engine is a good toy for a beginner to attempt. One whole matchbox and the middle half of a second box are needed. Take out the inside half and cut off one end, leaving about a quarter of an inch of the sides and base remaining on it. Gum the inside edges of the box, and slip the end in until it is in line with the outer cover; the front of the boiler is made. For the construction of the tender the second, inside half of the match box will serve. Leave the bottom intact when making the tender, cut all the sides away, excepting about five-eights of an inch at one end of the side and one end. Then gum the under side of the long flat piece, and place on to the inside of the box which formed the boiler, then cut away sufficient of the top part of the upper box to enable to be insertion of a piece of the inside box, nearly one inch and a half long, so as to form the cab of the engine. The axles for the wheels are made of matches, rounded by glass-paper. The two pairs of front wheels should have their axles gummed on to another match, the exact width of the box, which is then gummed on to the bottom of the box. The third pair of wheels, being larger, do not require this extra piece of wood. The last pair, though large wheels are also used for them, require a piece of wood hardly half the thickness of a match, gummed on to the box first of all. Slip some small button moulds on the axles to form the two first pairs of wheels, and a larger size serves for the back pairs. Some narrow strips off a match box, long enough to reach from one set of wheels to the next set. Gum these strips firmly to the front of the axle, and leave to dry. In order to make the funnel, a hole must first

be made in the centre of the box, about half an inch from the front edge, and a roll of paper inserted. About one inch and a quarter from the funnel make a smaller hole, and slip into it a very tiny roll of paper, gumming a round of paper over the top.

A Model Aeroplane.

The outside of an ordinary-sized match box and the outside of a small-size box, four matches, an elastic band, and a bead about a quarter of an inch long will be required to make this model aeroplane.

First, cut away one side of the larger box, leaving about a quarter of an inch at either end: on the opposite side, leave a piece half an inch wide in the centre beside the two ends. Make a small hole in the middle of this piece. Then, prepare the small matchbox in the same way. The four matches should be rubbed with glass-paper until they are smooth and then gummed to the boxes on the opposite sides. On the bigger box the matches should be three-quarters of an inch from either end, and on the smaller one about five-eighths of an inch from the end. The propeller is made out of stiff notepaper and should be cut in the same shape as is shown in the illustration, measuring five inches in length and one and a quarter inches at its widest point. To strengthen the propeller gum to the centre of a piece of match about one inch long.

When all the parts are dry and firm, slip the elastic band over the middle of the propeller, threading the band through the bead, and then through the hole in the larger matchbox, passing it through both boxes and finally through the hole in the little box, slipping a small piece of wood through the loop. The aeroplane is now ready to fly, and to make it work, it should be held in the left hand, and the propeller gently turned with the right hand until the elastic is well twisted. Then the propeller should be let go.

Kicking the ball around

Australian boys play every imaginable ball game, from hard-at-it football to backyard cricket. We are often referred to as a 'sport's crazy' nation. Visiting any school, local playground, or sporting field will find boys kicking, bouncing, and hurling balls. A wise man said, 'Children learn as they play. Most importantly, in play, children learn how to learn.'

Illustrated Sydney News 30 August 1888

The backyard shed

Children, especially boys, enjoyed helping their fathers tinker in the backyard shed. Sheds have all but disappeared, and with the availability of hardware supermarkets, homemade anything is a rarity. During the lean years of the Great Depression and war years, the sound of sawing, hammering and welding were common across Australia. Many toys were made out of discarded timber and tin and found objects. Over the recent years, there has been a movement known as 'men's sheds' where communities host a shed where locals can potter. It's hoped some of the dads are taking their kids into this environment for creative hacking, sawing, sewing and hammering.

The following three toys were no doubt made in sheds. —the first two on wheels, the dancing or jumping man, and the Mickey Mouse character are part of a group of toys that could be activated to move.

These include dancing skeletons, animals, circus strongmen, and ballet dancers.

Wooden fighter plane. Powerhouse 1930s

Pep-O-Mint truck 1920s Powerhouse

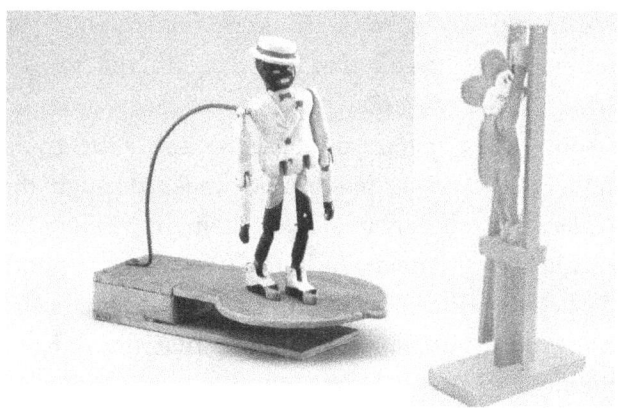

African-American Street Dancer (Australian) + Mickey Mouse mobile toy. *Powerhouse* 1930s

Getting into Mischief

The naughty boys thrashing machine in *Cole's Funny Picture Book*. Melbourne. 1879

Boys generally like to get into mischief territory, especially if they form a gang. These days, the very mention of the word 'gang' produces images of hoodlums or, to use a more appropriate word, larrikins. The old saying was, 'If there was trouble about, boys would find it.' I can recall that my gang in the 1950s regularly 'raided' the Chinese market gardens at Scarborough Park in Sydney's south. The gang would devise the strategy, target the carrots, and crawl on our hands and knees through the muddy canals to take about six carrots. The excitement was in talking about what the Chinese gardeners would do if they saw us and how they all had saltpetre rifles. Thinking back on such behaviour is embarrassing now, but there's no doubt that the danger was the main excitement.

John Haymes recalled how he and his mates built canoes out of corrugated iron, paddled around Dee Why lagoon, or made corrugated iron sleds to ride down the grass slope at Long Reef headland.[9]

Building cubby houses was definitely a secret boy's business. Cubby houses could be constructed from anything and placed anywhere: the back of the garden, in bushland, in parks and up a tree. They were partly constructed and part imagination. The first publicly known usage of a cubby house was in JM Barrie's *Peter Pan* in 1904. In the book, a lost boy in Neverland shoots Wendy Darling from the sky. Peter Pan and the Lost Boys built a small house around her to keep her safe. To this day, Wendy Houses are the English version of our cubby house. The idea was inspired by a little white shed behind JM Barrie's house where he grew up. These days, cubby houses are available commercially. The origin of the word cubby is controversial, but it most probably stems from the old English word *cub* for cow shed or stall.

IMAGINATION HAS no boundaries for children. A 2011 report from a three-year program where teams of fieldworkers visited selected primary schools around Australia for one to two weeks to observe and document children's play at lunchtime and recess described 75 forms of imaginary play. Many of these games involved props or toys brought from home (dolls, stuffed toys, etc.) or were based on characters that had broad appeal in popular culture, such as characters from the films *Harry Potter, Star Wars* and *Indiana Jones.* Some of the games had quite complicated 'plot lines' and used school infrastructure (as opposed to play equipment).[10]

> At one school, five Grade Three boys played a game based on the Indiana Jones series of movies about a hero who goes looking for ancient treasures and has adventures along the way. They all had character names and their task was to find the 'Crystal Skull'. They moved across the school oval according to the action of the game. The boys used the stormwater drains running under the oval in their

game. The drains have open metal grills, and in the game these were 'portals' – 'Portal One', 'Portal Two' and 'Portal Three' – their 'secret way to communicate'. The boys knelt on the covers of the drains and leant over to yell their messages to the others. The person on the middle drain had the job of relaying the message along to the people at the other end. Other older children witnessed the game and were impressed by its players' inventiveness.

10

DRESSING UP AND DOWN

Gumnut Children, Camdenville Public School. *State Archive NSW*

The late Edgar Penzig, historian, lecturer, actor and lover of Australian colonial history, often told audiences how every year he would visit the toy department of the big city department stores and ask where he could find a bushranger's outfit for his son and a convict maid's outfit for his daughter. Each year, he was politely told no such outfits existed; however, there were Robin Hood, Annie Oakley, Daniel Boone and countless other English and American outfits. He continued, reminding the poor sales assistants that we lived in Australia, not America or Britain. He had a point.

The author and his big sister ready for a holiday dress up party. 1950. *AFU*

Children enjoy dressing up and can make costumes out of the strangest materials. Imagination can lead to some wonderful costumes. Like most things in our lives, today's children are more inclined to look to popular culture for inspiration, resulting in them dressing up as mini rappers or pop dancers. The one exception appears to be the growing acceptance of Halloween. While it isn't particularly close to our culture, it is an opportunity for children to go all out with costumes and make-up. This seems better than dressing like junior pop stars and over-promoted celebrities. Bring on the spooks!

A Hop, a Skip and a Jump   327

Robyn Mayoh dressed as a chef with neighbouring children dressed as Dick Whittington and a scarecrow. St Peters, Sydney, Circa late 1950s. *AFU*

Costume Parties

Costume parties were popular entertainment in earlier times. Most women were capable dressmakers and adept at sewing elaborate costumes. The following photo montage, from 1917, shows children dressed as Charlie Chaplin, a cat, jockey, Napoleon, and an intriguing young 'canary' in a cage.

Children's Costume Party, Paddington, NSW, 1917. *Mirror* (Sydney)

Many children's birthday and holiday parties were in costume. Department stores typically only carried a handful of manufactured costumes, usually cowboys and Indians, and were mostly influenced by early motion picture features of serials. Wild Bill Hickock, Buffalo Bill, Pocahontas, Red Cross Nurse, Hopalong Cassidy, and Tarzan, being the most popular. Homemade costumes were far more inventive. It should be noted that adults also dressed up for costume parties, especially charity events. The First Lord Mayor of Sydney staged a costume ball in 1846, and around 300 attendees arrived in outrageous costumes, including one group dressed as 'La Perouse Aborigines'![1]

Colin & Gordon Bradbury, Swan Hill, 1921. *Museums Victoria*

DRESSING UP ALLOWS CHILDREN, and possibly adults, to enter the magic kingdom of make-believe. Dressed in costume allows easy access to a fantasy world. Children do it innocently, while some adults do it to escape reality, sometimes with rather peculiar results. Children do not necessarily need costumes to imagine they are a swashbuckling pirate, a spaceman on Mars, a cowboy or girl out on the range, a princess at the royal court or whatever. However, it does help them transport themselves, even if it is simply a salute to that uniform, a sword or a hat, or even a piece of plastic piping can all be re-imagined with success. Interestingly, most children can readily return to the same imaginary character and situation repeatedly. Adults who dream rarely get a chance to return to the same dream successfully.

Children dressed as daisies. Lillian Pitt Collection. 1910. *Museums Victoria*

junior swaggies. Dereel, 1930. *Museums Victoria*

Fairyland is another favourite place with endless possibilities for dressing up. The magic begins with a tulle tutu or similar dress, a sparkly Alice band, and a stick with a star on top. With the recent popularity of Harry Potter, many wardrobes have miraculously turned into wizard wear, and many broomsticks have carried quidditch players to glory.

Dressed as fairies in a tableau. *The Australasian*, 1931.

Halloween

Spooks. Unsurprisingly, Halloween has joined the list of Australian celebration days, including Father's Day, Mother's Day, Grandparent's Day, Red Nose Day, Secretary's Day, Turn Off The TV Day, Earth Day, Pink Ribbon Day and Australia Day. It is slightly dispiriting that all but one of these are British or American imports, while the sole Australian is now a matter of some controvery.

It has become difficult, if not impossible, to avoid Halloween when popular media highlights its arrival with Halloween episodes of popular television programs, particularly situation comedies, cartoons like *The Simpsons* and similar programs. Supermarkets have also climbed onto the bandwagon and offer stacks of pumpkins and haunted products, including, sadly, 'candy' packs. Google also presents itself with a Halloween image for the day. Facebook and Instagram are also full of Halloween messages, chats, and photographs. As a primarily English-speaking country, we are, of course, a prime target for anything produced by the American cultural machine. Some Australians are even celebrating Thanksgiving, which seems both inappropriate and incongruous.

Children ready for Halloween. *Hamersley News (Perth)*, Nov. 1978

Halloween is celebrated in America, Mexico, Canada and, to some degree, Britain and Ireland. Halloween (a shortening of All Hallows' Evening), also known as Hallowe'en or All Hallows' Eve, is a yearly holiday observed worldwide on October 31, the night before All Saints Day. It has left its Christian roots behind. Much like Day of the Dead celebrations, the Christian feast of All Hallows' Eve also incorporates traditions from pagan harvest festivals and festivals honouring the dead, particularly the Celtic Samhain. Typical festive Halloween activities include trick-or-treating (also known as "guising"), attending costume parties, carving jack-o'-lanterns, lighting bonfires, apple bobbing, visiting haunted attractions, playing pranks, telling scary stories and, more recently, watching horror films. Many Australian schools have embraced the celebration with a dress-up day.

2011 set a benchmark for Australian Halloween—two newsreaders finished with a 'Happy Halloween', and at least one television quiz show, Channel Ten's 'Deal or No Deal', saw the host, Andrew O'Keefe, dressed as a vampire for the entire program. It was embarrassing!

TRICK OR TREATING, a custom where costumed young children go door-to-door looking for handouts of sweets (or should I say 'lollies'?), is the most famous manifestation of Australian Halloween.

This is great fun for the kids, and it isn't easy to poo-poo the idea of dressing up. It is also fun for the adults to see their kids and neighbour's kids enjoying themselves. Halloween is the only sanctioned, even if unofficially, dress-up day in Australia, and for that reason alone, it should probably be encouraged. Perhaps the fact of its being of English origin rather than American makes it a wee bit more culturally acceptable. At the end of the day, or night in this case, it is fun to dress up, especially when so many others are costumed. Add to this the way 'scaring' has entered popular entertainment and, depending on how you view sweets, an opportunity for children to gather lollies (never candies!).

At least kids make the event their own with rhymes:

> Trick or treat - smell my feet.
> Give me something good to eat!
> Trick or treat, smell my feet.
> Give me something good to eat.
> If you don't, I won't be sad.
> I'll just make you wish you had!
> If you don't, I don't care.
> I'll pull down your underwear.

Dressing Up for the Nursery Rhyme Fair

Dressing up for the Christmas pageant.

In the late nineteenth and early twentieth centuries, it was fashionable for schools and community fetes to host an annual dress-up day, during which children were encouraged to dress as nursery rhyme characters. The following report is from 1929.[2]

Nursery Rhymes Fete.

Fun at Government House for a Nursery Rhymes fete on October 5 in aid of the creche and kindergarten. On behalf of the flower-stall staff, Miss Hal L'Estrange presented Lady. Goodwin with a posy of lily of the valley, delphiniums, and roses.

Both Sir John and Lady Goodwin were the recipients of souvenir programmes. Lady Goodwin's mottled blue crepe de chine dress was made with a side drapery. Her hat was a blue Baku swathed in silk. Mrs. P. W. Robinson, Miss Barbara Sisley, and Canon B. W. Robin. Messrs. W. L. Dowd and W. Stable marshalled the procession of Boy Scouts, Girl Guides, Junior Red Cross members and creche and kindergarten associates, with all the juvenile workers for the function, on the main drive, which was lined with stalls representing different nursery rhymes, the public entering by way of The House That Jack Built. Sir John Goodwin opened the fete and spoke enthusiastically of the organiser (Miss Bedford).

The 'Pied Piper' was presented by Miss Sisley, and dances by the junior pupils of Somerville House were given on the lawn.

Nursery Rhyme Fair 1937 Hobart

Costumed children, Lennox Head Public School. *State Archive NSW*

Another report, from 1938, followed the same theme headed - Nursery Rhymes and 'Popeye the Sailor' At Charity Fete[3]

"Mary, Mary, Quite Contrary," with silver bells and cockle shells; Popeye the Sailor-man with his traditional billycan of spinach; a flower patch where surprise packets were wrapped in pastel-coloured papers caught by posies of flowers; Treasure Island with gaily dressed pirates — these were all to be seen at the fete which was held at Government House this afternoon.

Orange Grove Public Schoolgirls dressed as 'pretty milkmaids all in a row'. *State Archive NSW*

A Hop, a Skip and a Jump

Coogee Public School students dressed as wheat for the agricultural display arranged for the Duke of Wales. *State Archive NSW*

OF COURSE, dress-ups can go sideways. The following photograph from a nursery day dress-up in Hobart, 1939, shows that 'the old woman who lived in a shoe' had so many golliwogs 'she didn't know what to do.'

Golliwogs in the Old Woman's Shoe. Hobart 1937. *AFU*

Greenwich Public School students dressed as Egyptians.
State Archive NSW

School World Culture Day

Many schools celebrate Australia's multicultural base with an annual World Culture Day. Students, and sometimes teachers and staff, are encouraged to attend school in a costume saluting their ethnic background. This includes people of Anglo-Irish descent, Indigenous groups and representatives of the nearly two hundred other national cultural groups in Australia. Schools encourage students to bring food or an object typical of their country and, sometimes, even a grandparent!

Understanding and appreciating differences is vital in a thriving society, and it is even more critical for it to be explored and celebrated at a young age. Children, in their innocence and sometimes influenced by the views of parents or siblings, are susceptible to forms of racism. Identifiers of differences like skin colour and dress can be easily explained with events such as World Culture Day - music, stories, costumes, and food are all wonderful ways to celebrate differences. Even experiencing traditional games from other countries should be seen as an opportunity to engage all children - it's hard to be racist when you're having fun.

Jolly Little Sailors

A sailor went to sea, sea, sea, To see what he could see, see, see. But all that he could see, see, see, Was the bottom of the deep blue sea, sea, sea.

The Victorian and Edwardian periods saw fashion for dressing young boys and girls in sailors' uniforms or, at least, clothing with a maritime flavour. Many portraits taken by commercial photographic studios of the time show young sailors, sometimes carrying a toy boat. The sea dominated daily life—transport, mail, emigration, military, etc., and this accounts for the fashion.

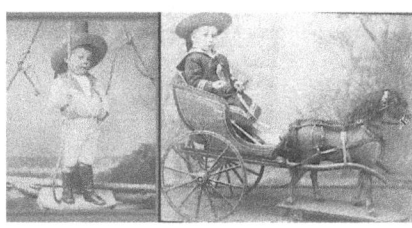

Unidentified boy sailors circa 1900

Little sailor boy, sheet music of 'Little Sailors' and a typical Edwardian costume.

Cowboys and Indians.

Dressing up like a cowboy or Indian became extremely popular worldwide throughout the 1940s and 50s because of the popularity of American westerns and film serials.

Kids made improvised wigwams from old sheets and blankets and imagined they were on the warpath or having a pow-wow with their tribe. Pocohontas and Hiawatha ruled the open prairies of Australian suburbs.

The costumes were relatively easy to make, and the associated game possibilities were endless—mostly involving wild chasing, whooping, and shooting. Cultural appropriation was a concept that didn't arise; it hadn't been invented then.

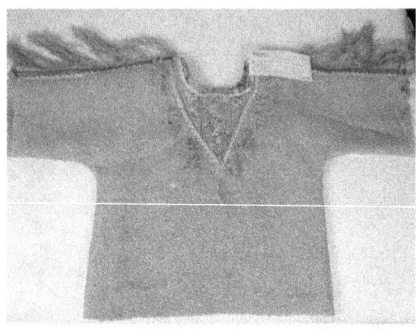

Indian shirt, William Boyd Collection 1950s. *Museums Victoria*

Indian feathered headress. William Boyd Collection 1950s. *Museums Victoria*

Mickey Mouse Club.

> Mickey Mouse (Donald Duck)
> Mickey Mouse!(Donald Duck)
> Forever let us hold our banner high
> High, high, high

Popular television programs also influenced children's costumes.

From 1954-58, Walt Disney's Disneyland was screened daily on Australian television and captured Australian children's hearts, souls, and wardrobes. With its themed segments of Tomorrowland, Frontierland, Fantasyland and Adventureland, all linked to the highly successful Disney marketing programs, Disney-themed costumes started appearing in retail outlets. Most successful of all was the spin-off program, The Mickey Mouse Club, led by its now famous line-up of Mouseketeers, which included Annette Funicello, Ryan Gosling, Justin Timberlake, Britney Spears and Christina Aguilera, to name a few. It was created in 1955 and ran until 1996. Who could forget the craze for wearing Mickey Mouse ears? In 1959, the cast of The Mouseketeers toured Australia, and mouse ears enthusiastically wriggled across the land.

The Mouseketeers touring Australia 1959

Australian radio catered for children with serials like *Biggles, The Air Adventures of Hop Harrigan, Kid Grayson Rides the Range* and *The Search for the Golden Boomerang*. ABC Radio hosted *The Children's Hour* and *The Argonauts*. The Argonauts Club was open to Australian boys and girls aged from 7 to 17. It proved hugely popular with young Australians: by 1950 there were over 50,000 members, with 10,000 new members joining each year through the 1950s (national membership reached 43,000 in 1953). Applications for membership were made by post. The new member was given a new identity - a ship name and number - and also received an enamelled badge and handsome membership certificate with the Pledge.

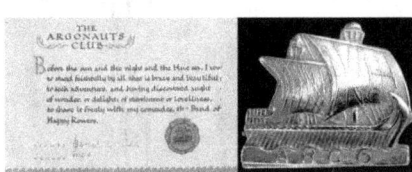

Argonauts Club pledge and badge.

Australian television introduced characters like Captain Fortune, Mr. Squiggle, Skippy, The Wiggles and Bluey, just to name a few.

Hero worship. Children like to emulate their heroes, and, in the past, we have seen tiny Robin Hoods, Davy Crocketts, Cinderellas,

Snow Whites and lots of Cowboys and Indians. Most were inspired by drawings in books or early television series and films. As popular entertainment became more sophisticated, complex and desperate, the focus moved from fantasy people to cartoon characters, monsters, stuffed animals and, lately, to show pony people, particularly singers. It was reasonably easy for a child to imagine him or herself as a version of a person, less so to assume the look of a cartoon or stuffed animal. Unfortunately, getting 'the look' of a teen or older celebrity has never been easier. Jewellery, clothing and make-up are all marketed so teens can look just like their latest obsession. This is nothing new; however, the fashion to dress up and look like Beyonce, Taylor Swift or whoever has become painfully young. Thankfully, the American horror pageant, where very young girls are dressed up like twenty-one-year-old showgirls, has not taken off in Australia - yet!

11

GETTING MOBILE

Lilo Bylton behind the wheel. Circa 1959. *AFU*

Tricycles & Bicycles

Tricycles are still the preferred first taste of self-propulsion for most toddlers. They sit safely on conventional tricycles; however, these days they are more likely giant ladybirds or mini fire-trucks, which they propel with their legs.

1936 pedal power. *Office of Public Record, Victoria*

Older children graduate to a bicycle. Receiving a bicycle was much anticipated and was seen as a sign of responsibility. You had to know road rules, respect for other riders, street navigation and parking security. You also had to 'look after it' with cleaning and oiling and, when necessary, know how to patch a busted tyre. It was a big adventure that screamed freedom.

ONE OF THE FAVOURITE MODIFICATIONS, especially for boys, was to clip a plastic playing card to the rear spoke wheel with a clothes peg to make the bicycle sound more like a motorbike. Multiple cards made the sound louder, especially the faster you pedalled. A simple trick for a loud effect.

Wheeled derby outside George Horton Shop, Ryde, NSW. *Photograph Geo. Horton. Ryde Library.*

Cyclops is a name familiar to many Australians who grew up with the company's scooters, tricycles, prams, and drivable model cars. Established in 1913 in the Sydney suburb of Leichhardt, Hunter Leisure still offers a range of branded bikes and scooters.

Advertisement for Australian manufacturer Cyclops.

Malvern Star Finnegan Bicycle Shop, Melbourne.

Undoubtedly, Australia's most famous bicycle was and still is the Malvern Star. Established by the Finnegan family in 1903 and named after the Melbourne suburb of the same name, the company now has over seventy different bicycles.

Cycling has been in the Finnegan family for nearly 150 years. The company's founder, Tom Finnegan, won the 1898 Austral Wheel Race of 240 gold sovereigns, one of the richest sporting prizes in Australia.

The Finnegan family on wheels. *Family site.*

Tom Finnegan winner of the 1898 Austral Wheel Race. *Finnegan family.*

IN THIS AGE of fast cars, motorbikes, speedboats, and aeroplanes, we have become blasé about speed. It was once not so normal, and many a child anticipated the first rush of speed and air against the face, all the more exciting if generated by leg power. Today's child has many options for self-propulsion, including surfboards, skateboards, skis, ice skates, and, of course, pushbikes.

Like most sporting accessories, skating shoes have significantly changed over the years. Single-blade skates that ride well on open roads and pavement, such as skate or laser bikes, are popular. Adults can even ride these lightweight skates.

Many new skateboards use more than leg power and include batteries and other means of extra propulsion.

. . .

Skating

Between 1885 and 1970, roller skating was a major pastime in Australia. There were hundreds of roller rinks where you could hire lace-up skates (few people could afford their own). The rinks were extremely popular with young children and teens. Many of the larger rinks had bands playing to accompany the skaters; later, records were played. The rinks typically had wooden slat floors and were extremely noisy as solo and partnered skaters did fancy steps, including skating backward. Some rinks organised weekly or monthly speed racing events with prizes.

Bruised knees and sore bums were commonplace for young or novice roller skating daredevils.

Roller-Skating and the laws of gravity. *The Pictorial Australian (Adelaide) April 1889*

The Northern Territory Times & Gazette (Darwin) March 1919,
suggested this as an aid to the roller skating craze.

SKATING WAS NOT for the faint-hearted!

In 1938, a Broken Hill newspaper reported[1] a few lines of encouragement.

A local girl has written the following poem, which will appeal to everyone taking up the noble art of skating.

> NOW THIS SPORT IS QUITE A FINISHED ART,
> But to me it's all brand new.
> And learning means a fall or two;
> This roller skating.
> I've tried to glide but hit the ground,
> My balance lost before it's found.
> Those others still go skating round -
> All roller skating.
> It seems to me a round of hefty bumps,
> Pushes and shoves and biffs, and thumps.
> I go home a lot of bruises and bumps -
> From roller skating.
> My clothes are all dirty, and grease right through,

> My shoulder-blade damaged (and other things too)
> My elbow is skinned and my knee bruised blue, -
> Through roller skating.
> It seems pretty hopeless, but maybe some day
> I'll learn how to do it the very best way,
> And then I'll be able to stand when they say -
> "Come roller skating."

Physician warns skating craze dangerous.[2]

A physician who has made a careful study of the effects of roller skating has shown that excessive indulgence in this sport frequently results in flat feet, defective development of the leg muscles, and impairment of the gait and carriage of the body. Roller skating is especially injurious to growing children, whose muscles, bones, and joints are still in the process of development. The muscles used in walking, especially those of the feet, remain inactive in roller skating, while other muscles are overworked. Hence the body becomes more or less deformed, especially in the case of young girls, who fail to acquire their normal grace and beauty of form.

Adelaide Glaciarium with dancers in fancy dress. 1906.

Skating, firstly roller-skating and later ice-skating, became extremely popular. Around 1910, there were rinks in all major cities and regional towns. Sydney was on wheels at the Royal Roller Rink

(Agricultural Showground, Moore Park), Manly Beach Rink, The Coliseum (North Sydney), The Vice-Regal Rink (Rushcutters Bay) and the Bondi Junction Rink Association with Centennial Park.

THE FIRST ICE rink was the Glaciarium chain, which had rinks in Adelaide, Melbourne, and Sydney. The Sydney Glaciarium on George Street West opened with much fanfare in 1907. The larger rinks had their own bands. Many rinks organised skating exhibitions, races and formal evenings - yes, skating in top hats and tails for men, gowns for women. Skating was considered a good exercise for children, and many schools arranged a weekly excursion to the closest rink, while others converted a section of the playground to accommodate weekly skating tournaments. Roller dancing was also popular with dances like the Jolly Miller and Monte Carlo. The primary rinks usually organised a 'children only' session on Saturday mornings.

THE SKATING CRAZE had all but disappeared by the 1960s.

Crystal Palace Skating Rink. Richmond, Victoria.

Billy Carts

Gone are the days of the billy cart. It fell victim to increased city and town traffic, po-faced councillors and the diversion of other entertainments.

Billycarts have been banished from our streets

It started as a cart drawn by a billygoat - hence the name. Goats had their problems; cantankerous by nature, always diverted by whatever was edible and problematic for the same po-faced councillors (goat droppings were a major health and traffic hazard on early streets). The new billy cart with wheels, mostly built from scrap, became popular in the gold rush when young children were usefully employed carting. As that century evolved, flashier models appeared, making good use of old pram wheels and sometimes the pram itself.

Coloured drawing cartoon card. A.F.U.

By the end of the century, the billy cart had established itself as a children's favourite, especially, but not exclusively, for boys. Most boys dreamt of owning a billy cart, and by the early part of the twentieth century, many did.

As road traffic increased, billy cart racing became a problem. Neither the early vehicles nor the billy carts were particularly responsive to steering out of approaching collisions—reports of billy cart derbies in the first decade of the twentieth century point to a craze. Most country towns and cities saw an explosion of sanctioned races.

Promotional cartoon for Ginger Meggs Billy Cart Derby, 1910.

IN 1910, the Ginger Megg's Billy Cart Derby was staged in front of a huge audience in Sydney's Centennial Park. Thousands came to witness the race which attracted 144 entrants.

By the 1920s, there were calls for banning billy carts in the cities, with headlines like "The roads are not playgrounds!". In the 1930s, there were continuing reports of fatal accidents and calls for prohibition. In the 1940s, billy cart racing seemed out of control, and in 1946, the *Newcastle Herald* declared war on "road hoglets in billy carts".[3]

Apart from the making of it and a sense of accomplishment, one of the joys of billy carts was the sense of freedom. Maybe teens who get their car licenses feel the same today. Having a mobile cart allowed you to move about and feel useful. You could transport your younger brothers and sisters, friends and, most importantly, 'things', collect refundable bottles, get the shopping, and collect rubbish for the annual Guy Fawkes bonfire.

In 1941, over 20,000 people watched a downhill derby in Newcastle, with boys aged between 10 and 15 in the driver's seat. Later that year, an estimated 30,000 watched the Centennial Park Billy Cart Derby. During WW2, boys and girls with billy carts formed brigades to collect scrap metal and other items useful in the war effort.

A billy goat cart, Newcastle, NSW, 1950s. *Australian Information Service.*

Originally a simple platform with four wheels and a moveable front steering column, the billy cart was adapted to become a self-powered vehicle that children would race. The challenge was to travel as fast and/or far as possible with the least initial momentum.

In 1931, one youngster, Alex Scott, wrote a poem about billy carts.[4]

THE BILLY CART

The windows of the Sydney shops

Are full of quite expensive toys;
Meccano sets, and trains, and tops,
And other birthday gifts for boys;
For bikes and trikes of varied sizes.
A lot of money might be paid;
Yet, more than these, our youngsters' prize
The billy-cart that Hector made.

The wheels, I fancy, once propelled me
Squalling infant in a pram;
The body (so it says) has held
Six dozen tins of apple jam.
From father's workshop, bits of wood,
And sundry nuts and bolts have strayed;
If tools could speak, they might be rude
About the cart that Hector made.

Now, up and down our peaceful street,
This car of Juggernaut careers;
And sober citizens retreat
With heart attacks and sudden fears
If pleasure can be gauged by noise.
Or happiness by din portrayed,
Its cargo is a thousand Joys
The billy-cart that Hector made.

Albert Dennis of Newtown, NSW, wrote to the Children's Sunbeams section of a Sydney newspaper in 1932 to tell the world how he built his billy cart.[5]

> "One day, I decided to make a Billy Cart. So, having found the box, I proceeded to nail the axles and wheels on. Then I put on a hastily made brake, and the cart was ready.
>
> I took it up the lane and tried it out. I was enjoying myself for half an hour when one of my mates came up and asked for a ride. Then came a couple more. After a while, one of them suggested that we all come down at once. The billy-cart was only built for two, but we all squeezed on. Soon we were off, but someone gave it an extra push, so that we started off much faster than I expected. We were going along all right, but a bit too fast for my liking, so I put on the brake; it eased it up a bit, but it suddenly came off in my hand. By this time, we were near the bottom of the lane, and at the bottom was a brick wall. I tried to turn round the corner sharply, but I misjudged the distance, and hit the kerb with a resounding smack. I was underneath the lot, but when I went to collect the cart all I saw were bits of iron wheels and wood scattered around. As I limped home I vowed that the next billy-cart I make I'll be the only one to ride in it.

Much later, in 2008, Max Prisk, in a nostalgic mood, summed up the excitement of billy carts as:[6]

> 'For generations, every Australian child knew that the wheel had been invented for just one reason: billy carts. There was no more splendid sight in their heyday - say the 1930s, '40s and '50s - than a concourse of billy carts, maybe 15 or 20 of them, perched at the top of a favourite hilly urban street, kids of all shapes and sizes holding the reins to the flexible front axle, waiting for the "ready, set, go".'

1912 Billycart kids, Malvern, Victoria. *State Library Victoria.*

Billy Carts came in all shapes and sizes, using whatever parts were available: pram wheels were highly sought after.

NOT ALL BILLY CARTS ARE CREATED EQUAL, and in 1949, twelve-year-old Richard Duimi of Enfield, NSW, had the inspiration to attach sails to his.[7]

Billycart with sails

'Richard gets a big kick out of riding a billy-cart downhill, but he hates the thought of pulling it up again.

Richard saw pictures of yachts in the Sydney-Hobart ocean classic and decided this sort of thing would be pretty good on a billy cart. So Richard, who talks with the soft brogue of Erin's County Westmeath, built a billy-cart that whizzes uphill under its own power.

Richard hoisted a sail to his cart. Now, he's the envy of all billy cart racers around the place.

Barry Stutsel, 14, one of Richard's racing mates, says the sailing billy-cart is really something. Pondered Barry: "I've been building 'em for five years, but I've never seen one like Richard's."

Billycart derby, Sydney, 1920s.

ELIZABETH HAWKES RECALLED her billy cart adventures.[8]

My brother was born an engineer, so he would build the most ingenious billy carts. One was the chassis of an old car; it had a seat, a steering wheel and a handbrake. We would gather a few local kids and set it up on the top of our sloping block, jump on the seat or the petrol tank at the back and let the hand brake off. We'd fly down the hill, and then the driver would have one opportunity to turn into a side track and yank on the handbrake to stop. If we continued down the hill we'd either smash into a tree or end up in the mud at the edge of the Georges River. Then, we all had to push it up the hill to do it again. I don't know how we survived.

Moves to ban the billy cart in Sydney commenced as early as 1932 when Ashfield Council made moves to clear their streets. The 76-year-old mayor interceded, and the billy cart raced down their streets for another 22 years.[9]

In their fight against banning billy carts in Ashfield parks, the youngsters have found a champion — he's the 76-year-old Mayor, Alderman Lapish - the only council member to vote against the ban. He said he'll do what he can to see the kids are not robbed of their fun by "old men who don't understand." "Tell them I'm all for them," said the white-haired Mayor, who still reads and likes the comic papers. "Tell them if I can help them, I will." He said it as a father of ten.

"Look here," he added; "I wouldn't place a ban on billy-carts any more than I'd steal the candy from a baby. I didn't vote for this thing. "You wouldn't catch me interfering with the fun of any youngster. I reared just short of a dozen of 'em, and, believe me, I know something about 'em."

Anyway, maintains Ald. Lavish, it's one thing to pass a resolution and it's another to enforce it. "It would take the entire police force of N.S.W. to keep the kids of Ashfield out of the parks with their billy-carts and scooters," he said.

"There's not a youngster in town who hasn't got a billy-cart, a scooter, or a 'trike' of some sort or other. Just wait and see. I didn't watch ten kids grow up without learning something."

Ald. C. I. Allum, who introduced the matter in council, says he is a father himself He has a boy, but his boy has neither a billy-cart nor a scooter. "These things have no right in the municipality," Ald. Allum said. "They get in the way. "They make too much noise. They don't look nice!"[10]

By the 1950s, the number of billy cart accidents had grown dramatically, and Sydney's Ashfield Council made the first move to ban billy carts from the streets. It was a very emotionally charged debate, but the national death toll and public concern decided for the Council. Billy carts were banned. Other councils followed suit.

Eric McLoughlin, writing in 1954, reacted to the decision with this lament:[11]

> Sad times are developing for boyhood, or at least they are in the eyes of the adult who remembers the days of cigarette cards, shanghais and billy-carts. Shanghais have long disappeared under the weight of adult disapproval, and the days of under-the-counter transactions sealed the fate of the cigarette card, designed as a sales draw.
>
> No more will harassed parents be apologising (and paying) for broken windows, and no more will boys treasure their "silkies", their war heroes, their champions of the race track Now, expressing the mood of the times, the Ashfield Council has banned the billycart, a decision which, one feels, will soon be followed by other councils, What a commentary on life! No doubt, the worthy aldermen had the welfare of the citizenry at heart when they pronounced the billycart dangerous, but many among them must have had moments of sadness as they recalled the joys of the billycarts of their boyhood.
>
> Memories of these headlong dashes from top to bottom of any hill (the steeper the better), with the spine-chilling sliding swerve at the end must still produce a thrill even when the years have frosted the thatch and expanded the waistcoat. Who of us cannot recall the great and complicated business of making the billycart — the shifts and manoeuvres to get the wheels (the most expensive component), the long and serious deliberations on the best type of box, the raid on mum's clothesline for steering gear, amid the surreptitious dips into the cooking fat to lubricate the moving parts!
>
> The joy of building — shared by every boy worthy of the name of boy in the neighbourhood — was eclipsed only by the joy of these wild rides. These billycarts are no trivial things in the world of boyhood. An unfashionable billycart, judged on the standards of its

background, is no less a disability than an outmoded car in expensive social circles.

You will recall how the billycart fashions changed. There was a day when a rough-and-ready iron wheel met requirements — just as Henry Ford's 'Tin Lizzie' was acceptable to an age in which, the internal combustion engine was still a novelty. Then came streamlining of the box and rubber tyres, just as in motor cars there was development of power, simplification of mechanical details, and improvement in appearance.

The modern boy, to be in the mode, must have ball races, which keep him low on the ground and make an engaging clatter when the contraption is at speed. Since the Redex trial there's been a fashion for markings on the bodywork (the more the merrier) of a type which proclaim the vehicle's notable qualities, and its capacity to stand up to any danger. Performances sometimes so sincerely fulfils these pronouncements that in the more crowded areas one must be nimble to avoid being tumbled.

It seems that if Ashfield's decision becomes general, boys will have to devote themselves to impressive model motor, cars, or elaborate scooters from the assembly line, which in the heyday of the billycart were no more than reserves. Or perhaps in these, days of nuclear fission, we may see the streets cluttered up with more and more kids disguised, as Spacemen or Frogmen, or as Hopalong Cassidys.

The era of the billy cart was over.

Hoop Rolling.

Hoop rolling popular in the nineteenth and early twentieth century, was another 'accident waiting to happen' and a road hazard.

Boy rolling hoop.

Essentially a child's activity in which a large cane, wooden or metal hoop is rolled along the ground, generally using an object like a stick, wielded by the player.

The game aims to keep the hoop upright for long periods or to do various tricks. Hoop trundling was popular with girls and boys;

however, it needed smooth surfaces, like roadways or grassy hills, to be effective. In the absence of a hoop, boys often rolled car tyres.

STILT-WALKING

Stilt walking, once popular, seems to have disappeared as a children's activity, probably another casualty of the 'fun police' or possibly something to do with the fact children rarely get an opportunity to build things. Yesterday's children found it simple to cut a pair of stilts from two small and straight saplings, the fork of a branch serving as a foothold. Of course, you had to learn how to walk on these stilts, and while learning, you had many spills, but that was part of the fun.

ANOTHER TYPE of stilt was made by piercing two holes in the end of a syrup tin or jam tin and threading strong strings through them. By grasping the ends of the strings you held the tins to your feet and, with a bit of practice, you could even run on the tins.

Here is a description from 1929[12]

Walking on stilts is an old form of recreation that appeals to many boys. Making stilts is quite simple.

Get two pieces of light, strong timber, about 4 inches square or thereabouts, and about the height of your shoulder, or longer if you want extra high stilts. It is desirable that the wood; should have a straight grain, and essential that it should be free from large knots. The foot rests should be placed about a foot from the ground, or higher for expert stilt walkers, but it is not advisable to have them above a couple of feet high. The distance between the foot rest and the top of the stilt should be the same as the distance between the foot and the elbow of the user.

The foot rest should be of the same thickness as the stilt, about 4 inches high and 3 inches along the top. It should he cut to a slope to fit into a notch cut at a corresponding angles in the upright. Strong screws (not nails) should be used to secure it in position, and to ensure that it will not break away under continuous pressure the upper end should be bound to the upright with wire. Better still, if you have a brace and bit to bore a hole through the wood, secure the upper end of the rest with a bolt. Then the wire binding will not he needed, and the job will be cleaner and stronger. The top of the stilt should be cut round, and smoothed with sandpaper, so that the handle will be free from splinters.

Nass schoolboys walking on stilts. *State Archive NSW*

~

Spinning Around

Australian postage stamp depicting child playing on a Hills Hoist.

The Hills Hoist was invented in Adelaide by Lance Hill in 1945. It isn't known whether he ever thought of it as a plaything. The Hills Hoist and similar rotary clothes hoists remain a standard fixture in many backyards in Australia. They are considered one of Australia's most recognisable icons and are used frequently by artists as a metaphor for Australian suburbia in the 1950s and 1960s. Before the Hills Hoist, washing was dried using a straight clothesline wire suspended by two long wooden poles called props. The props were a long wooden pole with a forked end, used to raise a line of washing to enable it to catch the breeze and very tempting for young children as a means of pole vaulting and playing Superman. When kids broke a clothes prop, they would head for the hills! Replacement poles were sold by clothes prop men who regularly shouted "clothesssss propppppps'.

Megan Grant and little Heather Grant in car seat. 1964

The Hills Hoist brought far more possibilities for playtime and, being metal, was far hardier. Holding on and spinning around was always fun, and it could also be used to hang long sheets and build a 'city' maze. You could even build a contraption or use a car baby seat to carry small children on the line. It offered unlimited play potential to any backyard play centre - as long as you weren't caught!

12

BOWERBIRDS

Some people are bowerbirds by nature. They collect everything, often to observe and catalogue, sometimes simply to fulfil a need to collect. Most children love to collect, and even infants enjoy gathering and assembling the simplest objects. As children get older, they often move on to more substantial collecting. It is curious how children migrate to certain collecting hobbies. Some collect model cars or planes, others particular styles of dolls, stamps, coins, bugs, autographs, clippings about film or recording celebrities, sea shells, postcards, tea cups, perfume bottles, bird's eggs, patches, pins, spoons, t-shirts, feathers, bottle-tops, bumper stickers and... well, there's no end of such a list. As always, if it is a commercial product, there's a manufacturer ready, willing and able to encourage the eager collector. The Barbie 'family' is the obvious leader in collectible doll marketing. Soft toys, especially Teddy Bears, remain popular. Children can become very attached to book series, and the recent success of *Harry Potter* books is a fine example, albeit tied to vigorous marketing campaigns. Yesterday's reader enthusiastically collected Enid Blyton's *Famous Five* and Secret Seven adventure stories and subscribed to the Girls and Boy's *Own Annuals*. Comics, especially those issued in series, were collected and often traded.

Collecting is also prone to fashion and mass-market manipulation. Fast food merchants like KFC and McDonald's know the commercial pressure they can exert by promoting a 'buy one get one' collector offer. In the last two years, supermarket giants Coles and Woolworths have mounted massive collectability promotions aimed at children. Disney is another company expert in enticing children into collecting, especially anything associated with its popular films like *Finding Nemo, Frozen* and *Toy Story*. Many marketers combine chocolate with their 'incentives' to sell Toy Story characters inside chocolate casings. Kinder Surprise is the world's most successful chocolate egg toy product. Anyone for a Pet Rock? Furby? or a Weebles family?

Pet Rock. An absolute must for the children!

Using Hands and Brains.

Construction Sets. Back in 1898, Frank Hornby was definitely onto something big when he created the Meccano Set with its system of reusable metal strips, plates, angle girders, wheels, axles and gears, and parts that are connected using nuts, bolts and set screws. Every boy's dream was to own a Meccano Set and build, build, build. Which also meant buy, buy, buy.

Meccano set and train.

Construction collectibles are still popular. Lego, the interlocking plastic brick created in Denmark in 1949, has sold over 800 million Lego parts worldwide, including millions in Australia. Unlike Meccano, its marketing is aimed at both girls and boys. This is possibly a key to its ongoing commercial success.

Collecting fashions come and go. The interest in coins and stamps, two of the most collected items over the centuries, has diminished, except for the dedicated few.

Stamp Collecting

Stamp collecting from around the globe.

Stamp Collecting was not only seen as fun but also had the potential to be financially rewarding. There were many stamp clubs across Australia, and most Sunday newspaper junior sections carried regular stamp-collecting tips and news. 'Aunty Mary', who wrote in the *Western Mail* (Perth) in 1936, was a keen advocate.[1]

> Stamp-collecting is one of the most pleasant of all pastimes, and I think, from your letters, that many of you have taken up this interesting hobby. Have you ever thought that, apart from its interesting side, stamp-collecting may also be a profitable and educational pastime?
>
> You know, boys and girls, one day, if you are patient enough, you may be lucky enough to pick up a rare specimen, and then, who knows, it may be worth a small gold mine. Sometimes, a set of stamps has a blemish, and when the next set is printed, this error is corrected. In such a case, the set with the blemish will be the more valuable of the two, for many of the incorrect ones are destroyed or lost. The value, too, will increase with age. Now, how would stamp-collecting advance your knowledge you ask in this way?. You get hold of a certain stamp, perhaps one which is not quite as familiar to you as some of your other specimens. Where is this unknown place, you wonder? You turn to your atlas, and if you continue with your hobby, there will soon be few places on the world about which you do not know. You may probably want to read about the countries of which you have the stamps. You will learn about the customs, the coinage, the people and so on. You will be led from stamp-collecting to natural history, geography, history, and you will love every minute spent on these subjects.

J.D.T., writing in the same newspaper in 1938, linked collecting stamps to Australian fauna.

> Stamp Collecting By J. T. D.[2]
>
> In subject collecting, one collects by design so that instead of labelling the album pages with the names of countries, they are headed with the titles of various subjects, such as birds, ships, explorers, etc. Such collections are always interesting because the dry-looking stamps are left out altogether.

. . .

Australian fauna stamps.

Let us imagine we are forming an animal collection, and what several cheap stamps show beasts. Why there are enough to fill pages from Australia alone. The new halfpenny stamp shows a fine kangaroo, a great improvement on those shown within a map of Australia on the earlier stamps. There is a 'roo, too, on all our King George V stamps at the side. Another one is shown on an issue of N.S.W., but it is rather hard to get, as this is the 1/ stamp of the series to commemorate that Colony's centenary in 1888. Our most important animal is the sheep; but, unlike the kangaroo which is found only on Australian stamps, he is honoured by several countries. Sheep appeared for the first time on our stamps in 1929, when the 3d. air mail issue showed a flock huddled together. while a plane passed over. Then in 1935, the Macarthur Centenary series showed a fine Merino sheep in a very similar design to our new 5d. stamp. The sheep industry is the most important in the Falkland Isles. The 1d. value of that Colony's Centenary issue pictures a fine Merino ram. More may be found on New Zealand and Argentine stamps.

Our Silver Jubilee issue showed King George V mounted on his favourite horse "Anzac." Other fine horses are on the stamps of Mongolia, Eritrea and Madagascar; but possibly the best is the Canadian 10 cent, showing a Mountie astride his fleet-footed horse; but we must pass on to the Koala, found only on our 4d. stamps. He is a loveable little fellow, and cries if he is hurt or frightened just like a baby. Completing animals on Australian stamps is the Platypus.

Well, this is a peculiar creature; it forms, in some respects, a link between the lighter mammals and the reptiles, a peculiarity being the hatching of its young from eggs laid in a burrow. Its bill is shaped like that of a duck, hence its other name of the Duckbill. This is only found in East Australia and Tasmania.

THIS LETTER from Jack Errington (Horsham, Vic.) Dec. 1928, is typical.

"Dear Pal. — This is the first time I have written to you. We get *The Weekly Times* regularly, and I always read the Australian Boys' Page, I am 11 years old and am in the 6th grade at school. I am recommended for my Qualifying Certificate. About 700 children are going to our school. I am collecting foreign stamps and would like to exchange about 10 stamps with another collector."

The word 'pen pal' was known to every Australian child born before the 1960s

Pen Pals

Exchanging stamps with other collectors encouraged letter-writing and, in its own way, experience in sharing and composing correspondence. Many children, especially those in remote communities, also collected 'pen friends', usually children of their own age and with similar interests. By all accounts, many were voracious writers. Newspapers often helped children find pen friends. Sadly, pen friends' hobbies have disappeared and been replaced by 'unsociable' social media.

COIN COLLECTING

Coin collecting was, obviously, more expensive for children than stamp collecting; however, many did, and some small fortunes were made. One feature of childhood, especially in the first half of the twentieth century, was saving small changes such as pocket money, possibly buying fireworks for 'Bonfire Night' or buying sample bags at the Easter Show. Collecting small change coins and notes from other countries was also popular, and most were pasted into albums, similar to stamp albums. Novelty money boxes, very collectible now, came in all shapes and sizes and were prized by young children to hoard their stash for a rainy day.

What better place to keep your pocket money?

Oxfam Kangaroo box and Koala Saver.

Politically incorrect and a reminder of past times.

LET'S MAKE A SWAP.

Collector Trading Cards. Collecting is often craze-driven, and swappable items had significant currency in schoolyards. In the early twentieth century, trading or swap cards featuring famous sportsmen and women were included in cigarette packs (that was a message in itself!), bubblegum, and biscuit packs, and were also available for purchase at department stores, motor garages, and news agencies.

Cards usually came in sets, and the aim was to collect the entire set. This meant swapping duplicates until a complete set was formed. The Godfrey Phillip's tobacco company produced several sets, including 54 cards featuring tennis greats. The card below features J. H. ('Gentleman Jack') Crawford, captain of the Australian team for the 1933 Davis Cup. He was the World's Number One player that same year.

G. Phillip's cigarette card featuring tennis player J. H. Crawford.
circa 1936-40

And to prove the early cards were an equal opportunity, another card, in the Turf cigarette 'personality Series' card No. 86, portrayed Marjorie Crawford, better known as 'Mrs Jack Crawford'!

She was also an Australian champion player. The fact Marjorie was listed on the card as 'Mrs Jack' suggests that she wasn't quite so 'equal'.

G. Phillip's cigarette card 'Mrs Jack Crawford'. Circa 1940. *Albury City Library.*

Nestle trading card circa 1930. *SLV*

The early cards, late nineteenth and early twentieth century, were predominantly for boys and mainly covered football, cricket, transportation, and military history. Fewer collector cards were marketed to girls and included historical and geographic cards. Children also collected the blank cards and jokers from standard card packs and used these for swaps.

A Hop, a Skip and a Jump 375

Dame Nellie Melba swap card. Ogden's Guinea Gold Cigarettes. 1900. *Museums Victoria*

The primary card issuers in Australia were usually associated with marketing products or services. Woolworths and Coles had their own ranges. Scanlan's Sweets, Mobil Oil, Sunicrust, Argus, Hoadley's, and Tip Top Bakery produced swap cards. Scanlen's sold theirs in milk bars from 1963 to 1991 and issued a yearly set.

A swap card from Coles. *Museum Victoria.*

In the Australian Children's Folklore Newsletter in 1991, James

Lambert discussed the difference between serious and non-serious cards.³

> I collected Weet-bix (and Vita-brits) cards when I was little, once even getting a whole set and sticking them onto one of those special posters ... The funny thing about these sorts of cards, as opposed to the cards obtained in packets of bubble-gum, was that there was not the same interest in them on a social level. No one ever brought them to school, no one ever swapped them or played games with them. You just seemed to have them at home. Come to think of it; they were usually of low interest regarding content - pictures of grubby old oil rigs or refineries, flax looms, an elephant in a zoo, some obscure butterfly - I think in an effort bro be 'educational'. Maybe this accounts for the seeming lack of interest as compared to footy cards, ABBA cards, and the most recent Neighbours and Teenage Mutant Ninja Turtles cards - the sorts of things you <u>don't</u> study at school.

Wrappers & Tops

The distinctive Juicy Fruit chewing gum package with the Wrigley's arrow. Introduced 1946. Mars.

Other manufacturers produced swappable items. The wrappers from 'Fantales', a chocolate-covered toffee introduced by Sweetacres in 1930, literally gave a brief biography of movie stars. The popularity of 'Fantales' has endured. In a straw poll of *The Canberra Times* newsroom in 1988, they emerged as the most popular childhood lolly, beating aniseed balls, humbugs, rainbow balls and cobbers. However, a Buzzfeed poll in 2014 put 'Fantales' at No.11, with 'Caramello Koala' coming out on top. Fantales wrappers still carry movie star biographies. One curiosity associated with wrappers was the wrapper of Wrigley's chewing gum range, especially Juicy Fruit and Spearmint, the two original products released by the American Wrigley company in 1892 and, later, P.K. gum, so called because of the initials of Philip K. Wrigley. Folklore had it that certain combinations of serial numbers printed on the wrappers could reveal a magic number, and if you found the winning combinations you received a lifetime's supply of chewing gum.

A modern Fantales wrapper with a biography of Tom Hanks.

After the School Milk Program was introduced in 1950, children started to collect aluminium bottle tops. They were not much good for anything except as Christmas decorations. Strung on a thread, they could be moulded to resemble Christmas bells. Collecting bottle tops off cordial and beer bottles offered more variety, and, as with all collecting, the further afield you collected, the more interesting the 'treasure' became. The *really* collectible milk bottle tops were produced to mark special events like Empire Day. These tops, featuring the British Union Jack, were treasured.

The fact that they were fairly useless as collectibles it didn't stop children collecting bottle tops and pressing them into different shapes. They were an early relative of the equally useless 'pet rock'.

Butterflies & Bugs.

Collecting butterflies and bugs is another hobby that has all but disappeared. Maybe it tells us something about ecology.

Yesterday's child would collect ants, locusts, butterflies, grubs, tadpoles and even flies, imprisoning them in old jam jars. While some bugs are caught and preserved for scientific purposes, some collections are just weird. One of the strangest must be the capture of tiny stink beetles and blowflies in a hollowed-out cork with pins pressed down to resemble a small prison cell.

Autograph Books

Collecting autographs was, and to some degree still is, a popular pastime for boys and girls. In this celebrity-driven world one could be excused in thinking autograph 'hunting' has become easier. But increased security has made big-name hunting more difficult. However, determined hunters know that persistence often pays off. In years gone by, children maintained an autograph book mainly for their friends. They were often used at school's end, and many entries are affectionate reminders of good times and forget-me-nots. Smartphones now capture these memorable moments.

Autograph albums first appeared in significant numbers in Australia in the 1830s and 40s, increasing in popularity in the sentimental seventies and elegant eighties when they were considered 'quite the fashion'. The custom appears to have originated in the mid-sixteenth century in Europe, with university students carrying a small leather-bound album to record the comments and hopefully approving sentiments of their patrons, protectors, companions and comrades. Students travelled widely then, and a book of hand-penned references was of practical value and a pleasant sentimental pastime. Albums then moved into the parlours of Europe, particularly Britain, and history.

An old man writing in a popular journal in 1873 reminisced:[4]

> Those who can look back for half a century will remember the rage there was in their youthful days for albums.... legion was not a name multitudinous enough for them; literary men crouched under their tyranny; young maidens wielded them as rods of iron... Splendid books they were in their day, bound in rich morocco and gold, and often containing contributions from Scott, Moore, Montgomery and Praed; whilst Prout's beautiful sketches adorned their pages side by side with other artists.

The anonymous observer names four of the most famous literary figures of the English-speaking world who were often quoted in diaries, newspapers, and magazines. They were seen as symbols of civilisation, and any respectable man or woman was expected to know their passages and witticisms. They were also quoted in autograph albums.

With the advancement of book printing and binding in the late nineteenth century, autograph albums became affordable and widespread. They were seen as a 'craze' and continued their popularity into the mid-twentieth century.

Albums came in all shapes and sizes; however, the standard was approximately 8" x 7" with a decorative cover, usually inscribed as 'Album' (remember these are pre-photographs), and containing blank pages. Autograph albums were considered quite personal and, unlike diaries, they were maintained to be viewed by others. Many owners made considerable effort to customise their albums, especially in decorating the covers and often the page borders. These sometimes included heavily stitched sewing, hand-coloured dyes and paintings.

Albums are relevant to folklore because they show us sentiments, and much of the verse is what we would classify as traditional. Many are drinking toasts that have found themselves on the paper page. They also tell us about the changing social times and often refer to significant events (like wars) or new inventions (like gas or electricity). Every album strove to be different to reflect its owner's tastes, circumstances and personality. The following autograph book was found in a garage sale in Darlinghurst, Sydney, and belonged to a young girl named 'Maggie'. The album commenced on 1st January 1908 and is inscribed 'To dear Maggie – from her loving sister Florrie'. The last entry was in 1916.[5]

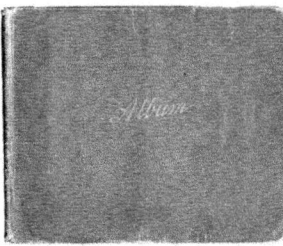

Maggie's (of Chatswood) autograph book. *AFU*

Maggie of Chatswood's album indeed tells us about Maggie and her friends. The following verses and comments have been included. It's worth noting the number of original verses, rather than the traditional florid and sentimental verses.

> If on this page you chance to look,
> Just think of the writer and shut the book.

The opening page advised the reader of the owner's intent:

> Yes, this is my album,
> But learn ere you look,

> That you are expected to add to my book;
> You are welcome to quiz it,
> The penalty is you add your own 'auto'
> For others to quiz.

Many of the verses were used repeatedly, and one assumes that some contributors simply wrote the same lines in every autograph book they were offered.

> You asked for something original,
> I scarcely know where to begin,
> For there's nothing original in me –
> Unless it's an original sin.

Understandably, expressions of friendship are a major subject.

> If scribbling in albums
> Friendship endures,
> With the greatest of pleasure,
> I'll scribble in yours.

> You'll find it will be best
> To meet with smiles, the pleasant glance
> And think all friends are true,
> And never trouble trouble, till trouble troubles you.

> Old friends are better than new ones
> Old faces are always the best –
> But a heart that battles with sorrow,
> Is better than all the rest.

> Make new friends but keep the old
> New ones are silver but old ones are gold.

> We live but in the present,

The future is unknown;
Tomorrow is a mystery,
Today is all our own.

The years roll by but friendship does not change.

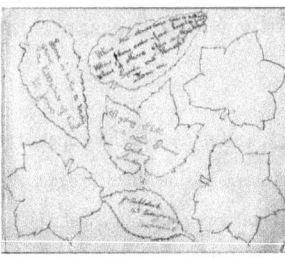

A typical 'leaf' page allowing further additions.

Witticisms, puns and old chestnuts were popular:

Here's to the love that lies,
In a woman's eyes,
And lies, and lies, and lies.

Laugh, and the world laughs with you
Weep, and you weep alone.

God made man
The man made money
God made bees
The bees made honey
God made the devil
The devil made sin
God made a place
To put the devil in.

Always speak well of the dead.
That's all very well as it goes,

> But why not extend it to these
> Who have not yet turned up their toes?

One of the most quoted ancients was Omar Khayyam:

> Come, fill the Cup, and in the Fire of Spring,
> The Winter Garment of Repentance fling;
> The Bird of Time has but a little way
> To fly – and lo! The Bird is on the Wing.

Euripides also got a guernsey:

> Were all certain nothing would be sure
> Joy would be joyless of misfortune-free
> Were we all wealthy, then we are all poor
> And death, not being life, would cease to be.

Henry Wadsworth Longfellow:

> Labour with zeal we will,
> Something still remains undone,
> Something uncompleted still,
> Waits the rising of the sun.
>
> Our God a tower of strength is he,
> A goodly walls and weapon,
> From all our need He helps us free,
> That now to us doth happen.

And, of course, 'anonymous' was ever-present to offer worldly advice:

> Straight is the line of duty
> Curved is the line of beauty,
> Follow the straight, and thou shall see

The curved line ever follows thee.

Try to do the little things as if
They were great and important
Try to do disagreeable things as if
They were pleasant.
Lived in this spirit, life becomes true service.

The above was typed on the page (which must have been difficult) and signed and dated 1915.

Three men went shooting one day –
The blind man saw them,
The man without arms shot them,
The man without clothes put them in his pocket.

The album's pages were printed in folio sheets of various pastel colours (light browns, greys, blues, greens, etc), and some pages had transparent sheets to separate drawings. There were 164 pages in the album (hand-numbered by the owner).

Original drawing accompanying verse

This world is full of beauty
As the other world above
And if we did our duty

It might be full of love.

There are many gods,
There are many creeds,
The paths they wind, and wind,
But the one old way,
Of being kind,
Is all this sad world needs.

The wise old crow lived in an oak
The more he heard the less he spoke,
The less he spoke the more he heard,
Why can't we all be like that bird?

There is no such thing as fighting on the winning side,
One fights to find out which side is the winning side.

Work as though you may live forever,
Live as though you may die today.

Traditional drinking toasts were often used:

Two's company but they were three,
The Girl, the parlour lamp and He,
Two's company there's no doubt,
That's why the parlour lamp went out.

Here's to the wings of true love,
May it never lose a feather,
Till your old boots and my old boots
Lay under the bed forever.

Many a shaft at random sent

Finds fully many a mark the archers never meant

And many a word at random spoken

May soothe or wound a heart that's broken.

Here's pain to our sham friends

But champagne to our real friends.

Here's to the man who kisses his wife

And kisses his wife alone,

For there's many a man kissing

Another man's wife

When he ought to be kissing his own.

May you live as long as you want to

And never want as long as you live.

Here's to a long life and a merry one

A quick death and a painless one,

A pretty girl and a loving one,

A cold, cold drink, and a then another one.

There is so much good

In the worst of us.

And so much bad

In the best of us,

That it hardly behoves

Any of us to talk

About the rest of us.

Here's to the heights of Heaven,

Here's to the depths of Hell,

Here's to the girl who can have a good time,

And has sense enough not to tell.

Boots go on feet; so do men,

Boots have soles; so do men,

Boots sometimes get tight; so do men,

A boot will shine, if polished, so does a man.

Some boots are imitation calf; so are some men.

Boots are tanned; so are men in their youth.

A boot when old gets wrinkled and hard, so does a man.

A boot to be of much account must have a mate;

So must a man.

The less understanding there is in a boot the bigger it feels,

So it is with a man.

And 'Shorter' responded with:

Chew me this, chew me that,

And chew me a pound of mutton fat.

A friend in need is a friend indeed.

And others played on words:

I have never met 'Miss Wisdom",

But I have often met misfortune.

The following verse appears to contain the names of several friends as plays on words:

Why doesn't Mabel Love me?

Why doesn't Phyllis Dare

Why can't Pauline Chase me?

We'd make a matchless pair.

I cannot Marie Studholme

She's rich, 'they say', I'm poor,

Now my trouble's doubled,

I cannot Carrie Moore.

Maggie's moments from her trip to England, 1913.

Some pages were drawn up to allow short contributions inside a border. These included pages with two-inch leaves or squares where several people could contribute. Some of these simply had a signature and date. These show how 'Maggie' had visited England just before WWI with Mr H J Miles, noting 'you left from Kent on the 28th February 1913, for Australia'.

THERE WERE SILLY VERSES TOO:

>Remember me in the river
>Remember me in the lake
>Remember me on your wedding day
>And don't forget the cake!

>It was in a restaurant they met,
>Romeo and Juliet.
>Rome(owed) what Juli(et).

> May your life be as sweet as roses
> And your husband as meek as Moses.

One trick in 'Maggie's' album was a turned corner of a page where a lock of Lillian R Robinson's hair was sewn into the page with a pink thread. The lock was then surrounded with drawn lilacs along with the following verse:

> You asked for something original
> Something out of my head,
> As I haven't got anything in it,
> I'll give you what's on it instead!

Maggie's book with human hair stuck on page.

Another trick involved writing verse or surprise endings upside down.

> Two in a hammock
> Attempted to kiss,
> But all in a moment
> (This last line written upside down)

They ended like this!

The following was written upside down:

> I'm the girl who ruined your book
> By writing upside down.

Circular verse was also used so that the poem was written spirally or in concentric circles. Some carried the following verse:

> Round is the ring that hath no end;
> So is my love for you, my friend.

Another popular autograph album trick involved turning down a page corner and writing 'Strictly Private – for ladies only'. When turned over the page reads 'Sticky Beak!'

It was not uncommon for autograph albums to contain pressed flowers and petals. Rose and poppy petals were the most popular. Sometimes, these petals were given an extra boost with scent.

> On this leaf, in memory pressed,
> May my name forever rest.

Several pages in the book featured hand-drawn, pencil, and charcoal illustrations, as well as wash and oil paintings. This meant lending the album to friends so they could render the work. Once again, this removes the album from the realm of diaries, which, understandably, were hardly ever given to friends to read.

A garden setting with watercolours.

This drawing, with charcoal, shows the steamship 'Lusitania' sinking. The inscription reads, 'When I think of the 'Lusitania' I will always think of you' (1915).

Historical reference with the sinking of the *Lusitania*.

Bawdy verses were sometimes included, but they were appropriately tame:

Mary had a little lamb, which was always full of fun,
 And every time she stroked its head, it murmured, "You're the one."

In contrast, the Reverend S. M. Baker of St Peter's Rectory offered:

> God has His best things for the few,
> That dares to stand the test;
> God has His second best for these
> Who will not have the best.

Limericks were also popular. This one, titled 'Ingenious Young Stubble', appeared with a pencil-drawn illustration of the 'young Stubble' in his motor vehicle selling soap. One assumes the word 'auto' was a play on the autograph and automobile.

> A handy young fellow named Stubble,
> Made an 'auto' without any trouble.
> He went 'round selling soap,
> And he murmured, 'I hope,
> I can patent my little soap 'bubble'

> There was a young man of Perth,
> Who was born on the day of his birth,
> He was married they say
> On his wife's wedding day,
> And died his last day on earth.

Conundrums:

> Be thou my star in reason's night,
> Be thou my rock, in danger's fright,
> Be thou my guide 'mid passion's sway;
> My moon by night, my sun by day.
> Who is it?
> Answer?

And so too the 'battle of the sexes':

> She's a right to be saucy, a right to be smart,
> But she hasn't any right to break a man's heart;
> To the 'breaches of promise' she has every claim,
> But 'wearing the breeches' is a far different game.

Then there was the 'art of the autograph':

> Some write for fortune,
> Some write for fame,
> But I write simply to –
> Sign my name.

> This little book is like a cabbage patch
> Where every little hen must have a scratch –
> And so must I.

> May each page of your album be brightened
> By the grace that a friend's hand will lend
> And each day of your life's journey be brightened
> By the touch of the hand of a friend.

Without a doubt, the prized position in any autograph album was the very back page:

> I've read these pages over and over
> To see what others have written before
> And in this quiet little spot
> I write the words 'forget me not'

> Back here just out of spite
> These two lines do I indite.

> By hook or by crook

I'll be the last in your book!

In the 1950s, autograph albums witnessed a dramatic change. While it was still expected that they would include the sentiments and autographs of friends, it was becoming more important to collect signatures of 'celebrities'. This was especially important for young girls, and coincided with the launch of television, which put faces to many stars. It was also the birth of rock and roll and a newfound freedom that encouraged young women to 'hunt' stars. Many youngsters, autograph book in hand, waited outside the gates of the old Sydney Stadium (Rushcutters Bay) when it was the venue for the first 'big shows' presented by impresario Lee Gordon. Gangs of young girls, some not so young, waited at the stage doors screaming, crying and desperately waving their autograph books at Johnny Ray, Crash Craddock, Johnny O'Keefe and other stars of the period. Today these books have become popular collector's items.

The past fifty years have seen Australians, like most of the world, become celebrity-obsessed to the point where entire television channels (E Television) and magazines (Who, National Enquirer, etc) are published weekly to satisfy the seemingly insatiable market. Does anyone want to trade a Paris Hilton for a Don Bradman signature?

I'LL LEAVE the last word to 'Maggie.'

IF ON THIS *page you chance to look*
 Just think of the writer and shut the book!

13

MERRILY AROUND THE MAYPOLE

Maypole dance PLC Melbourne 1923

If you ask baby boomers about their worst school experience many will say 'folk dancing'. A weekly folk dancing session was an integral part of primary school education from the beginning of the 1920s through until the late fifties. It most probably wasn't all that bad at the time. However, the music usually was, and, besides, it was all somewhat awkward. Dances had names like *'Gathering Nuts in May', 'Take Me To the Fair'* and *'Gathering Pea Pods'*. They were mainly English and Scottish dances accompanied by a piano or from a set of recordings sanctioned by the Education Department. The Australian Broadcasting Commission participated with a weekly folk dance broadcast and publishing the dance steps in *Sing* magazine. The program's main justification was a post-WW1 interest in youth fitness. The highlight of the folk dancing year was participation in the combined school's Health Week Folk Dancing displays.

Folk dancing for Health week. Newcastle Sun. Oct. 1952

The following account from 1921 stresses its cultural relevance and how "the child today derives such unrestrained joy."[1]

'Folk dancing. Recapturing grace - Value of Gesture

The revival of folk dancing during the last few years has attracted much attention in England and America, and the joys of these old-fashioned occupational and other dances have also been recaptured in Australia. Folk dancing now goes hand in hand with physical education everywhere, and at the Teachers' College Miss Edna Fyfe is in charge of the physical training of infant school teachers. The curriculum includes rhythmic work, games, and folk dancing. Much is to be gained of a purely physical nature from the frequent performance of these dances, but advocates of their revival have realised that the old-time national dance is, on its own merits, far too good to be forgotten and lost. To appreciate the meaning of the dances it is essential to understand the part played by gesture, as language, in the development of the race. It is often thought that the alphabet was the starting point for language, but man communicated with his fellows by gesture long before he used words. This explains, to some degree, folk dances, for they are the expression of moods and emotions or stories told through the medium of action.

The dances vary considerably in character, and the most outstanding types are the love dance, the lively war dance, the solemn and stately religious dance. The last named was often the dramatisation of the life or work of a god, and undoubtedly many of the old dances, which to us express merely a joyous or solemn mood, were originally part of the ritual of these earlier religions. In the occupation dances all the villagers used to gather on the green or common— the butcher, the shoemaker, the miller, &c.— and each as he danced gave expression to the actions and incidents of his day's work. Some people sang as they danced, uniting the actions of the dance with the words describing the actions. This is the origin of "Jolly is the Miller" and "Oats and Beans and Barley Grows." It is curious to reflect that many of the games played now only by children were at one time enjoyed by adults as well. Every child knows the game of "In and Out the Windows," but few people know that this was once a serious marriage ceremony. The residents of either side of a street used to come out of their homes and stand, while the bridal couple danced in and out and finally came to their own home. Games and folk dances now have a well-merited place in the school curriculum. The simple steps are within the ability of even small kindergarten children, and as the children go through the classes, their freedom and grace increase, and they find it easier to master the more advanced and difficult dances. Folk dance gives body control, as few things do, and it teaches courtesy and thought for others. For it must be remembered that these dances and games, from which the child today derives such unrestrained joy, were danced many years ago by people who, before giving expression to their moods, knew the joy and sorrow of work and existence.

Folk dancing in Hyde Park for Education Week. *State Archive NSW*

FOLK DANCING IS STILL PERFORMED in kindergartens and primary schools across Australia, and, of course, there is a keen interest in folk dancing for adults. Today, folk dances from many nations reflect our multicultural society. Many schools hold an annual all-nations day where children are encouraged to attend school in the national dress of their original or family homeland. Displays of dancing are often part of the program. There has also been a resurgence of interest in dances that reflect Australia's colonial past, and school 'bush dances' have become a popular annual event. When rural communities gathered, these old set and couples dances were extremely popular in the nineteenth century. Many of the dances were versions of old English, Scottish and Irish dances; however, like the bush songs, they were Australianised. There are now resources, including recorded music, instructions and even YouTube videos for schools to teach these dances.

. . .

Merrily Dance the Maypole

Maypole at Federation opposite the Royal Box & Exhibition Blg, Melbourne, 1901. Robert Brain, *SLV*

Today, the Maypole is considered a historic children's dance and curiosity. It was performed at schools, playgrounds, and fairs for many years with much rehearsal and choreography. Both Boys (who danced clockwise) and Girls (who danced counterclockwise) participated. Most girls' dream was to be selected for the Maypole dance.

As part of the year of Australian Federation celebration – on May 11th, 1901, The State School's Demonstration had 10,000 Victorian schoolchildren from 57 metropolitan schools, including a choir of 5000 students dressed in red, white and blue, participating in 'one of the most interesting fixtures of the official programme'. Costumes added to the impact of the maypole. There were also 'flower and Highland' dances. *The Melbourne Age* called the performance 'A work of art, a monument to discipline, and a living lesson on the capacity of the 'nation of tomorrow'.

Australian schoolchildren spent days making fancy ribbons and bouquets for May Day. Many Maypole dances were part of Maypole Fairs.

Girls dancing the Maypole, Ryde. 1908

How to make and dance The Maypole.[2]

For this, a stout pole is put firmly into the ground, and the visible part is covered with a coloured calico. The top is surmounted with greenery and flowers, and lengths of coloured braid are nailed securely to it; these require to be shorter than the pole, and ordinarily, 15 pieces are sufficient. The girls and boys take hold of the braid with one hand alternately right and left, so that a boy faces a girl. One hand is placed gracefully on the hip, and all keeping time, two steps are danced to the right and two to the left. If the children can sing some pretty songs it makes the game all the more enjoyable.

The infamous education manual for folk dance

The Folk Dance Syllabus published by the Physical Education Branch of the sinister-sounding Department of Public Instruction was well-known to Australian teachers. It contained the instructions for no less than 87 folk dances divided into age groups. Infant grades danced to action songs like *Washing Day, Climbing Up the Hillside, Wallaby Kangaroo, Soldier Boy* and *Springtime on the Farm*. The titles of the dances are a clue to what the actions would have been. There were also some time-honoured nursery rhyme dances including 'Three Blind Mice', 'London Bridge is Falling Down', 'Polly Put the Kettle On', 'Pop! Goes The Weasel', and 'Pat a Cake'. (Doubtless mention of these dances makes some readers cringe.)

Step ye lightly as ye go.... heel to heel, toe to toe

Middle grades were introduced to dances 'from many lands' including, *'The Shoemaker's Dance'* (Danish), *'La Vinca'* (Italy), *'Village Fair'* (Dutch), *'Peasant Dance'* (French), *'Gathering Pea Pods'* (English), *'Reap the Flax'* (Swedish) and *'Circassian Circle'* (English). The Anglophile compliers of the syllabus seemed to have omitted any Irish or Scottish dances!

Upper grades tackled the *'Polka Piquce', 'Swedish Clap Dance', 'Durham Reel', 'Sailor's Hornpipe', 'Varsovienne', 'Brahm's Waltz', 'Rigs of Marlow', 'Bean Setting'* and something called *'The Rospiggspolka'*. In case you were wondering - no Australian bush dances were in the syllabus.

Morris Dance

The ancient English ritualist set dances of the Morris were also performed by schools (and adults) in the late nineteenth and early twentieth centuries. The dances were performed individually or as part of the Mummer's Play, where characters portrayed the 'doctor', St George, 'lawyer', etc., according to traditional stories.[3]

Morris Dance Team Albury High School 1905

In the 1960s bush dances were revived by their association with the Bush Music Club, Victorian Folk Song & Dance Society and the annual National Folk Festival. Groups like The Bushwackers, Mucky Duck Bush Band, The Colonials, Cobbers, Bushwazee and The Larrikins, further popularised the dancing and the revival of interest in Australian folk songs. Folk dancing, including bush dancing, continues to be popular at the annual National Folk Festival and other folk festivals across Australia.

Dancing the Highland Fling

CHILDREN ARE STILL DANCING their way across Australia. Dancing is pleasurable, sociable and healthy. Long may we swing, jump, sway and promenade.

Children's Gavotte. 1938 *Ipswich (Qld) Library Collection.*

14

VERY AUSTRALIAN SONGS, WAR CRIES & STORIES

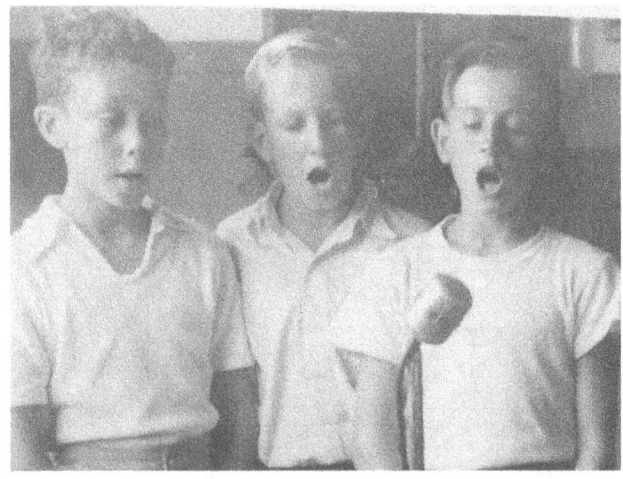

Coogee Public School singers. *State Archive NSW*

Yesterday's child would likely have sung 'Hoppity-hop, the kangaroo' or a song about the laughing kookaburra or Willy the Wombat. Today's child is likelier to sing a song from Disney's *Frozen* or Pinkfong's *Baby Shark*. Our world, of course, has changed dramatically, especially in the sense that we are inevitably caught up in what is loosely called 'world culture'. For many people this equates to a loss of individual national culture. A simple song about a kangaroo, however cute and handed down through the family, doesn't cut the mustard anymore. One of the worst outcomes of transient popular culture has been the devaluing of old songs, replaced with pop sound-alike tunes with mostly inane words that betray innocence. Frighteningly, the top ten children's songs of the last few years on the iTunes international chart were Kidzbop compilations with titles like 'Feel It Still', 'We Don't Talk Anymore' and 'I Don't Wanna Live Forever'. It's bad enough that the American labels cannot spell, but it's worse that Australian children are growing up with over-produced pop music that has little to do with storytelling or our own cultural story. This is also a story familiar to many adults. While it is impossible to bury your head, or in this case, ears, in the sand to escape the ever-rolling one-world culture (predominantly and often aggressively American), adults and children must remember that our Australian culture was and is different from America. Singing pop songs accompanied by tiny hips swinging seductively, aping the latest teen idol, may be innocent enough in a 'monkey see, monkey does' fashion. Still, surely children are better off singing about more child-appropriate subjects. Even the word 'childish' has been reduced to a put-down, as if being childish is somehow undesirable. The whole issue of young children growing up too soon is becoming increasingly sensitive. Thankfully, Australia hasn't adopted the American passion for pageants, a frightening concept where young children, mainly girls, are dressed like adult dolls, complete with ridiculously heavy makeup. One suspects these pageant entrants are an extension of the parents. Undoubtedly, the inimitable Dr. Freud would have had a field day with these folk.

Writing songs for children is quite a skill. What appears simple is often complicated. Children and adults generally react to songs differently than adults. Sure, adults get cynical or, more often than not, don't listen to the words. Many of today's songs are melody-heavy, designed for dancing or, at least, creating a particular atmosphere so the song itself fits a format, a pigeonhole for radio, internet description of the three-second 'grab', etc. Obviously, children's music changes to meet their needs as they age. Very young children like action songs. Then come story songs, followed by silly songs, then pop songs. Dancing songs are part of the progression; however, most boys bow out of these earlier than girls.

CHILDREN'S SONGS are also faddish. Australian children's music superstars, The Wiggles, have become successful because they have a stock of very workable songs, including action songs, and have maintained a healthy balance between celebrity and music. The songs are as popular as the personalities. Their bright primary colours have also been a key to their success. Before The Wiggles, Australian children's recording artists tended to be solo performers, whose personality tended to dominate the songs. Patsy Biscoe, Mike Jackson, Don Spencer and Peter Combe, all fine performers, were typically musically self-accompanied in a folk style, and their song repertoires, ranging from children's standards to original compositions, usually told Australian stories. The Wiggles came from a rock and roll background, formed from a band called The Cockroaches, and play a more rock-based style of children's music.

Much of The Wiggles appeal comes from their songs incorporating body movements - imitating the movements taught by the band members. It is a hugely successful formula and the group is regarded as an exceptional Australian exports. To witness a performance by the group is quite an event and the audience excitement undeniable.

Students of the Farrer School for the Deaf tune up their band. *State Records NSW*

Music has undoubtedly been influenced by television. *Sesame Street*, launched in 1969, prided itself of its contribution to aiding numeracy and spelling through phonetic games and humour. It also tackled social issues by reinforcing social differences using a range of wacky characters in sometimes even wackier situations. The Australian Broadcasting Corporation's *Play School* pre-dated *Sesame Street* by three years. Established in 1966, it is estimated that 80% of Australian preschool children under six watch the show at least once a week, and most watch daily. It has also been a positive force in childhood development and continues its role as a preschool educator. Incidentally, the show's theme music, 'There's a Bear In There', is an Australian composition by Rosemary Milne and Richard Connolly.

However the songs are presented, it is generally agreed that children's participation in music, especially active participation, can be extremely beneficial in improving behavioural and emotional development. Music is bonding, uplifting, and improves self-esteem. It can also aid numeracy and vocabulary development.

The roo jumped over the moon.

Stepping back in time one hundred and fifty years, way before recorded music and the radio, Australians were singing about Australian subjects. These were mainly story songs, many referencing Australian animals. Like the old bush songs, we rarely know who composed these, but we do know they were passed around by popularity, and, like the folk songs, they changed as they went from singer to singer. Some were published in newspapers and songbooks. They sound quaint by 'Bananas in Pyjamas' standards; however, they are a reminder that today's composers of songs for children continue a line that started long ago when people realised Australian children needed Australian stories in their world.

Students of Lochinvar Public School with their violins. *State Archive NSW*

Here's a sampling of *very* Australian children's songs.

NOAH'S ARK. [1]

(Tune: 'When Johnny Comes Marching Home Again')

Now, good old Noah he built an ark,

Hurrah ! hurrah!

And like a good old patriarch, Hurrah, hurrah!

He thatched it all over with stringy bark,

And pitched it all round to keep it dark,

And we'll all feel gay

When Noah comes marching home,

Now Noah the ark began to cram,

Hurrah! hurrah!

Assisted by Japheth, Shem and Ham,

Hurrah ! hurrah !

They put in the animals two by two,

From the polar bear to the kangaroo,

And we'll all feel gay

When Noah comes marching home.

There was the hippopotamus and the flea,
Hurrah! hurrah!
The elephant and the bumble bee,
Hurrah ! hurrah !
There was the cow with the crumpled horn,
And the cock that crowed them up in the morn,
And we'll all feel gay
When Noah comes marching home.

Hares, and rabbits, and foxes, and pheasants,
Hurrah ! hurrah!
And tigers, and adders, to make things pleasant,
Hurrah ! hurrah !
There was the glow-worm all serene,
And the lady's chignon with the Gregorian,
And we'll all feel gay
When Noah comes marching home.

There were owls, and bats, and mice, and rats,
Hurrah! hurrah!
Cockroaches, black beetles, dogs, and cats,
Hurrah! hurrah !
The fowls from above, and sharks from beneath,
With a couple of donkeys from Hampstead Heath,
And we'll all feel gay
When Noah comes marching home,

One day two bullocks were having a lark,
Hurrah ! hurrah!
When they butted a hole in the side of the ark,
Hurrahl hurrah!
Noah took a dog's nose to stop up the hole,
Which from that very night has been wet and cold,

And we'll all feel gay

When Noah comes marching home.

THE OLD MACQUARIE[2]

(Tune: 'One More River To Cross'.)

Noah, he built himself an ark

There's one more river to cross

He built it out of gumtree bark

There's one more river to cross.

Chorus: One more river

And that's the old Macquarie

One more river,

There's one more river to cross

The animals went in one by one

They all wanted to have some fun

The animals went in two by two

The wombat and the kangaroo

The animals went in three by three

The little bug and the frisky flea

The animals went in four by four

The buffaloes they got stuck in the door

The animals went in five by five

Some had children, and some had wives

The animals went in six by six

Some carried swags, and some carried sticks

The animals went in seven by seven

Some talked of hell, and some of heaven

The animals went in eight by eight

Some were early, and some were late

The animals went in nine by nine

Some in a circle and some in a line

The animals went in ten by ten

They had so much fun they said, 'Let's do it again'

Perhaps you think there's another verse - but there isn't!

Like the previous songs, this tall tale has a biblical reference; this time, it's Jonah and the whale.

The Wonderful Crocodile[3]

(Tune: 'End For End, Jack'.)

Now list, ye landsmen, all to me,
To tell you the truth I am bound,
What happened to me by going to sea,
And of the wonders there that I found.
Shipwreck'd I once was off La Perouse,
And cast upon the shore,
So I resolved to take a cruise,
And the country to explore.

Fol de rol, da riddle of a ray day
For the riddle of the ray day
With me for der rol da riddle of a ray day
For the riddle of a ray day.

But far I had not scudded out,
When, close alongside the ocean,
I saw something move, which at first I thought
Was all the earth in motion;
But steering close up along side,
I found 'twas a Crocodile—
And from his nose to the tip of his tail
He measured five hundred mile.
Fol de rol, etc.

This Crocodile, I could plainly see,
Was not of the common race;
For I was obliged to climb a jolly high tree
Before I could see his face,
And when he lifted up his jaw
(though perhaps you'll think it's a lie)

It reached above the clouds for miles three score,
And his nose nearly touched the sky.
Fol de rol, etc.

Whilst up aloft in this tree so high
It blew a gale from the south;
I lost my hold and away did fl
Bang into the Crocodile's mouth.
He quickly closed his jaws on me,
And thought to grab a victim,
But I popped down his throat, d'ye see,
And that's the way I tricked him.
Fol de rol, etc.

I travelled on for a mile or two,
Till I got into his maw,
Where I found of rum kegs not a few,
And a thousand bullocks in store.
Of life I banished all my cares,
For in grub I wasn't stinted—
In the Crocodile I lived ten years,
Very well contented.
Fol de rol, etc.

The Crocodile was getting old,
One day, alas! he died;
But he was three years in getting cold,
He was so long and wide.
Big skin was ten miles thick, I'm sure,
Or somewhere there about,
For I was full six months, or more,
In cutting my way out.
Fol de rol, etc.

But now once more I've got on earth,

> I'm resolved no more to roam,
>
> In a ship that pass'd I got a berth,
>
> And now I'm safe at home.
>
> Lest my story you should doubt,
>
> Should you ever travel near the Nile,
>
> Just where he fell, you'll find the tail,
>
> Of this wonderful Crocodile.
>
> fol de rol, etc

The next song was written in the 1950s by Stan Wakefield, a member of the Bush Music Club, Sydney.

THE SPARROW AND THE EMU EGG[4]

> There was a little sparrow, and he was out of work
>
> So he humped his bluey on his back and he set out for Burke
>
> He walked till he had bunions, then thought he would enquire
>
> And found that he had only got as far as Nevertire.
>
> He was hungry and so weary, he could hardly drag a leg
>
> When suddenly beside the track he spied an emu's egg,
>
> He popped it in his billy can to boil it for his tea,
>
> And by his Waterbury watch, he counted minutes three.
>
> And when the minutes three were up, he thought it time to stop
>
> So he took his little tomahawk and he cut off the top
>
> 'Twas a pity he boiled it, 'twould have been much better fried
>
> For when he stooped to sup it up, he tumbled down inside.
>
> And when he fell in to the egg, he to his sorrow found
>
> Three minutes wasn't long enough, and the poor little chap was drowned:
>
> The moral of this story is: if emu eggs you seek
>
> For supper, you should take great care and boil them for a week.

The next song is an Australianised version of an old British folk song. The British version has three huntsmen: English, Welsh, and

Irish. Only an Australian could have introduced a verse about a 'meadow cake'. Kids love a seemingly innocent song when something disgusting is introduced. [5]

THREE MEN WENT A-HUNTING

Three men went a-hunting to see what they could find,

The first the saw was a kangaroo that somebody had left behind,

The Aussie said, "It's a kangaroo" The Scotsman he said, "Nae"

"My god!" said Pat, "It's the biggest rat I've seen for many a year."

Three men went a-hunting to see what they could find,

The next they found was a porcupine that somebody left behind,

The Aussie said, "It's a porcupine"

The Scotsman he said, "Nae"

"My God"! said Pat, "It's a pin cushion, with pins stuck in the wrong way."

Three men went a -hunting to see what they could find,

The next they found was an elephant, that somebody left behind,

The Aussie said, "It's an elephant".

The Scotsman he said, "Nae"

"My god!" said Pat, "It's an animal, with its tail stuck in the wrong way."

Three men went a-hunting to see what they could find,

The next they found was a mother-in-law somebody had left behind,

The Aussie said, "It's a mother-in-law'"

The Scotsman he said, "Nae"

"My god!" said Pat, "It's a talking machine, and it's talking all night and day."

Three men went a-hunting to see what they could find,

The last they found was cow manure that somebody left behind

The Aussie said, "It's cow manure"

The Scotsman he said, "Nae"

"My god!" said Pat, "It's a rhubarb pie, with the crust all eaten away!"

Some imported songs, like the following, are relevant to the Australian story. The fear of young children disappearing in the wild bush was a real threat to early settlers. The bush was seen as a frightening place, especially for a child. It was possibly sung to children as a warning.[6] The song was published in England in 1866 and is based on the story of the Duff children lost in the bush near Horsham, Victoria, in 1864 and found alive nine days later.

BABES IN THE WOODS

Oh, my friends, don't you know
How a long time ago
There were two little children
Whose names I don't know?
They were taken away
On a cold winter's day
And left in the woods
I heard some folks say.
And they sobbed and they sighed
And they bitterly cried
'Til at last they grew weary
And lay down and died.
And the robins so red,
When they saw they were dead,
Took strawberry leaves
And over them spread.
Oh babes in the woods,
Poor babes in the woods,
How sad is this story?
Little babes in the woods.

The following song, recorded by Rob Willis from Lola Wright, was most probably learned at school. The original version was published in *McGuffey's Original Eclectic Reader* in 1830.

THE MERRY BROWN THRUSH

There's a merry brown thrush sitting up in a tree;
"He's singing to me! He's singing to me!"

And what does he say, little girl, little boy?
"Oh, the world's running over with joy!
Don't You hear? Don't you see?
Hush! look! In my tree,
I'm as happy as happy can be!"

And the brown thrush keeps singing,
"A nest do you see,
And five eggs hid by me in the juniper tree?
Don't meddle! don't touch! little girl, little boy,
Or the world will lose some of its joy!
Now I'm glad! now I'm free!
And I always shall be,
If you never bring sorrow to me."

So the merry brown thrush sings away in the tree,
To you and to me, to you and to me;
And he sings all the day, little girl, little boy,
"Oh, the world's running over with joy!
But long it won't be,
Don't you know? Don't you see?
Unless we're as good as can be."

AND IN A SIMILAR VEIN.

OH, LITTLE CUDDLY NATIVE BEAR

You're big brown eyes just stare and stare
And gum leaves are your favourite fare
Oh, little cuddly native bear
Trees you climb and perching there,
You go to sleep with never a care
To do the same I would not dare
Oh, little cuddly native bear.

I had a tree with blossoms rare
I have a garden you can share

So everyday I say this prayer
Give me a cuddly native bear.

MAGGIE, MAGGIE MAGPIE
Perched up in the tree,
High above the branches
Whistling merrily
Do you whistle early,
In the morning cool,
To wake us up for breakfast
And in time for school.

Here's another very Australian action song, 'Cuddly Koalas' set to the tune of 'Frere Jacques'

1 Cuddly Koalas,
Cuddly Koalas.
2. Possums, too,
Possums, too.
3. Wallabies and Wombats,
Wallabies and Wombats.
4. Kangaroos,
Kangaroos.

And what could be more Australian than the well-known singing commercial for Aeroplane Jelly? The product was launched with the commercial in 1937, and the song is still known. Parents teach it to their children, and it is sometimes even used as a lullaby. At least folks know the words!

I like Aeroplane Jelly, Aeroplane Jelly for me.
I like it for dinner, I like it for tea,
A little each day is a good recipe!
The quality's high, as the name will imply,
It's made from pure fruit, one more good reason why

A Hop, a Skip and a Jump 419

I like Aeroplane Jelly, Aeroplane Jelly for me.

SINGING IS ACKNOWLEDGED as a healthy and rewarding school activity. It is communal yet allows individuality, encourages comradeship, concentration, and memory, assists in understanding and appreciating melody, provides evidence of the potential of music, and, above all, is highly enjoyable regardless of ability.

We now acknowledge many music styles; however, this has not always been the case. Most school music was set by the syllabus 'mafia' and, frankly, in earlier times, was mostly dull, dull, dull. It largely consisted of twee English songs of a semi-classical style. This, of course, echoed the popular belief of the late nineteenth and early twentieth centuries that such classically-originated music was the only 'healthy' listening music and so-called 'popular music', especially vaudeville and, surprisingly, later, jazz, were evil music best left to the debauched. This might explain why so many school songs, sometimes known as school anthems or, in some religious schools, as school hymns, are texts praise God and encourage students to follow the righteous path of Christianity. One could comment that such intent is slightly misguided in today's multi-cultural and rationalist Australia.

Many ex-students recall their school songs with horror rather than affection. The musical settings were often turgid, and the verses were old-fashioned and difficult to remember. They didn't roll off the tongue, nor were they particularly enjoyable to sing. Most songs were sung at assemblies or special events, like the school year welcome or the annual prize-giving.

Occasionally, school songs divert from the norm using tunes like 'Click Go the Shears' or 'The Farmer's Boy'; however, the settings are usually hymns, marching songs or something like 'Jupiter' from the suite *The Planets* by Gustav Holst.

On the other hand, war cries grab anything from pop songs to bawdy army songs as their tune base and are all the more effective for it. Some songs and cries are short, others lengthy.

IT SEEMS that this collection is the first attempt to gather Australian school songs and war cries. If nothing else, it is representative. The school song tradition continues, albeit mainly for primary schools, where singing is still acceptable and not considered 'awkward'. Some senior-year private schools also persevere. War cries are another thing altogether as they are far more robust, often changed, sometimes bawdy, and primarily used in more raucous situations like sporting events. Some large schools have war cries for their different house colours or teams.

Not much has been written about school songs and war cries, but this personal account from 1927 contains many familiar themes.

SCHOOL SPIRIT FOUNDED by school songs and cries.[7]

> When a raw, first-year boy comes to a school, meets, for the first time, hundreds of new faces, and sees a totally new set of surroundings, it is some time before he becomes acclimatised and thoroughly contented. We can all remember that first nervousness, and how it was overcome. The Head smiled and told us of the spirit of the school. We, who had previously been most derisive of such things, were feeling the surge as patriots. The sports master told us of previous years, the successes and failures, and, unconsciously, we

assimilated the school background. He told us of the present first team; how they came; raw recruits, and were gradually moulded into good players. Not only were they good players, but they were good students. The first day we were taught the school song. Nervously at first but with increasing lustiness, we sang the song. One hundred boys, we were practically all strangers in the morning. In the afternoon, under the effect of community singing, the lusty shouting of the war cries, we hundred boys had a common feeling. We had been imbued with the spirit of the school. We had lost our diffidence, and we had started on our way to become good schoolfellows. What was the reason? Principally the school song and the war cry.

School Songs

School songs are patriotic-style songs typically sung at school assemblies, particularly on special occasions. They are primarily Victorian in origin and, therefore, sound rather twee to our blasé 21st-century tastes. Their words are also contrived, as is some of the poetic rhyme.

Most school songs still being performed appear to be those of girls' schools. It is common knowledge that boys feel uncomfortable singing, especially teenagers whose voices change with adolescence.

Unlike the war cries, these songs are usually taught in the school music program.

Teachers, typically on the frontlines of schools, recognise the importance of having Australian songs available. It is impossible to establish whether this request in 1910 was granted, but their suggestion is admirable.

SONGBOOK TO SMELL **of wattle and eucalyptus.**[8]

'The council of the Teachers' Association has decided to ask the Department of Public Instruction to compile a songbook under the supervision of a specially appointed committee for use in schools. These people who have had the privilege of going through our schools or who have listened to the songs sung on State and other occasions by our schoolchildren will readily, even jerkily, perhaps, admit that there is room for such an innovation.

The idea is to make the book smell of the wattle and the eucalyptus and to give Australian genius a chance. Let me write the nation's songs, and I care not who makes their laws, said someone a hundred years ago, and it still holds good.'

Stock and Station Journal's 1910 article suggesting school songs should 'smell of the wattle and the eucalyptus' was a great idea, but most school songs appear bogged down with meaningless, well-meaning cliches and dull tunes. There are a few exceptions and some even went as far as using folk song tunes - Lismore High School (A Thousand Miles Away), Tamworth High School (The Farmer's Boy), Andurama Public School (Click Go the Shears) and Hornsby Girls High (Vicar of Bray).

For an extensive sampling of Australian school songs, go to https://warrenfahey.com.au and search for Australian School Songs & War Cries.

WAR CRIES ARE FAR MORE GROUNDED, earthy and have a purpose.

Here are two war cries from my school days. They were sung at sporting events when I was a student at Marist Brothers Kogarah.

> One, two, three, four,
> Who do you think we're barracking for?
> Five, six, seven, eight,
> Who do we appreciate?
> Go…
> Hurstville, Hurstville,
> Yah, yah, yah,
> Ought to be, ought to be,
> Dipped in tar.

> Kogarah, Kogarah,
>
> Rah, rah, rah,
>
> Ought to be, ought to be,
>
> Dipped in gold

A war cry is a chant Australian schools use, typically in conjunction with sporting events. They are usually reserved for competitions outside of the school. Most cries are short, around eight lines. The shortness allows the war cry to be repeated ad nauseam – usually whenever the school scores or wins an event.

During the game, the war cry is often performed by the audience, rather than the players. The shortness also provides easy learning. Most war cries are not "taught" by schools and are an oral tradition.

The term "war cry" originated from the Maori tradition of New Zealand. When Australia was first settled, the Maori strongly- often violently -opposed the British and would employ their traditional war cries to scare the British away. This tradition lives on in the Haka, as performed by the ALL Blacks rugby team. These war cries must have made quite an impression on the British, who took them back to England and Australia and seemingly adopted them for their schools.

Many Australian school war cries still incorporate Maori-sounding words, although they are not necessarily real words. There are also Australian war cries incorporating Aboriginal-sounding language, which probably translates into bunkum.

Learning and performing a school war cry is an empowering experience for most children. It is communal, loud, exciting and bonding.

SCHOOL WAR CRIES were seen as vital to success in competitive sports, and supporters and players benefited from the endless cries. This rather exaggerated description from the nineteen-twenties summed up the feelings of the time.

. . .

School war-cry is vital factor in sport.[9]

School sport offers a study in psychology. Humans are always influenced by other human beings, both mentally and physically. The chain of influence stretches around the world in a continuous cycle that never ceases, something on the style of the sea serpent that the ancient sailors believed to be curled around the edges of the flat world with its tail in its mouth.

Not only school sport, but every sport is affected by lusty partisanship, though the school barracking has the most effect, as the players know intimately those who are vocally siding with them.

When Tom Jones, of XYZ College, first appears on the field for his side in the big match, with several thousand students, and their parents or friends either with him or against him, many conflicting emotions tend to make him a nervous wreck. There are those who are eager to seize upon his slightest mistake to jeer, and then there is the agonising nervousness due to the fear that he will make a fool of himself before his fellow collegians.

The game starts, and he is very very nervous, and liable to bungle; then the college cheer assails his ears, and his chest swells with the thought that he is one of a few to represent the dear old school. He is filled with a glorious patriotism, spurious perhaps, but it does its work. He plunges into the battle, not caring what happens to him as long as he carries the leather sphere over the line for the glory of the school.

When the glamour wears off after his first few games, a personal note intrudes — although he is still fighting for his school colours. Mary Smith and a multitude of the fair sex are watching him, and he swells his muscles and grits his teeth, inspired, similarly as the peacock, who struts his glorious plumage before the fascinated eyes of his lady love.

Still, first and foremost is the effect of other human minds on his, lending him strength to win. Tom Jones is the average school or college boy. — D.A.D.

A Hop, a Skip and a Jump

HERE IS a selection of Australian war cries.

Because they are primarily from the oral tradition, words might vary. It is not unusual to find a war cry, or at least a close variant, used in several schools, with only slight changes to identify the school.

> **War-Cry**
> Ero, Wero, Wero rum
>   Um stick a bubble on a zip bang colly wobble
> Stick to the green, white and blue.
>   Ecka Pecka wangi, eka dora whiskey
> Chillaloo, chillaloo wah
>   Wigga wogga, wigga wogga, zip bom bah.
> St Pat's, St Pat's. Yah, yah, yah.
> Who are — who are — who are we?
>   We are — We are SPC.
> Ginger beer; Ginger beer, pop, pop, pop,
>   St Pat's, St Pat's. Always on the top.
>   1938

St Patrick's Ballarat 1938.

SOUTHPORT SCHOOL, *Qld 10*

Tokio! Tokio!

Shav-en-us, gavin,

Pe Kinny, nish nah,

Lay Kinny Shin.

Kinny, Kinny, wuff-wuff,

Kinny, Kinny, Shah.

Southport! Southport!

Rah, Rah, Rah.

Tokio - Tokio!

Shavenus kavoo,

Come on Southport -

Red, White, Blue,

S-O-U-T-H-P-O-R-T;

Southport!

Tokio! Tokio! Tokio! "

NORTH SHORE MARIST BROTHERS, *NSW 11*

Igo Sego Opigo Ango

Chorem Chorem ante far

Race 'em chase 'em

We're the boys to pace 'em

Marist North Shore rah rah rah

North Shore rah.

DE LA SALLE COLLEGE, *Kingsgrove, NSW 12*

King Gee,

Col la!

Here we are!

We are the boys from La Salle – a

Bexley, Beverly, Riverwood, Nar -

We are the greatest near and far!

K-I-N-G-S we are!

Salle – a!

SYDNEY GRAMMAR. *NSW 13*

Alligator mince meat,

Crocodile pie,

V-I-C-T-O-R-Y!

Are we in it?

We say YES!

We are the boys from the S-G-S

G-R-A-M-M-A-R Grammar!

ENMORE BOYS HIGH. *NSW 14*

1, 2, 3, 4, We're the boys from En-more

ST. ALOYSIUS' COLLEGE, *Sydney. NSW 15*

Prefects: Aloysius One, Two, Three.

All: Who are, who are, who are we?

We are, we are, S-A-C,

Wallah, wallah, yes we are,

Aloysius, Yah, Yah, Yah,

B-L-U-E. Blue!

TENTEFIELD HIGH SCHOOL. *NSW 16*

Alligator, Crocodile, mince meat pie.

VICTORY.

Are we very good?

We say yes!!

We represent the T. H. S.

T. E. N. T. E. R. F. I. E. L. D.

Tenterfield

NARRABUNDA HIGH SCHOOL, *NSW 17*

Yah Yah, Ego Yah

Ego Warrego Ego Yah.

Ango Popigo Turramurra Wopigo

Orky Orky Blah Blah Blah.

Hoopra Hoopra Yak Yak Yak

Narrabundah, Narrabundah, Black Gold Black!

THE SCOTS COLLEGE, *Sydney.* *NSW 18*

Boom chicka boom!

Boom chicka boom!

Boom chicka chicka chicka

Boom boom boom!

TSC TSC here we are!

S-C-O-T-S

SCOTS!

SCOTS COLLEGE, FAIRFAX HOUSE. *NSW 19*

One a gamma, two a gamma, three a gamma, bang!

Winners or losers we don't give a hang!

Ninga ninja, hot potato, half-caste alligator.

Fairfax Fairfax, rami zen

F-A-I-R-F-A-X FAIRFAX!

ST JOSEPH'S COLLEGE, *Sydney. NSW 20*

Hoggity, Hoggity, Wish, Bam, Wop

Give it to 'em Buddy, Buddy

Give it to 'em hot

Pass the ball, Pass the ball

Tackle 'em true

Joeys, Joeys, Cerise and Blue.

J O E Y S Joeys!!!

> **NO "WAR CRIES"**
>
> Yesterday's G.P.S. sports did not produce the enthusiasm of past years— and no wonder!
> Schools were advised during the week that "war cries" were taboo. Consequently there was a chilled atmosphere.

Sydney Sun, 1929. Whatever happened? A ban on war cries?

AINSLIE PRIMARY SCHOOL, *Canberra. ACT 21*

Ainslie, Ainslie brave and bold

Ainslie, Ainslie dipped in gold

Telopea, Telopea dipped in tar

Telopea, Telopea, yah yah yah!

MILTON CENTRAL SCHOOL, *NSW 22*

Ulladulla, Boolangatta, Narrawallee, Yatte Yattah

Yatte Yattah, Yatte Yattah, Yah! Yah! Yah!

We see the big breeze down among the pine trees

M -I-L-T-O-N – Milton!

GOULBURN HIGH SCHOOL. *NSW 23*

Boom chicka boom, Boom chicka boom

Boom chicka chicka boom boom

Ha Ha Ha Here we are

High School High Schooll Ya Ya Ya

Digga digga hot potater, half caste alligator

Ram sham combinator Ha Me Sa

High School , high school

Ya Ya Ya

G O U L B U R N, GOULBURN

State Commercial School, *Brisbane. Qld 24*

Yahoo Eck, Yahoo Eck,

We are the girls of the Central Tech,

Yahoo Eck, Yahoo Eck,

Bee Tee Cee,

Yes we are.

Bomba Barramunda, Saratoga- shah

Balmarina Bandazima Wanganui-rah

Murra Murra Mittagonga, Wangaratta-rue

Come on commercial, White, Mauve, Blue.

Wesley College, Perth

Zeemalah Hah!

Ika bakka Ikka Bakka Ikka Bakka Da

Wesley Wesley Ra Ra Ra Ra!

We've got the house, (clap, clap)

We've got the team, (clap, clap)

We've got the Pep, (clap, clap)

We've got the steam (toot toot)

We've got the house, team, Pep, steam,

Cheering off the other teams.

RAH RAH RAH RAH-RAH RAH RAH RAH

Yeah, team !

Yanco High School

Woomera, Woomera,

Babilloo, Boomerang,

Crocodile, Kookaburra, Wombat, Orangutan,

Wee-HO! WAY-HO! Turrumunga Mine.

Quandong, Billabong, Gundabluey Pine.

Platipus, Emu, Wallaby, Roo,

Ibis, Vulga, the White Cockatoo!

Murraburra, Cowra, Colamine, Banko,

Bogavine, Narrabeen, Never say Wanko!

HOOPLA! HOOPLA! HA! HA! HA!

YANKO HIGH SCHOOL -

YAA! YAA! YAA!

CORRICK, CHRISTIAN BROTHERS HIGH SCHOOL.

Corrick, corrick corrickerika-era.

Here we are, here we are,

CBHS we are.

Tumbarumba, Gundagai, Murrumbidgee, bindieye.

REDLANDS SCHOOL

Who do you think we are?

Redlands the best by far,

We give our best in all we do,

Watch out, it is the Redlands crew.

HOLY CROSS, *Woollahra, NSW. 25*

Whereever we go,

People want to know

Who we are

So we tell them

We are Woollahra, might, mighty, Woollahra.

ST PATRICK'S COLLEGE, *Strathfield. NSW 26*

St Patrick's 1, 2, 3,

Rick Rack Rickety Rack

SPC are on the track

Blue black blue black blue black Gold

A Hop, a Skip and a Jump

Warrambee! Warrambee!

Strathfield Strathfield SPC

SPC

Who are, who are, who are we?

We are the boys from SPC

Yah Yah here we are

Pats boys Pats boys

Rah rah rah

SPC.

St. Patrick's College, *Strathfield, NSW.* 27

Rack Rack,

Rickety Rack

SPC are on the track

Blue Black

Blue Black Gold

Blue Black Blue Black Blue Black Gold

Worry Me, Worry Me

Strathfield, Strathfield, SPC

S - P - C

> **Sydney Boys High.** *NSW* 28
>
> Koomiti, Koomiti, Kara, Kara
>
> Koomiti, Koomiti, Kara, Kara
>
> Eh-up, Eh-up
>
> Up, Up, Koomiti – High!

> **Sydney High School.** *NSW* 29
>
> Koomati Koomati Kara Kara
>
> Koomati Koomati Kara Kara
>
> Higgerty Piggerty Hoop-a-roo
>
> Higgerty ,Piggerty, Mufferty, Wiggerty
>
> Koomati Koomati.
>
> HIGH

Albury High School, *NSW30*

Oompah oompah

Yacki, Yacki, Oompah,

Bluemella, Bluemella, Yah, Yah, Yah;

Ego yah, ego yah,

Anargi, Popargi, Urananagi,

Albury High School, yah, yah, yah;

Pom-tita pom, pom tita pom,

Hullah, hullah, umpa, hah,

Albury High School, yah, yah, yah.

Brisbane Boy's High

Aloomba Kaloomba by-a-duco

Winya Winya go go go

Karigal Karigal Nany-o-mar

Nurumbeta Burundarra tarra-kara-la

Go on College Green White Black

Ray Ray Ray

Rockhampton Grammar School, *Qld 31*

Kar-medi Kar-medi,

Kara Kara

Tin-ee-eye Tin-ee-eye

Tin-gan-gara

Hop-ee-go Hop-We-Go

Two to one Whop-ee-go

Whoska Whoska

Ya Ya Boska

Ork-eye Ork-eye

Bah Bah Bah

Grammar boys, grammar boys,

Yes we are.

Penrith Intermediate High School. *NSW32*

Kumata kumagaya rara kara

A Hop, a Skip and a Jump

Tinkita tonketa

Hura you mahara mahiti ta

Foketa fiti ta ra

Hoo-mate kumati tefiti ta ra

The precise origin of the war cry is not clear but it seems to be a corruption of a well-known Maori haka composed by the famous Maori Chief, Te Rauparaha, of Ngaati Toa (1768-1849). The haka is translated as follows:

> (Leader) it is death, death!
>
> (Refrain) It is life, life!
>
> (Leader) It is death, death!
>
> (Refrain) It is life, life!
>
> Here is the hairy man whose deed it is to make
>
> the sun shine!
>
> Together, all together! Together, all together!
>
> The sun shines!

The newspaper went on to publish the following explanation of the song verses and use of indigenous words.

> Penrith, Penrith, Penrith High!
>
> Warragamba, Yah!
>
> Wollondilly, Warragamba, Penrith on
>
> Nepean,
>
> Ooka, ooka, Kooka, Kooka—'roo—
>
> roo—roo!
>
> Kookaburra, Kangaroo, Warrngamba,
>
> Wallaroo,
>
> Toongabbie, Burrawang, Werrington,
>
> and Kurrajong,
>
> Hop, hop, hop! Jump, jump, jump!
>
> Altlora Altlora! Penrith High! Yah!

NARANDERA HIGH SCHOOL, *NSW 33*

Maijuma Maijuma. Ha, Ma Luan.

Ngara Ngara Wodangian

Gana Guridjar. Ni Garami Va?

Narungdoora, Narungdoora,

Narrandera.

Pronunciation:

Meyejooma, Meyejoona. Har! Mar Looann.

Oongarra, Oongarra Woddangiann.

Garner Uooridjar, Nee Garrarmee Var?

Marroondoora, Narroondoora,

Narrandera.

"As soon as I see my foe, he falls dead. This is because we stand together. My foe, I can't see you. Have you fled?" 'The text was put together by a member of the staff and the first three lines are genuine Aboriginal from Arnhem Land. The language of the local aborigines is unfortunately lost, except for a few doubtful phrases. Had the local tongue been available, it would have been used. As the war cry stands, two very slight phonetic alterations have been made in lines 2 and 3, to render the phrases easier to pronounce. Line 4 is the traditional spelling of the supposed origin of our word "Narrandera" "Narungdoora" has been variously translated, and the sad truth is that the meaning cannot now be stated definitely. Mr. George Gow derives it from "narung" — "lizard' and "doora" — 'spear,' and gives the well known legend of the native who speared a lizard in this vicinity. Surveyor Woolrych is quite definite that 'narung' means 'jew-lizard' and 'derra ' means 'place of.' An Australian Museum ethnologist says that 'narrandera' means simply 'goanna.' Doubtless still other interpretations have been given, but we have not seen them. It is merely worth noting that trained linguistic observers were very scarce last century and that tradition in these matters is seldom reliable.'

St. Mary's High School, *Penrith. NSW 34*

Alcheringa, Wairiapendi.

Blor Gum Jones,

Blor Gum Jones.

Minnie Smitha, Willie Schmidta.

Podkachooka, Podkachooka.

Kuala Lumpur, Kuala Lumpur.

Kim Khoo Ka.

Pod-E-Eartha, Pod-E, Eartha. Allawah.

The first line represents the name of a boy, Bill Jones, which becomes "Gum" Jones in typical Australian nickname style.

"Alcheringa" and Wariapendi" are Australian aboriginal (Arunta' tribe) for "spirit land" and "we , go seeking".

Then come the English Minnie Smith and the German Willie Schmidt (with the poetic licence "a" added to provide rhythm.

"Podkachooka" is a combination of Central European names, similar to a combination of names belonging to students who have attended the school.

"Kuala Lumpur" is Asian, as is "Kim Khoo Ka, which uses the name of a Malayan exchange student who was first dux of St. Marys High School.

"Pod-E-Eartha" represents the "seed of the earth" that comes to rest at St. Marys (denoted by the last, drawn-out word, "Allawah"—Australian aborigine for "camp here").

HURLSTONE, *Sydney. NSW*

Hurlstone, Hurlstone, yes we are

Cheer-o-woka, cheer-o-woka ego hah,

Anthrophotheguy, Kings of Hurlstone

Warrah, warrah, yah yah yah

Cheers for the hoopra, hoopra, hoopra

Tap-a-go-yah!

HURLSTONE AGRICULTURAL COLLEGE, *NSW35*

Anthropopagai. Taranaka Wopagai.

Orkie Orkai.

Here we are. ....

Yah Yah Yah

GRAMMAR MELBOURNE. *Vic.*

Jingle bells, jingle bells

Grammar boys are here,

We're here to fuck your women

And drink up all your beer

So come on all you fuck wits

Come put us to the test

'cause we're the boys from Grammar

And we are the fucking best!

MT BEAUTY, *Vic.*

Leader: Where do we come from?

All: Mt. Beauty!

Leader: Wadda we sleep on?

All: Thistles!

Wadda we eat?

All: Snakes!

Leader: How do we eat 'em?

All: Alive!

All: Beauty! Beauty! ya, ya, ya,

Eat 'em, beat 'em, ha, ha, ha,

Green, Gold, always bold,

Knock 'em, drop 'em, leave 'em cold,

Beauty, Beauty, yaaaa!

MCCAUGHEY YANCO AGRICULTURAL MEMORIAL HIGH, *Yanco, NSW.* 36

Woomera Woomera babaluke boomerang,

Crocodile, Kookaburra, Wombat, Orangoutang;

Wheeho, Whayho, Terramungamine,

Quondong, billabong, gundabluey, pine;

Platypus, Emu, Wallaby and Roo,

Ibis, Brolga, White Cockatoo;

Murrumburrah, Cowra, Coolamon, Banko,

Boggabri, Narromine, Nevertire, Yanco;

Hoopra, Hoopra, Ha, Ha, Ha,

Yanco High School, Ya, Ya, Ya.

BRISBANE STATE HIGH SCHOOL, *Qld* 37

Shhhhhhhhh . . . Wooo . . .

High school, war cry, 1, 2, 3!

High high,

High, high, high,

Oompa oompa

Ya ya ya,

Rik rik rik-a-tik,

High, high, high

Pilly willy wing, ping pong ti groo

High school, high school,

Blue, red, blue!

Oompah, oompah,

Stick it up your jumper.

Umpire, umpire,

Stick it up your jumper.

VAUCLUSE HIGH SCHOOL. *NSW 38*

Listen all and all beware,

Come and meet us if you dare,

We fear no one, we play fair.

Listen and we'll tell you why,

Loud and clear you hear our cry,

VAUCLUSE, VAUCLUSE, VAUCLUSE HIGH.

Kaitingi Kaitunga Puana Katu !

Kia-Ora ! Kia-Ora ! Kia-Ora Katu !

Kumani Kumani ! Kia-Ora ! Kia-Ora !

Kumani Kumani ! Kia-Ora ! Kia-Ora !

Hoopnatai Koopnatai ! Hoopnatai Koopnatai !

K-O-G-A-R-A-H, Kogaraaaaaaah!!!!

LOYOLA COLLEGE, Melbourne. Vic

Loyola is hot to go!

H-O-T-T-O-G-O

Awoo! Hot to go!

Awoo! Hot to go!

Laaaaaaaame.

Bombala Public School, *NSW 39*

Bom, bom, bom ; bom, bom, bom;

Bombala, Bombala, School on the hill ;

Bombala bom, we work with a will;

Bombala bom, we never stand still.

Who are, who are, who are we?

Bombala, Bombala, torn, bom, bom.

Waverley Christian Brothers, *Sydney NSW 40*

Lemonade! Lemonade!

Drink it from a tin!

Every time the "blues' go out

The 'Blues' go out to win!

Fort Street High School, *Sydney, NSW 41*

Rick!~ Rick! Rickety Rick!, And a Hooster, Hooster, Hey!

Hi Billy Wonga -

Hi Billy Wonga !

Hooster! Hooster! Hey!

Riz Raz! Riz Raz! Six Sam Bah!

Fort-street Fort-street

Yah! Yah! Yah!

Footscray Technical School, *Vic 42*

(Solo) Hey - . -- hey!

(Chorus) Hey! e - e - e - el

(Solo) Too no ma too carro meena !

(Chorus) Kia ora ! Kia ora he he hah!

(Solo) Oo - o- o - o -mpah!

(Chorus) Oo - o - o - o - mpah! Yacca

Yacca Ooo - o - o - mpah!

Bloo a metta bloo a metta

Yoh! Yoh! Yah!

A Hop, a Skip and a Jump

JUNEE DISTRICT SCHOOL, *NSW 43*

Yah Yah Yah! He, he, he

Marinna, Ivor. Old Junee,

Eurongilly, Wantabadgery,

Junee students all are we.

Murrulebalo. lllabo. Yathella

Junee District School, hah, bah.

Wattle. boomerang, kangaroo,

You will see what we can do.

Harefield, Reefs, and Wantiool,

Junee. Junee District School,

Kurrajong, billabong, Murrumbidgee,

Yah!

CROOKWELL RURAL CENTRAL SCHOOL, *NSW. 44*

Booma lacka, booma lacka,

bow wow wow

Chicka lacka," chlcka lacka

Chow chow chow, ...

With a ha ha ha, here we are,

CROOKWELL RURAL, ya ya ya.

Hi-to S.W.O.M. is nigh

Ricki tickt pop-i-gi

Yarra Yarra wobt wobt

Whiskers on his gobba gob

Ya...a...a

Yi go ya, yi go ya

Crook-well Rural, ya ya ya.

WAGGA WAGGA HIGH SCHOOL, *NSW*

Yacki Yacki, Ooprah,

Yacki Yacki, Oopray,

Yacki Yacki, Oopray.

Blue, Blue Blue.

Wagga High, Wagga High, yes, we are,

Tooma, Gumly, Heega, Yah.

Burrandana, Humula,

Currawarna, Rah.

We are Wagga High

Wagga Wagga HIGH.

St Anthony's School Toowoomba, Qld.

St. Anthony's School on Memory Street,

For God and School we do compete,

Our aim is to win, fair and square,

Faith and ability will get us there.

We all compete, fair and true.

St. Anthony's! St. Anthony's!

BLUE! WHITE! BLUE!

Sydney Tech High School, Bexley. NSW45

Boomalaka, boomalaka bow wow wow

Chingalaka, chingalaka chow chow chow

(Something...something) Who are we?

STHS Can't you see?

T-E-C-H Tech!!!

St Columban's College, Albion. NSW 46

Gogra Gogra Tanga

Looka Boolie Yamba Ga

Tayanuka tuka tuka

Go Columbans yah

Forwards backs tanga lock

Boolie boolie Yamba Rock

Boolie boolie Yamba ga

Blue Gold Blue

Streeton Primary, Melbourne, Vic. 47

Turn on the radio, what do you hear?

Condor, Condor, give us a cheer!

We're gonna beat them, bust 'em, that's our custom,

Gooooooo Condor!

SANDGATE DISTRICT STATE HIGH *Brisbane Qld 48*

Warra warra where are we,

Sandgate Sandgate by the sea,

Maroon and Gold

Colours glorious,

Flying bold and victorious,

IBIS IBIS never die

I believe in Sandgate High.

SUNBURY WEST *W.A. 49*

West is the best

All the others are a pest.

XAVIER COLLEGE. *Vic 50*

X.A.V.I.E.R.

Xavier, Xavier, 'Rah! 'Rah! 'Rah!

Rivo, rivo, 'Rick, 'Rick, 'Rah!

Xavier, Xavier

YAAARRR!

Hoorick Hoorah

When Xavier plays the Public Schools, excitement quite intense

Prevails amongst our barracks assembled round the fence;

They watch with blazing eyes the shifting fortunes of the fray

And urge their struggling comrades on, and this is what they say:

(Chorus) Hoorick! Hoorah! Hoorick! Hoorick! Hoorah!

Xavier! Xavier! Hoorick! Hoorah!

The battle may be hot - but whether 'tis or not,

It matters not a jot, O Sons of Xavier.

The Xavier players, when they hear their comrades' rousing call,

Buck in with all their dash and vim, and drive along the ball;
The barrackers, they feel a thrill that quivers through their soul,
As they behold the double flag spring up behind the goal:

The fortunes of the battle change, the Red and Black gives way,
Our broken ranks are driven back before the foe's array;
The hostile war cry surges up like thunder in the sky -
But quick we take the challenge up, and this is our reply:

The toiling ranks of Xavier hear again the battle cry,
And rouse themselves like warriors prepared to do or die;
They fling themselves into the fight, and soon the old refrain
Announces that they've lifted up the pair of flags again:

And so our noisy barracks behold their comrades play;
their wild emotions reflect the fortunes of the fray;
At times a whirling storm of joy comes sweeping through the throng.
And then their feelings find relief in a burst of their war song:

The tumult of the struggle dies, the fight at last is o'er,
Our sturdy representatives are marching back once more.
A rousing welcome let us give to those who fought so well,
By sending out one parting shout that beats the old school bell:

>Aaaaaaaaaaaa…..way in a manger,
>No crib for a bed,
>The little Lord Jesus,
>Stood up and He said,
>X.A.V…I.E.R
>Xavier, Xavier, 'Rah!, 'Rah!, 'Rah!
>OOOOOooooooo
>Xavier, Xavier, 'Rah!, 'Rah!, 'Rah!
>AAAHHHH

LEWISHAM CHRISTIAN BROTHERS HIGH SCHOOL, *Sydney. NSW* 51

Yarangabie Yarangabie Yarangabie Yaronga

Tarrawarra Tarrawarra Tarrawarra Tonga,

Mullimbimby Mullimbimby Ya mun Doo

Lewisham Lewisham Blue Gold Blue.

Ya Ya ingo Ya,

Ingo popigo Tullawarra wopigo

Ya BOSCO!

C, B, H, S, Lewisham.

St. Joseph's College, *Nudgee, Brisbane. Qld*52

Hokatika Hokatika – wish bam whap

Ingo buddy buddy – give it to 'em hot

Pour the boot, Pour the boot

Tackle 'em true

Nudgee, Nudgee – blue white blue.

Wesley College. *Melbourne. Vic*53

Wesley Wesley zim-bah

Wesley Wesley yah yah

Wesley, Wesley, Wesley, Wesley,

Yah yah yah!

(But is was said so fast it usually came out:)

Wezza wezzazim-bah

Wezza wezza yah yah

Wezza wezzawezzawezza yah yah yah!

St Pious, *Chatswood. NSW*

Wood Chatta Wood.

Wood Chatta Wood.

Wood Chatta, Chatta Chatta,

Wood Wood Wood.

Sizza Boom Bah.

Sizza Boom Bah.

Chatswood, Chatswood,

Rah Rah Rah

Canna Canna Woof Woof,

Ricka-Racka-Roo

Chatswood, Chatswood,

Blue – Gold – Blue

C-H-A-T-S-W-double O – D,

CHATSWOOD!

Kurri Kurri, NSW

Hopetoun Colour

We're Hopetoun,

We're Hopetoun,

We're royal blue,

We're gonna hypnotise

And paralyse the other crew.

H o p e t o u n

Hopetoun - yeaaaaah.

Lismore High School

Yay yay ibba ibba wagga wagga

Whiskers on ya gobba gobba

Santa hoppa ganda,

Rick rick rickety rick,

Rick rick hooray.

Longreach School of Distance, *Queensland*

Billabong Billabong far and wide

Boree Coolibah side by side

Yackamunda Yackamunda Rah Rah Rah

Distance Ed, Distance Ed, Best by far - L - S - 0 - D - E

Distance Ed Boree Om Om Om Chicka Bom

Om Chicka Bom Chicka Bom Bom Bom

Standing tall above the rest

We will always do our best Sizza bom bar

Sizza bom bar Boree ! Boree !

Best by far B - 0 - R - E - E

Coolibah Coolibah, Coolibah, rah, rah, rah

Look out everyone here we are

Boom - Chukka, Boom - Chukka,

Coolibah Boom - Chukka,

Boom - Chukka, best by far

Bahicool, Bahicool, Bahicool bah

We are the coolest, so ha! ha! ha

REDLANDS, *NSW*

Here we go!

Redlands

Here we go!

(clap, clap, clap)

(repeat again and again and a again....
(Chorus) Redlands, let's hear you shout

Telling all what we're about;

Come on Redlands, let's hear you scream!

Strive to achieve what others dream.

(Response)

Do you know what we're about?

Or do we need to give a shout?

Redlands HEYA Redlands HEYA

Redlands the best by far!

KATOOMBA HIGH SCHOOL[54]

(Tune: Hurrah! Hurrah!)

Ice cream, chocolate, banana split

We think <insert other team's name> is up to...

SHIFT to the left and shift to the right

Stand up, sit down, fight fight fight.

STUARTHOLME SCHOOL, *Toowong, Qld*[55]

(Parody - Stuartholme Girls On Gaou)

All through the city

All through the city, there's been a lot of talk,

About the Stuartholme girls and the wa-ay they walk.

Wooowoooo!

They walk through the city,

Lookin mighty pretty,

Talkin 'bout the mighty, mighty re-ed and gold!

I said: Hey, On Gaou, hey, hey, the power

Hey, hey, the beats gonna step on your feet..

Wooooooooooo

Step on your feet …Wooooooo.

Clap your hands (two claps)

Stomp your feet (two feet stomps)

Get on down to the Stuarthome beat

(body/hand percussion on legs)

RAMSGATE PUBLIC, *NSW*

Ramsgate, Ramsgate, don't be slow,

Be like Elvis and go, man, go.

KOGARAH HIGH SCHOOL. *Sydney. NSW.* 56

One , two, three, four,

Who do you think we're barracking for?

Five, six, seven, eight,

Who do you think we appreciate?

KOGARAH!

Kogarah, Kogarah, yar yar yar

Ought-a be, oughta be,

Dipped in tar.

Ramsgate, Ramsgate, brave and bold

Oughta be, oughta be

Dipped in gold.

BLUE MOUNTAINS GRAMMAR

B.M.

B.M.G.

B.M.G.S.

LETS GO!!!

(sung to the tune of 'Botany Bay')

If had the wings of an eagle

And an arse that's as black as a crow

I'd fly to the top of the goal post

And shit on the (boys school name) below.

Miscellaneous taunts

Catholics, Catholics,

Ring the bell

While the Proddies[57] go to hell

(response)

Publics, publics,

Ring the bell,

While the Catholics go to hell.

(yell) Catholics stink!

(Sung to the tune of 'Botany Bay')

If we had the wings of an eagle,

And an arse that's as black as a crow,

We'd fly to the top of the goal post

And shit on Grammar below.

similarly

My old man, he told me,

Beda started HIV

With a nick nack paddy whack... etc

(similarly *to tune of This Old Man*)

My old man he told me

(the boy's school) started HIV

With a nick nack paddy whack... etc

Jingle bells, Jingle bells

grammar boys are here

we're here to fuck your women

And drink up all your beer

So come on all you fuckwits

Come put us to the test

'cause we're the boys from Grammar

And we are the fucking best

House Colours

School teams are typically grouped under team names and colours, with blue, red, and gold being the most commonly used colours. Each colour has its own war cry and chants used in competition. Inevitably, especially with older students, some unsanctioned and bawdy verses appear.

Here is an example of a school House War Cry. For an extensive sampling of Australian school house war cries go to https://warrenfahey.com.au and search for Australian School Songs & War Cries

Wagga Wagga High School, *NSW*

One, two, three, four,

Who do you think we're barracking for?

Five, six, seven, eight,

Who do we appreciate?

(shout) House Name

Rah rah ree,

Kick 'em in the knee

Rah Rah rass

Kick 'em in the other knee

What do we eat?

What do we eat?

Wolf meat! Wolf meat!

How do we like it?

How do we like it?

RAW! RAW! RAW!

Pork chops, pork chops

Greasy, greasy

We can beat *(other team)*

Easy, easy!

Don't mess with the best coz the best don't mess

Don't fool with the cool coz the cool don't fool

Go yellow o o o go yellow

Sittin' on a bandstand, bangin' on a tin can,

Who can? We can.

Nobody else can win (clap-clap-clap)

Win (clap-clap-clap)

Come on (team name), let's win (clap-clap-clap)!"

Oxley, Oxley,

In the bin,

Macquarie Macquarie further in,

Cook Cook on the top,

Here comes Sturt to squash the lot.

Insults

Children delight in insults, especially if chanted in unison. Any point of difference is good fodder. These days, most insults would be deemed bullying, although, in yesterday's Australia, they were mostly considered good-natured fun. These rhymes, for obvious reasons, were not condoned by the schools! In the third chant, the reference to 'frogs' most probably meant condoms - 'French letters', 'frangers' or 'frogs'.

Catholic dogs

Swim like frogs

(a dish of holy water)

Proddie dogs

Jump like frogs

Trying to get out of the water

Catholic dogs

Sit on logs

Eating chocolate out of frogs.

Protestant cats

Sit on mats

Eating maggots out of rats.

In and out of the water.

Sargent's Pies 58

Sargent's pies are full of flies,

With maggots in the middle.

Anything that runs, jumps, crawls or flies,

That's what they put in Sargent's pies.

PMG 59

PMG Pig's meat and gravy

PMG pigs must grunt

Marching into school.

Most readers will remember marching into class either to the sound of the school band or a taped recording. The whistle or bell would sound, and you were expected to rush to your designated area on the parade ground, ready to be called to attention. Often, the headmaster or a senior teacher would address the school before a whistle blew or the music commenced, and the school would march off to class. The music ranged from the predictable Sousa to Wagner.

The 'Colonel Bogey March', a British composition of 1914, appears to have been a favourite for many primary and secondary schools. Students, of course, are ready to parody them all.

> Bullshit, that's all the band could play..
> Bullshit!
> They play it night and day,
> Bullshit, it's always bullshit
> It's only bullshit our band can play.

Reg Byrnes recalled the same tune at Bass Hill Primary with the following verse.

> Hitler had only one left ball,
> Goering had two but they were small
> Himmler had something similar
> And poor old Goebbels had no balls at all.

Jane Harding also reported the same tune with the following text as sung at Mentone Girl's Grammar, Victoria. David Allan Dunbar had the same rhyme; however, Listerine was replaced with kerosene. Comet was a powder cleanser similar to Bon Ami.

> Comet, it makes your teeth go green,
> Comet it tastes of Listerine,
> Comet it makes you vomit,
> So have some Comet and vomit today

Sound Off!. Christine Zaninovic-Mesic's school, St Michael's Infants, Casino, NSW, used a parody of the American song, usually associated with the USA Marines, 'Sound Off'.

> Got a good job for twenty-five bob
> And I kicked the manager up the gob, and I
> Left, left, left right left!

Sharon Casey reported that in the 1980s, the high school band would always play *Darth Vader's March* from *Star Wars* whenever the school principal appeared at assembly. It was a standing joke instigated by the school's music teacher and the band members. One wonders if the principal was ever in on the joke.

THE CONTINUING story of pop and parody.

Singing and dancing to pop songs has become a normal part of childhood amusement. In years gone by (and that generally means before television) children listened to children's songs. They were mostly folk-style story songs, rounds and songs about childhood things. A lot of them were rather meaningless and uninspiring. They were also not designed for 'serious' dancing. With television came programs that introduced kid's pop, sometimes referred to as kidz pop, which, in essence, was very similar to what teenagers and adults were listening to, but with less raunch. Music video programs and, later, entire music networks like MTV, took the music further. Certainly, looking back to the beginning of television and groups like The Beatles, the fans at concerts, airports and other screaming points looked very young. Over time, the raunchiness factor seems to have increased dramatically to the point where children as young as six bump and grind along with Beyonce, Harry Styles or Rihanna. Some of the lyrics they mimic would make the rest of us blush. Not that they always understand what they are singing.

Much of today's pop music is marketed to very young children. They are an important factor in music sales. Music, of course, is fashion and impressionable youngsters readily adopt the fashion of their idols. Some artists even design and merchandise clothing specifically to target children. Mini-Me is alive and kicking. Both girls and boys, usually not in the same group, will sing, do the dance steps and wear the fashion of their latest idol. Playgrounds are alive with the sound of junior dance, rap and hip-hop.

Pop songs are also parodied by children, possibly because they misheard sentences across the cultural divide between ghetto

America and our backyard. Sometimes, the songs are localised because they are far too American to be comfortable. Idols also go out of fashion and become the butt of jokes and parody songs. Parodies can also be taken from the internet, like 'Which BackStreet Boy is Gay?', a 1999 parody of the band's hit 'I Want It That Way'. Sometimes incorrectly credited to Weird Al Yankovic, the song had a widespread circulation in Australian playgrounds.

> **WHICH BACKSTREET BOY IS GAY?**
>
> I am, a liar, I should retire
>
> Believe when I say
>
> This Backstreet Boy is gay
>
> But fans don't wanna believe
>
> That I'm really gay
>
> But I say
>
> That this Backstreet Boy is gay
>
> CHORUS:
>
> Tell me why
>
> No one believes that I'm gay
>
> Tell me why
>
> The girls still wanna love me
>
> Tell me why
>
> I just want you to know that
>
> This Backstreet Boy is gay
>
>
> Am I a flamer
>
> Yes I am really
>
> I'm screwing AJ
>
> And this Backstreet Boy is gay
>
>
> Now can't you see I like big, tough, strong men
>
> All these girls just don't turn me on, no-oh
>
> I don't like women
>
> I need you to see that
>
> Deep down inside my heart

It's for my sweet boy

He's such a big stud

He is, he is, he is, he is

Don't wanna hear you say

He must be talking crazy

My Nick cannot be gay

I just want you to please say

Nick is a flamer

Tell me how

You think that I am not gay

Tell me why

You girls still wanna love me

Tell me what

What will convince you I'm gay

Don't say I can't be gay

Tell me why

You still won't believe I'm gay

You just saw me kiss AJ

Tell me why

You wanna be my girlfriend

When this Backstreet boy is gay

But wait, we're ALL gay!

15

PLAY SONGS, TAUNTS AND PARODIES

Ginger Meggs tambourine 1930s Leckie & Gray Toys. Photo: Mark Spalvin. *Courtesy Luke Jones, Australian Toys. A Collection (Melbourne Books 2019)*

The Australian playground is still alive with the sound of skipping, running, jumping and singing. A cynic would be tempted to add the sound of smartphones or, at least, children talking into them and messages being pinged.

It is up to state governments and individual schools to decide whether or not to allow access to smartphones during school hours.

Some require students to hand them in at the start of the school day, whereas others have relaxed rules. Some encourage the use of devices as learning aids. It is an unresolved debate.

Many schools implement a BYOD policy — Bring Your Own Device. The rationale is that smartphones have become an important tool for learning, and banning them would set education back a decade. Defenders argue that devices are now part of everyday life and early adoption strengthens the understanding of the user. Furthermore, devices have already become the primary teaching tool in most schools and are used for information gathering, documentation and connectivity.

The issue of cyberbullying is also relevant to any discussion of the use of these devices, especially during designated breaks and playtime. A quick survey of the local school will probably show that many students either use their smartphones or share videos, photographs, and games with their group. The older the child becomes, the more prevalent the use of devices in the playground is. The big questions relate to age—at what age do the majority jump from playing to becoming connected?

There is no question that we live in the information age; smart devices are integral to our lives, with more than half the world's population being connected to the Internet as of 2018. However, the real question is whether our enthusiasm to adopt all things 'smart' has made us dumber. In the case of children, when is the appropriate age to hand over the device? We now know that children are putting their hands out for mobile phones, tablets, etc, at an extremely young age. The fact that interactive games and storybooks are completely seductive must be considered. This decision, of course, is parental.

There is little doubt that the growth of smart devices is changing how children play. Some would suggest they rob children of essential aspects of their childhood, such as that they are growing up too quickly. Of course, the same accusations are made about other aspects of childhood, like the too-early adoption of fashion, make-up, tattoos, and piercings.

When smart devices started to become affordable and popular, most schools banned them; however, many relented under pressure, including from parents who wanted to 'be connected at all times (this is also a reflection of how adults have also succumbed to smartphones and other devices). Developments in education also called for wider use of devices in schools for teaching purposes. Nothing much was said about the playground, which, as we know, tends to be an organic development based on - leave it be, and it will eventually sort itself out.

Schools where smartphones have been banned during recess periods report the level of noise has increased dramatically as students return to interacting. Smartphone dependence has led to introversion and loss of social communication skills, which, in turn, have led to other social problems. Teachers, always at the frontline, know how crucial early socialising is to development and how, with peer pressure and subtle guidance, playtime, in its own way, is a vital part of the school learning experience.

So, what about the songs, rhymes and games? Yes, they survive, and yes, they are threatened, and yes, they are disappearing. There is no doubt we are becoming more passive in our day-to-day activities. While we were once a nation of people who entertained ourselves and each other, we are now accustomed to being passively entertained, mainly by the electronic media. It is also true that Australians do not sing as much as they used to. We have a history of singing, all sorts of singing, including at home around the kitchen table, piano or wherever, but this has been replaced in many homes by televsion. Although we do still (sometimes) sing, most children grow up with very little home music. Of course, there are exceptions to the rule, but generally, singing has been replaced by listening to broadcast music. Thankfully, kids are still encouraged to sing at pre-schools, kindergarten and primary schools. It has to be remembered that today's children's parents most likely grew up in the same situation, where recorded music was the norm.

Children want to sing and play, be physical, and be challenged. The younger the child, the more active the behaviour. Some would say this is simply part of the ageing process, but the fact remains that the transition age from playing to device-land is shrinking.

We also know that physical activity has reduced in proportion to the growth of Internet use. This is a problem for all Australians, not just children; however, it is particularly relevant to younger Australians who are developing problems of social interaction and obesity.

Most of today's playground songs are associated with activity games. Rhymes and chants for perennial favourites like skipping and clapping rhymes and rhythm keepers can still be heard; however, the creation and oral transmission of other songs is disappearing.

Collecting children's play rhymes in Australia started in the late nineteenth century when newspaper contributors, including letters to the editor, diarists and others, included rhymes from their own family history as curios. One significant contribution was Victor Daley's collection *Song-Games in Sydney* in the 1890s, published in *The Bulletin* in 1898. The first concerted collecting came with the visit of American Fulbright scholar Dorothy Howard in the nineteen-fifties and was then taken on, randomly, by amateur folklorists from the same period, primarily as their overall sweep of recording old songs. The major contribution was the 1969 publication of *Cinderella Dressed in Yella: Australian children's play-rhymes*[1]. This collection included many rhymes collected by other people, including the pioneer oral historian Wendy Lowenstein. Incidentally, Wendy, miffed that Turner had omitted several bawdy verses from the collection, privately published these in *Shocking, Shocking, Shocking*.[2] Later Australian collectors, many inspired by previous work and the 1969 publication of Iona and Peter Opie's now classic work *Children's Games in Street and Playground*,[3] actively notated Australian children's rhymes. The next major step was the publication of several collections edited by Dr. June Factor, commencing with *Far Out, Brussel Sprout*[4].

Playground rhymes are often mysterious things. Wendy Lowenstein, writing in the introduction to *Shocking, Shocking, Shocking*, noted, "As far as rhymes are concerned, children are both conservative and creative, in that they may pass on the rhymes of their ancestors, often virtually unaltered, and yet a new parody or rhyme will sweep from one end of the continent to the other with amazing rapidity, and relevant lines from one rhyme will become incorporated into others which continue to co-exist with the originals."

Bawdy or rude children's rhymes have been collected from Australian children for decades. Children like to shock and, as we know, pick up on words that adults often frown upon. Many are scatological; what was rude then is not necessarily considered rude now. These rhymes, often circulated in playtime and then repeated at home, mostly to amuse and shock parents, are like jokes that appear, disappear and eventually return for another round.

Wendy Lowenstein comments on children's ribald rhymes, " A child's idea of what is rude and what is amusing varies with age and personality. The Fat and Skinny rhymes appeal greatly to six to eight-year-olds, who tend to consider bottoms, panties and lavatorial matters both daring and amusing, but as they grow older, kids become more and more blasé until in their mid-teens, it is difficult to divide their rude rhymes and jokes from the adult tradition."

FATTY AND SKINNY

Fatty and Skinny had a bath

Fatty fell in and broke his arse.

Fatty and Skinny went to war

Fatty got shot by an apple core,

Skinny went home to tell his mom

But all he got was a kick up the bum.

Wendy Lowenstein explained that most children appreciate the distinguishing line between adult material and that which belongs to them. However, they do not usually agree on where such a line should be drawn.

Ian Turner, in the introduction of *Cinderella Dressed in Yella*, addresses bawdy playground material, saying, "What the rhymes in this collection reveal is that children, both boys and girls, from eleven or twelve onwards have ...a rough theoretical knowledge of sex, know that it is a taboo subject, and delight in mocking both the taboo and the adult preoccupation with sex."

Sadly, and this seems to be a reoccurring theme in this book, the reality that children are now growing up too fast, and much of what Turner and Lowenstein said about bawdy rhymes has changed. Children post nine or ten have virtually stopped reciting rhymes. Children also know about sex far earlier than children of the seventies, when both collections were published. Today, children think nothing of using words like butt, bum and fart and some of the best-selling books are about those very unsubtle subjects. Andy Griffith's *The Day My Bum Went Psycho, The Bum Book* by Kate Mayes & Andrew Joyner, then there's *The Fart Book, Fart Monster & Me, There's a Monster Under My Bed Who Farts, Walter the Farting Dog* etc.

Here is a small selection of playground rhymes, chiefly noted down by the compiler of this book, over the past fifty-five years. Like all folklore, they change over time and through transmission. Apologies if they are not quite the same as the ones you know.

BLOWING UP THE SCHOOL.

These rhymes are traditionally sung on the last day of term before holidays.

SCHOOLS OUT

schools out

teachers let the fools out

one went east

one went west

one went up the teacher's dress.

GLORY, GLORY, HALLELUJAH 5

We hit the teacher with a ruler;

The ruler broke in two,

So we hit him with a shoe,

And now he's black and blue.

No more teachers

No more books

No more teacher's dirty looks.

GLORY, GLORY HALLELUJAH 2

Teacher hit me with a ruler,

I hid behind the door

With a loaded .44

..and now there's no teacher anymore.

No more English no more French,

No more sitting on a cardboard bench.

No more spelling, no more sums,

No more whacks across our bums.

KICK THE TEACHER OUT THE DOOR.[6]

Twelve and twelve are twenty-four,

Kick the teacher out the door.

If she tries to come back in,

Throw her in the rubbish bin.

If she says, "Don't do that!"

Hit her with a cricket bat.

DECK THE HALLS WITH GASOLINE, 7

Fa la la la la, la la la la. Light a match and watch it gleam,

Fa la la la la, la la la la.

Watch the school burn down to ashes,

Fa la la la la, la la la la.

Aren't you glad you played with matches,

Fa la la la la, la la la la.

DECK THE HALLS WITH DYNAMITE.

Fa la la la la, la la la la.

Press the plunger, see the lights.

Fa la la la la, la la la la.

Now the school's a bunch of rubble.
Fa la la, la la la, la la la.
Aren't you glad you stirred up trouble?
Fa la la la la, la la la la.
Fa la la la la, la la la la.

ROW, ROW, ROW YOUR BOAT. 8
Gently down the stream,
Kick your teachers overboard
And listen to them scream

JOY TO THE WORLD 9
The school burned down
And all the teachers too
The principle is dead
We shot him in the head
And flushed him down the loo
And all the teachers too
And as all of this is very true.

JOY TO THE WORLD 2
the school burned down
And all the teachers died...
If you're looking for the principal
He's hanging from the flag-post
With a rope around his neck (etc)

ON TOP OF OLD SMOKEY 10
All covered in sand
I shot my poor teacher
With a green lackey band
I shot her with pleasure
I shot her with pride
I couldn't have missed her
She was 40 feet wide

I went to her funeral

I went to her grave

When people throw flowers

I threw a grenade

I went to her coffin she didn't look dead

I got my bazooka

And blew off her head

Her head went up

Her head went down

Her head went splat!

All over the ground

ON TOP OF OLD SMOKEY,

All covered with blood,

I shot my poor teacher with a .44 slug.

ROW ROW ROW YOUR BOAT 2

Gently down the stream

Tip your teacher overboard

And listen to her scream

NO MORE ENGLISH NO MORE FRENCH,

No more sitting on a cardboard bench.

No more spelling, no more sums,

No more whacks across our bums.

COME TO OUR SCHOOL, COME TO OUR SCHOOL. 11

It's a place of misery,

There's a teacher in the doorway

Saying, "Welcome unto thee."

Don't believe it, don't believe it,

It's a pack of dirty lies,

If it wasn't for the teachers

It would be a paradise.

BUILD A BONFIRE, BUILD A BONFIRE,

Put the teachers on the top,

Put the prefects on the bottom

And burn the bloody lot.

SCHOOLS OUT, SCHOOLS OUT, 2

Teachers let the fools out.

One went east, one went west,

One went up the teacher's dress.

KICK THE TEACHER OUT THE DOOR. 12

Twelve and twelve are twenty-four,

Kick the teacher out the door.

If she tries to come back in,

Throw her in the rubbish bin.

If she says, "Don't do that!"

Hit her with a cricket bat.

Bodily functions.

Children appear obsessed with scatological themes and entire books have been written on the subject. These are but a few examples of playground rhymes about bodily functions.

Ink, pink, pen and ink;

I smell a great big stink,

And it comes from Y-O-U.

HERE **I** STAND ALL BROKEN-HEARTED,

Pooed my pants and then I farted.

ARTY **F**ARTY HAD A PARTY

All his friends were there.

When Tutti Fruitti did a beauty

They all went out for air.

TAR RA RA BOOM DI YAY. 13

I'll take your pants away

And while your standing there

I'll take your underwear
And while your eating honey
I'll flush you down the dunny
And you'll come up again
A chocolate aeroplane

DIARRHOEA, DIARRHOEA
People think its funny
But it's really brown and runny
Diarrhoea, diarrhoea
No pain, no strain
Just sit, and let it drain

POOS AND WEES 14
Poos and wees
Jobbies and plops
Jobbies and plops
Poos and wees and jobbies
Poos and wees and jobbies
Jobbies and plops
Jobbies and plops.

MUM IS IN THE KITCHEN COOKING FISH AND CHIPS 15
Dad is in the bathroom sinking battleships

IF YOU'RE HAPPY AND YOU KNOW IT PICK YOUR NOSE 16
If you're happy and you know it pick your nose
First you pick it then you lick it and you roll it and you flick it
If you're happy and you know it pick your nose

A LITTLE PUFF OF WIND, STRAIGHT FROM THE HEART,
Travels down the backbone and generates a fart.
Now a fart is very useful,
it give the body ease.
Warms the bed in winter,

And suffocates the fleas.

WE WANNA WE WANNA WE WANNA WEE
If you don't stop for us we'll do it on the bus.
And in a little while it'll trickle down the isle.
And you'll get your feeeet wet

Oo ah oo ah oo ah
A man fell down the sewer
He pulled the chain and up he came
In a chocolate aeroplane

BEANS, BEANS THE MUSICAL FRUIT (THEY'RE GOOD FOR YOUR HEART) 17
The more you eat the more you toot (fart)
The more you toot (fart) the better you feel
So lets eat beans for every meal

AGA DOO DOO DOO. 18
Pick your nose and have a chew
If its nice pick it twice!
It is very good for you.

HAVING FUN FUN FUN
Flicking boogers at the sun
If the sun gets too hot
Then your boogers turn to snot!

Popular culture.

Today's children are influenced by popular culture - surprise, surprise - so were *yesterday's* children.

> **JAWS**
> *Peter had a fishing boat; the boat began to rock.*
> *Up jumped JAWS and bit him on the....*
> *Cocktails, ginger ales, 5c a glass,*

If you don't like it, shove it up your.....
Ask me no questions, tell me no lies
I saw five men doing up their
Flies are dangerous; bees are worse
this is the end of my dirty little verse

Television and radio commercials have a habit of entering folklore. A current example is 'Gummy Bears Are Chasing Me'. Based on a commercial for a children's jelly bear confectionary, this song has received widespread circulation.

Gummy bears are after me
One is red one is blue,
yellow one just stole my shoe.
When I get it back I'll sue.
Then I'll come and talk to you.
A B C D E F G
Gummy bears are after me,
One is red, one is blue,
One is peeing on my shoe.
Now i'm running for my life
Because the red one has a knife.
(Alternate verse)
Now i'm running even faster
Because the blue one has a blaster.
A B C D E F G
Gummi Bears are chasing me
One is red, one is blue
One is peeing on my shoe
Now I'm running for my life
'Cos the red one's got a knife

Waltzing Matilda
Who bloody killed her?
Found her in the grass

With a shovel up her arse

GINGER MEGGS, GINGER MEGGS,

What have you between your legs?

One fat sausage, two boiled eggs,

That's what you've got between your legs.

I'M POPEYE THE SAILOR MAN,

I live in a caravan,

With a hole in the middle,

Where i do my piddle,

I'm Popeye the sailor man.

I'M POPEYE THE SAILOR MAN, 2

I come from the isle of Japan,

I live with my Granny and tickle her fanny,

I'M POPEYE THE SAILOR MAN. *3*

I'm Popeye the sailor man,

I live in a jar of jam.

The jam is so sticky

It sticks to my dicky,

I'm Popeye the sailor man.

TEMPTATION, TEMPTATION, TEMPTATION,

Dick Tracy went to the station

Marilyn Monroe was there

Marilyn Monroe was bare

Temptation, temptation, temptation.

THE BOY STOOD ON THE BURNING DECK 19

The witness sat in the witness box,

Picking his nose in a fury;

He rolled it into little balls,

And flicked it at the jury.

I SAW YOUR MUM;

She opened up her legs;
I saw her bum;
It was hairy;
Not to mention scary.

ADDAM'S FAMILY

The Adams family started
When Uncle Festa farted,
The children were disgusted,
They stuck their dicks in custard,
The Adams family. Drop dead!

COLONEL SANDERS CAME TO TOWN
Riding on a chicken,
Stuck his finger up its bum
And said "It's finger-licking"

Captain Cook Rhymes.

CAPTAIN COOK CHASED A CHOOK
All around Australia
He lost his pants in the middle of France
And continued in his underpants.

CAPTAIN COOK DID A POOP,
Behind the kitchen door,
A cat came up and licked it up,
And asked him for some more.

CAPTAIN COOK HAD A POOP
On the coast of France,
His father tried to do the same
But did it in his pants.

Captain Cook chased a chook
All around Australia
Lost his pants in the middle of France
And found them in Tasmania.

Captain Cook, the dirty chook,
Went sailing up the river,
He struck a rock and spilt his cock
And left his balls to shiver.

Captain Cook chased a chook
Along the Murray River
He hit his cock upon a rock
and had the balls for dinner.

Captain Cook did a poop
Behind the apple tree;
A piece of grass tickled his arse
and made him do a pee.

Racist[22]

Children can be very cruel. Do they pick up on what they have heard their parents say? Is it an unconscious fear of the unfamiliar? Whatever the case children have used racist rhymes for decades.

Ching Chong Chinaman
Went to milk a cow,
Ching Chong Chinaman
Didn't know how,
Ching Chong Chinaman
Pulled the wrong tit,
Ching Chong Chinaman
Was covered with shit.

Me Chinese, me play joke,

A Hop, a Skip and a Jump

Me do wee-wee in your Coke.

THE NEXT ITEM is typical of physical racist insults.

> MY MOM IS CHINESE *(holds eyes up at the corners)*
> *My dad is Japanese (holding eyes down at the corners)*
> *But look at me! (holding one eye up and one down)*

INSULTS..

Children can be extremely cruel to each other. Yesterday, it was schoolyard taunts, and today, it extends to horrific cyberbullying. Schools and the government are developing programs to combat such antisocial behaviour, but one must question the negative influences on children when they regularly hear/see adults behaving badly, particularly on film. We all need to be nicer.

> ROSES ARE RED,
> *Cabbages are green;*
> *My face is funny;*
> *But yours is a scream.*

> I AM RUBBER
> *You are glue*
> *Anything you say bounces off me*
> *And sticks to you!*
> IP, DIP, DOG SHIT .
> *You're 'it'.*

Birds and Bees and other amusements.

Kids use rhymes because they are fun, and there's something magical and musical in parodies, ditties, and chants. Many, like Knock Knock jokes, are timeless, while others come and go and come back again in a changed format. Anything that can shock an adult is fun.

> TAR RA RA BOOM DI YAY,
> *I'll take your pants away,*
> *And while your standing there,*

I'll take your underwear,
And while your eating honey,
I'll flush you down the dunny,
And you'll come up again -
A chocolate aeroplane!

TAR RA RA BOOM DI YAY, 2

I met a boy one day,
He gave me sixty cents,
To lie behind the fence.
And there he laid me down,
And pulled my nickers down,
My mummy was surprised,
To see my tummy rise,
My daddy jumped for joy,
It was a baby boy.]

OLD MOTHER HUBBARD,

Went to the cupboard,
To fetch her poor doggy a bone,
But when she bent over ,
Rover took over,
And gave her a bone of his own!

LADY OF SPAIN

I implore ya
Pull down your pants
I'll explore ya
Lady of Spain, I love you.

THE LITTLE FLY. 23

There was a little fly and he flew into a store,
And he pooped on the ceiling and he pooped on the floor,
And he pooped on the lollies and pooped on the jam,
and he pooped all over the grocery man.

The grocery man he got his little gun,
To shoot that little fly on his little brown bum,
But before he could count t to five or ten,
The little brown fly poop-pooped again.

Milk, milk,

Lemonade.
Around the corner
Chocolate's made
(while pointing to your various body parts)

If you're happy and you know it pick your nose

If you're happy and you know it pick your nose
First you pick it then you lick it,
And you roll it and you flick it.
If you're happy and you know it, pick your nose

Ding dong dell,

Pussy's in the well.
If you don't believe me,
Go and have a smell.

Knock knock!

Who's there?
Bear.
Bear who?
Bare bum!

Knock knock. 2

Who's there?
A little old lady.
A little old lady who?
All this time, I had no idea you could yodel.

Knock! Knock 3

Who's there?

Voodoo.

Voodoo who?

Voodoo you think you are, asking all these questions?

KNOCK KNOCK 4.

Who's there?

Boo.

Boo who?

No need to cry, it's only a joke.

IF YOU GO DOWN TO THE WOODS TODAY 24

You better close your eyes

If you go down to the woods today

Your in for a big surprise

Cos mum and dad are having a jab

Uncle Bob is sucking his knob

And Aunty Sue is having a screw with Graaaandpa

WE MUST, WE MUST, WE MUST INCREASE OUR BUSTS

The bigger, the better, the tighter the sweater,

The boys depend on us

Up your nose with a rubber hose

Twice as far with a chocolate bar

Further than that with a cricket bat

CHEERS, BIG EARS

Same goes, big nose

Well said, dickhead"

And for a response in the affirmative

"You betcha bitchin' butt cheeks, babe"

Literary minds. From bawdy to puns.

This example was also used as a skipping rhyme.

Chapter 1, chapter 1, let's have fun

Chapter 2, chapter 2, I'll strip you

Chapter 3, chapter 3, you strip me

Chapter 4, chapter 4, lay on the floor

Chapter 5, chapter 5, open legs wide

Chapter 6, chapter 6, connection of the dick

Chapter 7, chapter 7, feels like heaven

Chapter 8, chapter 8, doctor at the gate

Chapter 9, chapter 9, nappies on the line

Chapter 10, chapter 10, do it all again!

Book Titles

The Yellow River by I. P. Daley

Something's Smelly by Who Flung Dung

The Baby's Revenge by Nora Titsoff

The Russian Doctor by Karl Kutchanakersov

The Pregnant Nun by Clerical Error

The Rush to the Toilet by Willy Makit (illustrated by Betty Dohnt)

The Cyclist by Isabella Necessary-on-a-bike

Timber by Teresa Green

Flooded by Helen High-water

INDEX

Explanation of index. This is not a definitive index. It is simply a reference guide to keywords. It does not mention games and amusements individually, although some, where they are part of the book's storyline, are referenced. The page number often refers to the first mention of the word. Otherwise, it would have driven the compiler crazy.

A-C

action games 171 - adams, eleanor 62, 70 - anderson, maybanke 195, 196 - australian children's folklore collection (AFFC) 80 - autograph books 378 - backyard wars 314 ball games 226, 234, 319 backyard shed 320 - - barnardo's 49 - basedow, herbert 56 - bates, daisy 65 - *banella*, baby ship 42 - bicycles, tricycles 342 - bib-bob 98 - big brother movement 49 - billycarts 351 - biloela industrial school for girls 33 - blake, aubrey 250 - blind man's buff, the bellman 88 - blind, deaf & dumb institute 38 - blood, marita, living rosary 252 - bloomfield, william 13 - blyton, lilo 98, 385 - board games 179 - bonfire night, guy fawkes, fireworks 255 - bottle tops game 377 - boogeymen 145 - books/reading 33, 179 - boomerang toys 72 - boreham, vonnie 98, 161 - boulton, rebecca 6 - brown paper games 107 - bush jewellery 292 - bush picnics 102- bushies and bobbies 93- butterfly, bug collecting 377

- campfire games, indigenous 64 - *canberra p&o* 47, 55 - chalk 28 - chasing, tag 91 - child convicts 2, 12 - child welfare organisations 55-58 - children on stage 327 - children's friend society 37 - children's pages in newspapers 157 - chomley, eliza 82, 249 - chuck penny, chuck farthing, chuck hole 25 - cockfighting, high cockalorum 313 - collecting 366 - coin collecting 371 - cole's funny picture book 104, 162 - collector trading cards 373 construction collectibles 367 - cork dolls 286 - conundrums 167, - corn dollies 288 - costume parties 327 - counting out rhymes 148, 230- - cowboys & indians 214, 337— crack the whip 220 - crossing the equator, crossing the line 40 - cubby house 322 - cup & ball game 29 - *cutty sark* 25

D-F

dancing, maypoles, folk 37, 78, 440-450 - davey, gwenda 81, 122 - digital play devices 301-310 - dawn magazine 116 - diaries 18 - dongers, clive james 202 - doll houses 278 - dolls 275, 290 - dressing up 326, 332 - edwards, ken 52, 60, 69, 70 - elastics 240 - elliott, arthur 219 - ellis, peter 379 - emigrant settlers 15 - *empress of ireland* 24 - facial games 173 - factor, june 122, 198, 238 - fairbridge children 48 - fairyland 329 - father christmas 42, 53 - finger knitting 292 - female factory 7 - female orphan institution 10, 39 - fetes 333 - finger games 172 - folk and other dance 398 - fortune-telling fish 243 - fowler, f 23 - fuller, meredith 104 - fullerton, mary 107-108

G-J

games for indoors 159 - ginger meggs 353 - gilmour, mary 55 -

golliwogs 280 - halloween 330 - hand games 225, 234 - hawkes, elizabeth 106, 357 215 - haycock, mary 3 - hayward, elizabeth 3 - haymes, john 322 - hide and seek 86 - hightown primary school study 237 - hills hoist 364 - hero worship 340 - hernandez, t 66 - holdswoth, willam 6 - holidays, christmas, easter 264 - honey game, indigenous 62 - hoop rolling 360 - hopalong cassidy 114-115 - hopscotch 29, 229 - howard, dorothy 81, 235, 458 - howell, robyn 54, 69 - - hudson, john 4 - hughes, michael 38, 92 -hula hoops 224 - hunting, treasure hunt 241 - i spy with my little eye 90, 156 - indigenous play 50 - insults 449 - *isle de france* 28 - jacks, knucklebones 97, 297 - james, clive 202 - jig-saw puzzles 98

K-M

kaleidoscopes 241 - kelly, doug 84 - kites 262 - knitted animals 293 - knitting, finger knitting, nancy, 292 - kookaburra sits on the old gumtree 152 - *lady Penrhyn* 6 - lambert, james 375 - land of make-believe 82, 84 - land of nod 188 - lees, meg 108 - little sailors 38, 337 - love, lyn 67 - lowenstein, wendy 458, 459 lullabies 120 - living rosary 252 - laurie, robyn 106 - magic lanterns 35, 246 - magic, hypnotism 248, 250 - making models 316 - mather, Anne 3 - marbles 304 - marching into school 450 - *marco polo* 21 - marshall, alan 56 - mary, juditha 84 - maypole 395 - mazzarino family 47 - memories of a queensland childhood 215 - meredith, john 93 - mickey mouse club, mouseketeers 338 - migrant ships 4 - milburn. thomas 8 - models & matchbox toys 317 - mischief 322 - moore, patrick 13 - monkey bars 261-262 - morris dance 402 - mountain devils 284 - mumblety-peg & knife games 310 - multiculturalism in play 153, 198, 236, 336 - musical toys 110

N-R

name play 174 - *new australia* 34 - *new himalaya* 43 - nonsense rhymes 230 - northern territory games 112 - nursery rhyme fair dressing up 332 - nursery rhymes 151 - outdoor games - paper toys 295, 296 - parlour games 212 - peg dolls 282 - park, thomas 49 - pen pals 423 - penzig, edgar 325 - pemberton's pools 100 - pig latin 176 - pen pals 371 - pet rocks 367 - physical games 93 - pin finger 312 - playtime in lean times 106 - play songs, taunts, parodies 508-576 - playground 190, 228 - playground diversity 254 - - playground movement 197 - playsongs, taunts & parodies 455 - port puer institution 10-11 - potato people 109 - preventorium institution for ailing children 31 - punch & judy 22, 244 - point puer 7 - ragged children's society 38 - rock paper scissors 226 - riddles 166 - roth, walter 58, 62 - reading 27, 186 - rhyming alphabets 176 - *royal mail alameda* 21 - russell, heather 226 - ryan, melanie 161, 203

S-T

sandman 145 - school songs and war cries 404, 420 - school at sea 50 - school world culture day 386-387 - seaside amusements 98 - secret language 175 - shadow puppets 244 - shanghai slingshot 211, 310 - ship's alphabet game 27 - simon says 218 - skating 347 - skipping 79, 99, 205, 229, 231 - spinning tops 224 - sport (indigenous) 69 - stamp collecting 369 - stanley, g, 60 - stilt walking 362 - sword fights 312 - storytelling, 188 - string games 206, 298 - string, string games, indigenous 59 - sunday school play 2, 18, 30, 35 - tableaus 251 - tag games 203, 222 - tag, british bulldog, cockylora, red rover - see tag games - technology 265 - teddy bears 280 - thomas, s 68 - tongue-twisters 169 - there was an old soldier from botany bay 171 - thomas, sue 83 - thornton, w. p. 96 - thumb fights 226 - tin plate toys 111 - tooth fairy 146 - toys, indigenous 66 - toyshops 104 - trick questions 185 - turner, ian 121 - twig toys 289

V-Z

vernon training ship 32 video games 265 — walker, alan 219- waltz, bernard 45- war cries 404 - white city pleasure gardens 101 - wignell, edel 233 -willis, rob 92 - wells, r 163 - wonder and excitement 240 - wonderland 101 - word games 155 - wrappers, lolly 376 - wroth, john acton 5

NOTES

1. All At Sea

1. Letter, Edinburgh University Library, Scotland,
2. http://purl.slwa.wa.gov.au/download/slwa_b1717677_1.pdf
3. https://convictrecords.com.au/convicts/boulton/rebecca/129143
4. Further reading: P MacFie & N Hargraves, 'The empire's first stolen generation', *THS* 6/2, 1999
5. J. L. Hotsky, M. D, Castlereagh-Street. *The Sydney* Oct 1834
6. *Sydney Gazette & NSW Advertiser,* Nov 1818
7. The Sydney Gazette and New South Wales Advertiser Jan 1833
8. Various advertisements from *Sydney Gazette & General Advertiser,* 1825
9. https://www.thesocialhistorian.com/female-emigration-australia/
10. https://www.parliament.vic.gov.au/vufind/Record/78265
11. *Daily Telegraph* Sydney, March 1897
12. *Sydney Sun,* Jan 1928,
13. *Southern Lights and Shadows: Being Brief Notes of Three Years' Experience of Social, Political and Literary Life in Australia,* London 1859
14. Northern Star, Lismore, 26 March 1906
15. Sydney Gazette 21 August 1808
16. A manuscript *Book of Games* compiled between 1635 and 1672 by Francis Willughby
17. *Book of Games* compiled between 1635 and 1672 by Francis Willughby
18. Sydney Gazette & Advertiser. Dec 1804
19. *Sunday Times*, Perth, September 1950
20. *Recorder* (Port Pirie Aug 1949
21. British migrants Robert and Maureen Hallam, 1969. Museum of Immigration, Victoria.
22. Interview with Warren Fahey onboard Seven Seas Voyager, 2018
23. *Moree Gwydir Examiner and General Advertiser* ,NSW, May 1914
24. *Weekly Times,* Melbourne Oct 1928
25. *Daily Telegraph,* Sydney Jan 1950
26. *The Argus,* October 1940
27. *The Courier Mail*, Brisbane, October 1937

2. Indigenous Play

1. Edwards, Ken. A Typology of the Traditional Games of Australian Aboriginal and Torres Strait Islander Peoples, 2012
2. Howell, Robyn "The History and Culture of the Ashford District". D. West. Government Printer 1983
3. Sydney Morning Herald, 15/3/1934

4. Gilmore, Mary. 'Old Days, Old Ways' A&R 1934
5. Basedow, Herbert, The Australian Aboriginal, compiled and edited by David M. Welch, second edition, Australian Aboriginal Culture Series no.8, 2012
6. Marshal, Alan. *The Dark People.* In Farwell and Johnston *This land of ours... Australia*, Angus and Robertson, London.
7. Roth, Walter, *Games, Sports and Amusements of the Northern Queensland Aboriginals*, 1902
8. Gilmore, Mary. ibid.
9. Howell, R. ibid.
10. Edwards, Ken. ibid
11. *Gundagai Independent and Pastoral, Agricultural and Mining Advocate*, Dec. 1926
12. *The Australasian* June 1902
13. Roth, W. ibid
14. Adams, Eleanor. Course extract reproduced in Australian Children's Folklore issue 9. November 1985.
15. Adams, Eleanor. Ibid 1985
16. Edwards, Ken. ibid
17. Mountford C. P. Nomads of the Australian Desert. Adelaide Rigby. 1976
18. Edwards, Ken. Ibid
19. Bates, D. Songs, Dances, Games etc. Daisy Bates Collection. National Library of Australia, Canberra, A.C.T., 1929.
20. Hernandez. T. ibid
21. Howell, Robyn "The History and Culture of the Ashford District". D. West. Government Printer 1983
22. A selection of Aboriginal children's games. Lyn Love. 1983. Anthropological Society of Queensland newsletter 1983
23. Thomas, Sue. Cited in Australian Children's Folklore newsletter Issue 19 December 1990
24. Love, Lyn. ibid
25. Howell, R. ibid
26. Edwards, Ken. Ibid
27. Love, Lyn. ibid
28. Damas, Eleanor. Ibid 1985
29. AIAIS Origins of AFL and Aboriginal ball games.
30. The Australasian. 17 August 1935
31. *The Register News Pictorial* (Adelaide) 26 Sept 1929
32. *The Daily Mail* (Brisbane) 16 Aug 1924

3. Playtime In The Bush and City

1. Museums Victoria website Australian Children's Folklore Collection - introduction written by Dr Moya McFadzean, Senior Curator of Migration & Cultural Diversity at Museums Victoria.
2. Eliza Chomley , *My Memories,* unpublished manuscript, La Trobe Library
3. Internet correspondence with Warren Fahey 2019.
4. Internet correspondence with Warren Fahey 2019.
5. Internet correspondence with Warren Fahey 2019.

6. internet correspondence with Warren Fahey 2019
7. Conversation with Warren Fahey 2019
8. Mary Fullerton, *Bark House Days,* Melbourne University Press 1964 (1921)
9. Mary Fullerton, *Bark House Days,* Melbourne University Press 1964 (1921)
10. oral history interview 2018
11. Lees, Meg. Private correspondence with Warren Fahey 2019
12. Meredith, John, recorded by Rob Willis, Thirlmere, NSW, August, 1992. Oral recording housed in the Rob & Olya Willis Collection, National Library of Australia.
13. Sydney Morning Herald, January 31 1953 W. P. Thornton
14. *The Queenslander* March 1911
15. Ibid
16. Boreham, Vonnie. Private correspondence with Warren Fahey 2019.
17. Internet correspondence with Warren Fahey 2019.
18. The Cumberland Argus Parramatta 14 Dec 1960
19. *Daily Telegraph*, Sydney, December 1915
20. Shepparton Advertiser, 28 February 1940
21. Australasian 26 April 1913
22. Australasian Melbourne 20 April 1918
23. *Northern Territory Times,* May 1919
24. https://en.wikipedia.org/wiki/The_Dawn_(feminist_magazine)
25. *The Dawn,* December 1904
26. *Albury Banner & Wodonga Express*, Jan 1919
27. *Australian Town & Country Journal,* Jan 1893.
28. Ibid
29. *Northern Star* Lismore NSW, 24 December 1920

4. Singing The Baby To Sleep

1. Cinderella Dressed in Yella: Australian Children's Play-rhymes.
2. Mss Collection. Mitchell Library/State Library of New South Wales.
3. *The Age*, Melbourne, 19 December 1942. Also known as 'Rock-a-bye-baby'
4. The Bulletin Magazine, Sydney, 30 August 1917
5. Perroux was a well-known photographer from Toowoomba, and Souter author of several books, including the 1933 publication *Bush Babies of Australia.*
6. *The Brisbane Courier.* September 5. 1931
7. By Eileen Clinch. *The Worker* (Wagga Wagga) 24 July 1913.
8. Maitland Mercury & Hunter River General Advertiser 15 Sept 1891
9. Daily Standard (Brisbane) 21 Jan 1928. The English 'Black Paternoster' seems to have spread widely in Australia and prompted several parodies and variants, always a sign of the tradition at work!
10. The Bulletin, Sydney, 3 June 1959. 'School Rhymes of 40 years ago'
11. The Sydney Mail & New South Wales Advertiser 15 Feb 1911
    J. L. Ranken
    Northern Territory Times Darwin 19 Aug 1930
12. By Eugene Field. *Illustrated Books*, Dept of Education South Australia, 1909. Deakin University.

13. written by American writer and poet Eugene Field and published in 1889. The original title was "Dutch Lullaby". The poem is a fantasy bedtime story about three children sailing and fishing among the stars from a wooden shoe boat. The names suggest a sleepy child's blinking eyes and nodding head. The spelling of the names and the "wooden shoe" suggest the Dutch language and names, as hinted in the original title. It has had numerous musical settings and circulation in Australia. This appears to be an abbreviated version.
14. *Australian slang (obsolete)* Excellent; wonderful. Related to bonzer.
15. The Central Queensland Herald (Rockhampton), Queensland, 31 December 1931
16. *The Bulletin* magazine, 1910
17. Truth, Sydney, 19 January 1936
18. The Daily Mail, Brisbane 26 July 1923
19. Townsville Daily Bulletin. 1 September 1928
20. Australian Woman's Weekly, 24 Dec 1938 Colin Wills.
21. West Coast Sentinel, Streaky Bay, SA, 25 Feb 1927
22. Bathurst Free Press & Mining Journal, 23 Oct 1852 ("from Punch")
23. The Bulletin, Sydney, October 1917.
24. University of Kentucky Press
25. A pretend action song
26. The Kookaburra Case. See www.warrenfahey.com.au
27. Davey, Gwenda. Australian Children's Folklore newsletter Issue 14 June 1998

5. Word Games

1. Internet correspondence with Warren Fahey 2019.
2. The Bulletin had a policy of accepting short contributions, under 300 words, for consideration in the magazine. Seeing your name in print in The Bulletin was a cause for celebration.
3. *The Weekly Times* (Melbourne) 1939
4. *Old Times* 15th January 191
5. *The Australasian*, Melbourne, 1904,
6. Old Times, Sydney, 1911
7. Boreham, Vonnie. Private correspondence with Warren Fahey 2019
8. Ryan, Melanie. Private correspondence with Warren Fahey 2019
9. *The Australian Journal*, June 1860-70
10. *Huon Times* (Tasmania) March 1933
11. Broadcast 15 January 1987 on ABC Radio National (2FC) Talking History program.
12. CID 15031.
13. Mudie, Ian. The Bulletin Magazine, Sydney. 3 June 1959
14. McAKerchar, S., Fremantle, WA. cited in Australian Children's Folklore newsletter Issue 22, 1992
15. Denis Tracey edited this book's manuscript! His mother's version, possibly from a film, included Q for the bus.
16. Australian Folklore Unit Collection 1974-9
17. (NLA)
18. a small spinning top spun with the fingers, especially one with four sides lettered to determine whether the spinner has won or lost.

19. NLA.
20. NLA.
21. NLA Collection
22. Private collection
23. Private collection
24. boardgamegeek.com
25. https://www.warrenfahey.com.au/rookwood-cemeterys-notable-residents/

6. The Playground

1. the *Evening News*, Sydney, August 1910,
2. the *Bendigonian*, Bendigo, Victoria, December 1917
3. *Brisbane Courier,* September 1912.
4. *The Sydney Morning Herald*, November 1913.
5. Maybanke Anderson, *The Sydney Morning Herald*, November 12, 1913:
6. *Daily Standard*, Brisbane, June 1918
7. The Age, Melbourne, May 1927
8. *Play & Friendships in a Multi-cultural Playground,* Heather Russell with Gwenda Davey and June Factor, 1986,
9. *The Age*, Melbourne, Mr Eager
10. Clive James, *Unreliable Memoirs*. Pan Books, London, 1980
11. Ryan, Melanie. Private correspondence with Warren Fahey 2019
12. Steve Roud in *The Lore of the Playground*
13. *Australian Town & Country Journal,* Sydney, 7 January 1903
14. *The Argus* (Melbourne) 13 August 1937
15.
16. the *Brisbane Courier Mail*. November, 1932
17. *The Argus* (Melbourne) February 1925
18. *Victorian Parlour Games.*
19. *Freeman's Journal*, Sydney, 10 December 1931
20. Hawkes, Elizabeth. Private correspondence with Warren Fahey 2019.
21. The Brisbane Courier, Queensland, 15 March 1911. Unattributed authorship.
22. *Hoc est corpus,* Latin for 'This is my body'. It may reflect the words of the priest pronouncing the consecration during Mass.
23. Correspondence Australian Folklore Unit
24. ibid
25. Ellis, Peter, Bendigo, Victoria. Cited in article 'Recollections of Bendigo High School in the 1950s'. Play & Folklore Issue 53 April 2010
26. Wikipedia entry
27. Published in Australian Children's Folklore Issue 9. 1985
28. 1,2,3 Hit It! Play & Folklore Issue 54 2010
29. Cinda 11026
30. Cin 12004
31. CIN. syd 1945
32. COIN 12006a Melb
33. CID 12009B.

34. Wignell, Edel, Burwood, Victoria. Cited in Australian Children's Folklore newsletter Issue 4. May 1983.
35. For examples of complete stump speeches refer to Warren Fahey's Australian Folklore Unit www.warrenfahey.com.au
36. CIN 13007a.
37. CIN The Witchdoctor 1962
38. CID 14010A Howard 1957
39. CID 14013 Howard 57
40. 2007-2010 Childhood, Tradition and Change. Funded by the Australian Research Council, with assistance from the National Library of Australia, Museum Victoria, the University of Melbourne and Deakin and Curtin Universities:
41. Extracts from the report: Australian Children's Folklore Publication, Institute of Early Childhood Development, Melbourne. Authors Heather Russell, assisted by Gwenda Davey and June Factor.

7. Wonder And Excitement

1. *The Queenslander* March 1911
2. Rosen, Bruce. Tasmania. http://vichist.blogspot.com/2006/09/punch-and-judy_25.html
3. Henry Mayhew London Poor
4. https://warrenfahey.com.au/bushranging-and-other-crimes/ Joe Watson sings 'The Ballad of the Kelly Gang' - Warren Fahey Collection, NLA
5. Eliza Chomley, *'My Memories'*, unpublished manuscript, La Trobe Library, pp.9-10,12-13,15-16
6. Audrey Blake, *A Proletarian Life*, Kibble Books, Malmsbury, 1984
7. How To learn Hypnotism, How To Be An Escapologist. Pamphlet sized booklets were frequently advertised in Australian newspapers and songsters.
8. *Newcastle Morning Herald and Miner's Advocate*, Feb 1954:
9. *Evening Star* (Adelaide) Nov. 1912
10. *Sydney Gazette 1924, Sydney Monitor May, 1928.*
11. *The Commercial Journal and Advertiser* (Sydney) Nov 1839
12. *The Cornwall Chronicle* (Launceston) Nov 1845
13. *The Australasian* (Melbourne) 5th Feb. 1921
14. *Sunday Times* (Perth) 3 Nov. 1940. Attributed to 'The Hobo'.
15. *Newcastle Morning Herald & Miner's Advocate*, May 1954
16. *The Sun*, Sydney, 12 January 38
17. *The Australasian* May 1929
18. *Draft Australian Sedentary Behaviour Guidelines for Children.*
19. Digital Australia. https://igea.net › Research › IGEA Research Reports
20. Scientific America, magazine. https://www.scientificamerican.com
21. https://en.wikipedia.org/wiki/Minecraft
22. https://en.wikipedia.org/wiki/World_of_Warcraft
23. https://en.wikipedia.org/wiki/Fortnite_Battle_Royale
24. Interview by Warren Fahey with Justice Single. Palm Beach 5.2018

8. Girls Will Be Girls

1. Collected from Meredith Lucas, Paddington, by Warren Fahey, Australian Folklore Unit Films
2. *Observer* (Adelaide S.A. in 1930.
3. *The Herald* (Melbourne) 1939.
4. Sydney Morning Herald, 31 January 1953. W P Thornton
5. *The Sydney Morning Herald*, November 1952
6. *The Evening News* (Sydney) March, 1926,
7. *The Brisbane Courier* (Queensland) April 1922
8. Queensland Times Ipswich 16 April 1929
9. Chronicle, Adelaide, 12 August 1943
10. The Sun, Sydney, 3 Sept 1944
11. The Queenslander. 24 January 1905
12. Australian Children's Folklore newsletter Issue 3 Aug 1982 - the account was given by Kathleen Gawler

9. Secret Boy's Business

1. Ellis Peter, Cited in Play & Folklore Issue 55 April 2011
2. (R. Rutherford, *Sunday Herald,* (Sydney) June, 1949)
3. Mary Fullerton, *Bark House Days,* (1921) Melbourne University Press 1964
4. According to this reference from *The Melbourne Punch,* June, 1872,
5. From Sir Joseph Verco, unpublished manuscript, Mortlock Library. S.A.
6. Lambert, James, Pennant Hills, NSW. Cited in Australian Children's Folklore newsletter. issue 20, September 1991.
7. *The Queenslander* April 1915
8. The Age Melbourne 28 Feb 1930
9. Haymes, John. private correspondence with Warren Fahey January 2020
10. Still Playing: Australian children's play, tradition and change in the early 21st century. Reported by Kate Darian-Smith in Play & Folklore Issue 56. October 2011.

10. Dressing Up And Down

1. See https://warrenfahey.com.au/dance/ Lord Mayor's Fancy Dress Ball, for a complete list of costumes.
2. The Australasian, Melbourne. 19 Oct 1929
3. The Telegraph Brisbane 7 May 1938

11. Getting Mobile

1. *Barrier Miner,* Broken Hill, June 1938.
2. *Evening News*, Sydney, April 1910.
3. The Newcastle Sun, 1946
4. Sydney Morning Herald, August 1931
5. *The Sun* (Sydney) May 1932

6. *The Sydney Morning Herald*, June, 2008
7. *The Sun* (Sydney), Jan. 1949
8. Hawkes, Elizabeth. private correspondence with Warren Fahey. January, 2020.
9. *Daily Telegraph* (Sydney) June 1932
10. Ibid
11. *The Sun* (Sydney) August 1954
12. Melbourne Age. 8 November 1929

12. Bowerbirds

1. *Western Mail* (Perth) Dec 1936
2. *Western Mail* (Perth) Junior, Dec 1938
3. Lambert, James, Pennant Hills, NSW, letter to editors of Australian Children's Folklore newsletter 1991.
4. *Chamber's Journal* (Saturday, August 30, 1873),
5. Australian Folklore Collection.

13. Merrily Around the Maypole

1. *The Sun* (Sydney) December 1921
2. *The Week* (Brisbane) Dec 1890.
3. See www.warrenfahey.com.au for a complete script of an Australian version of a Mummer's Play.

14. Very Australian Songs, War Cries & Stories

1. *Australian Melodist Songster* 1875-85. Vol 14. J. Messina & Co.
2. Recorded from Mrs Susan Colley, Bathurst, in 1973, by Warren Fahey. Australian National Library Collection.
3. *Australian Melodist*,
    published in 1875-85
4. Published in *Singabout Magazine*. Bush Music Club, Sydney, 1950. EXACT
5. This is a version cobbled together from verses collected by Warren Fahey from children.
6. An old British sentimental song which gained folk song status. An Australian version was published in
7. *Sunday Times* (Sydney) August 1927
8. *The Sydney Stock & Station Journal* March 1910
9. *Sunday Times*, Sydney, Sun 21, Aug 1927
10. (Contributed by Rob Gill)
11. (contributed by Stuart McCarthy)
12. (contributed by Nick Weare)
13. (contributed by Dr Emanuel Vlahakis)
14. contributed by Dean Thomas
15. (Contributed by Adrian Bartels)
16. (Contributed by Stephen Condrick)

Notes

17. (contributed by Bob Fagan)
18. (Contributed by John Goodyear. TSC meaning The Scots College and pronounced 'tessi')
19. (Contributed John Goodyear)
20. Internet via old boy's network. During the early 60's, under a new headmaster, the school dropped '*Joeys, Joeys*' and used *College, College*. When he left '*Joey's, Joey's*' came back and is now used widely.)
21. (contributed by Elizabeth Jamieson. Telopea being the other public primary school in Canberra at the time)
22. (contributed by Judy Pinder)
23. (Contributed by Graham Chalker)
24. Contributed by Merle Heiner. Contributor added, The first is circa 1915 and the second from before the school closed in the 1970s.)
25. Contributed by 'Megan' who added, "repeat twice, getting steadily louder each time".
26. Internet with added notes. 'Created in 1936 for the Metropolitan Catholic Colleges Combined Athletics Carnival at S.C.G.. Suggested by Br. Coughlan and composed by Br. Butler. During WW2 it was sung by a group from First XIII to a popular tune 'Three Little Fishies')
27. (As half remembered by 'Billy' ACT)
28. (Contributed by Chris Maltby, who added, "The "Eh-up" is a long "aaaaaay", short "oop" sound. Who knows what it may mean? It was just as common to make loud and rude raspberry noises during the polite war cries of the private schools...")
29. (contributed by Russ Hannah)
30. (contributed by Geoffrey Weule)
31. (contributed by Ian Dearden)
32. *The Nepean Times*, September 1927. *A Sydney regional newspaper* reported that the Penrith school had adopted this war cry:—
33. *Narrandera Argus & Riverina Advertiser,* October 1948. 'The School Union has recently adopted an official war cry for the school. The correct text, pronunciation, and translation are as follows. '
34. *Nepean Times* (Penrith) August 1962. New School War-Cry To Greet Visitors

    A new school war cry will greet 145 High school students from near Newcastle when they arrive at St. Marys High School today for two days of pre-Education Week activities.

    Typical of the international atmosphere engendered by St. Mary's principal, Mr. W. J. Eason, the war cry' embodies flavours of Australia, England, Asia, Central Europe, Germany, and Asia
35. Contributed by Robin Weston. Contributor added, "My father spent some miserable years at Hurlstone Agricultural College in the forties. He played Rugby and regarded this chant as the only worthwhile thing about that era. We suggested it for Cowell Area School when we lived in Cowell. So it became *Cowell Cowell, here we are*.)
36. (*The Argus*, Melbourne, Feb. 1941, including text. 'The Yanco Agricultural High School War Cry is sung with gusto by students at every opportunity. It has become popular for the school's winning sports teams to sing this war cry loudly while the huddle of players hops around in a circle.
37. (Contributed by Robyn Kinne)

38. (Contributed by Tony Suttor). Written by teacher H. E. Gill.
39. (Reported in *The Bombala Times*, NSW Dec 1931)
40.
41. (Reported in *Sunday Times* (Sydney) August 1927)
42. (Reported *Advertiser* Footscray (Vic) October 1916
43. (Reported *Daily Advertiser* August 1927)
44. (Reported *Crookwell Gazette* April 1951)
45. (Contributed Ross Barnard)
46. (Contributed by Patrick Whitmen)
47. (Contributed by Ruth Hazelton). Parody of 'Radio Ga Ga' by Queen)
48. (Contributed by Bruce Watson) who added IBIS meant... I believe in Sandgate)
49. (Contributed by Carol Reffold)
50. From Catharine , school librarian. "Two war cries. The 'Rick' and 'Rah' are the shortened, 'Hoorick' and 'Hoorah' derived from one of the earliest school sports songs, '*Hoorick Hoorah*'. 1950s version followed by the original 1916 version - described as a 'Barracker's Song' - is a rousing cry to barracks. The final section - 1990s to now (parody of 'Away in a Manger', and sung very staccato):
51. (Contributed by Peter Cafe)
52. (Contributed by David Gool)
53. (Contributed by Bruce Watson) who added, "We also had a simple little thing we would say aimed at rival school Melbourne Grammar":
    > Who are? We are! Gram-ma.....Poof-tah!
54. Contributed by Max Cullen
55. (From Natasha Dearden, then in Grade 9). This is a contemporary parody, and considering Stuartholme is a Catholic private girls' school, it is no doubt an unofficial school song. It has body percussion actions.

    On Gaou is a slang word made popular by the Ivorian group Magic System in their 2001 song '*1er Gaou*'.
56. The author of this book went to Marist Brothers High School Kogarah and lived in Ramsgate.
57. Proddies - protestants
58. Sargent's Pies still exist, but many would argue they don't taste the same. Their Sydney factory, at Darlinghurst, covered a block, and you could smell the delicious aromas for blocks away. The pies were round, had thin, crunchy pastry, and tasted wonderful. According to this rhyme, they were also mysterious.
59. Kids raised post-WWI2 will remember the importance of the Postmaster General and the department's headquarters, the capital city main post, and the telegraph office. It was a simple step from the abbreviated PMG to Pig's Meat and Gravy, although no one knew the reasoning. It was a good reason to chant

15. Play Songs, Taunts And Parodies

1. *Cinderella Dressed in Yella: Australian childrens' play-rhymes*, collected by Ian Turner (Heinemann Educational, Melbourne).
2. a folklore occasional paper (Ram's Skull Press, 1974).
3. (Oxford University Press, UK),
4. Dr June factor. (Penguin Books, Melbourne)

5. *Sydney Morning Herald,* September 1967. 'Children playing at Lavender Bay wharf yesterday were cheerfully singing this parody of *'John Brown's Body'* at the top of their treble voices.'
6. AFU 1973
7. Deck the Halls. Christmas song
8. Round
9. Joy to the World hymn
10. On Top of Old Smoky - as popularised by The Weavers in the 1950s
11. Cinderella Dressed in Yella, Coll. Canberra 1962. Tune: Clementine
12. AFU 1973
13. Ta Ra Boom Ti Aye popular song in Australia circa 1880s
14. Frères Jacquaca
15. Parody of sea shanty Hog's Eye Man
16. Parody If you're happy and You Know It, Clap Your Hands
17. Heinz beans commercial parody
18. -seasons in the sun parody
19. Nineties child - To tune of Ace of Base song "I saw the Sign"
20. Shocking wl 1973
21. AFU
22.
23. Macarthur, Kathleen, cited in 'Bread and Dripping Days: an Australian growing up in the 1920s' Kangaroo Press.
24. Teddy Bear's Picnic

www.ingramcontent.com/pod-product-compliance
Lightning Source LLC
Chambersburg PA
CBHW071309150426
43191CB00007B/552